# GROUND ZERO WARS

*The Fight to Reveal the Lies of the EPA in the Wake of*
*9/11*
*And Clean Up Lower Manhattan*

Jenna Orkin

# Acknowledgments

This account cannot do justice to any, let alone all, of the activists who worked so tirelessly to achieve cleanup of Lower Manhattan following 9/11, as well as health care for victims. Indeed, some are not even mentioned. A partial list includes 9/11 heroes Jonathan Sferazo, Marvin Bethea and Mike McCormack; cleanup workers Alex Sanchez and Manuel Checo; Micki Siegel de Hernandez, Director, CWA District 1 Occupational Safety and Health; Good Jobs New York; Chief of Staff Amy Rutkin, Press Secretary Eric Schmeltzer and now New York State Assemblymember Linda Rosenthal, from the office of Congressman Jerrold Nadler; World Trade Center Environmental Health Center; Joel Shufro and Jonathan Bennett of the New York Committee on Occupational Safety and Health; Marcy Benstock from the Clean Air Campaign; Office of Staff Analysts' Rob Spencer; former Chief of Staff for Congresswoman Carolyn Maloney, coordinating her leading efforts on the James Zadroga 9/11 Health and Compensation Act, Ben Chevat; Congresspersons Carolyn Maloney and Peter King; Alison Johnson, Chairman of the Chemical Sensitivity Foundation; David Kallick, Senior Fellow at Fiscal Policy Institute[i]; artist Columbia Fiero; Professor David Kotelchuck; Dr. Steve Markowitz; Dr. Jeanne Stellman; Dr. Jacqueline Moline; Dr. Robin Herbert; accordionist/activist/songwriter Paul Stein; Dr. David Carpenter; volunteer Rachel Hughes; Dr. John Howard; residents Kelly Colangelo, Pat Dillon, Mariama James, Harriet Grimm, Diane Stein (both of them – there were two activists by this name;) Michael Cook, Craig Hall, Kathleen Moore and Esther Regelson; Lawyer and now New York County Supreme Court Justice Ellen Gesmer; Lisa Baum, Occupational Health and Safety Representative for the New York State Nurses

Association; Stan Mark of the Asian American Legal Defense and Education Fund; Margaret Hughes, Director of the Good Old Lower East Side; Jackson Chin, Puerto Rican Legal Defense and Education Fund; Dr. Adrienne Buffaloe Sprouse; filmmaker Heidi Dehncke without whose insight and many talents this book could not have seen the light of day; filmmakers Penny Little and Todd Darling; Stuyparents Partha Banerjee, Kiki Dinos, Lissette Velez de Intriago, David Strauss, Ellen Bilofsky, Jonathan Jakobi, Lori Pandolfo, Marty Davis, Sumiko Takeda, Lauren Lochner, Constance Rodgers, Gary Lincoff, Marcia Wertheimer, Gillian Smith Robinson, Ed Griffith, Elizabeth Lee and Vicky Healy as well as numerous others; teachers Milton Diaz and Pat Niglio; Angela Benfield of PS 89. This book represents but a hint of the monumental efforts they and others undertook to fight a giant from whom to snatch some improbable yet important victories.

# Dedication

*To my son, Adele and my family and students*

# TABLE OF CONTENTS

# Introduction

September 11 marked a turning point in modern history, analogous to the fall of the Roman Empire and the arrival of the Dark Ages. For some of us in the trenches of the "war" that was declared by the United States Environmental Protection Agency with the words, "The air is safe to breathe," it represents a birth of consciousness.

That is not meant in any Buddhistic sense; quite the contrary. This consciousness took the form of a distrust that knows no depths. What we became conscious of – and our suspicions took on only fuller form and substance over the subsequent years – was a degree of callousness that allows untold suffering and death in the name of "the greater good" which is to say, the economy.

In a few cases, the seeds of this consciousness were sown immediately. The tragedy of the environmental disaster, as opposed to the attacks themselves, is that it unfolded in slow motion over three to four months while the fires burned and smoldered downtown, releasing thousands of contaminants into the air, including dioxins which are among the most toxic substances known to man, in combinations some of which had never existed before. (The second phase unfolded over the remaining five months of the cleanup and the third, while activists and politicians fought for responsible demolition of contaminated buildings in the surrounding area. The last phase is going on now, as Ground Zero workers and others fall ill and die of their exposures.)

The release itself wasn't slow; it was at first explosive, then continued on a vast scale, relentlessly. What *was* agonizingly slow was the emergence of data to prove conditions that were obvious to anyone not blinded by wishful thinking. It looked like hell; it smelled like hell. But the government says it's OK and why on earth would they lie? *They*'re not the bad guys here. Whether subtly or not, the zeitgeist suggested that to question the government in its darkest hour was just not good form. Patriotism demanded showing the terrorists and that meant acting as though Lower Manhattan was just fine, thank you.

This book is not a comprehensive overview of the disaster such as Juan Gonzalez' magnificent *Fallout* or the Sierra Club's equally hard-hitting *Air Pollution and Deception at Ground Zero: How the Bush Administration's Reckless Disregard of 9/11 Toxic Hazards Poses Long-Term Threats for New York City and the Nation.* Rather, it tells a story of the early days of the battle of Ground Zero; the efforts made to uncover the truth whether for personal reasons (in this writer's case, to convince my son or my ex-husband that our son should not remain in school downtown;) or for impersonal ones: because you're a scientist, environmental lawyer or activist who can see what lies ahead; or because once you find yourself engaged in such a war, and gain experience which newer arrivals send queries about, fighting it becomes an end in itself.

My father used to say, "Mistakes are made in the beginning." Nowhere is this more true than in an environmental disaster when an initial declaration of safety drives all subsequent actions because to change course is to open oneself up to litigation;[1] whereas on the individual scale, it can be unbearable to admit error even to oneself, particularly for parents who may have

---

[1] This conundrum surrounding initially misleading statements of safety – that to reverse course is to open oneself up to litigation – could be combatted by escalating the penalties with each subsequent lie.

2

put their children into jeopardy because they were unwilling to face the inconvenient truth with its attendant sacrifices. Some parents felt it important to foster the independence their children were exercising for the first time – and for better or for worse, Stuyvesant, the school located four blocks north of the World Trade Center that my son attended on 9/11, inspired an unusual degree of loyalty. Other parents worried about reducing their children's chances to attend a good college which they believed would provide the ticket to a happy adulthood. The dilemma was even more acute for immigrant parents to whom Stuyvesant represented the American dream for which they'd left their homes and families and worked their entire lives.

It was in the beginning that the greatest differences could have, should have and would have been made if right had prevailed.

That did not happen. But it has provided comfort to know that a handful of people recognized the scope of the con from day one. If you have to be in hell, it helps to have a few friends with you.

Contrary to articles and other books which have been written on this subject, the revolt of activists against the United States Environmental Protection Agency did not start months or even years after 9/11 itself. Those articles and books were written by journalists who conducted interviews with a select number of individuals long after the fact, most of them, victims. This bias fed the public appetite for human interest stories and perpetuated an image of helplessness. But those who went to work immediately after September 11 itself were not gaga or shell-shocked or any of the other clichés bandied about, purportedly to excuse flailing ineffectiveness in the early days.

It did, however, take time for us all to find each other. The environmental disaster of 9/11 was like the Big Bang: At first, we were all specks of dust in our separate niches of the universe, whose whole was only equal to the sum of its parts. It took months of City Council and State Assembly meetings for us to hear each other's testimony, recognize like minds, exchange cards, then information via email, finally to coalesce into coalitions.

In the beginning, the advocates fighting the battle of Ground Zero were a disparate band of comrades encompassing scientists such as Paul Bartlett and Dr. Marjorie Clarke; lawyer Joel Kupferman and his Policy Analyst, Kimberly Flynn; chemist Monona Rossol; City Councilwoman Kathryn Freed and a smattering of laymen culled from the ranks of Lower Manhattan residents, office workers and parents.

Our company grew rapidly, though not rapidly enough, as well as exponentially but this story, unlike most others that have thus far been published, focuses on the early days.

This account is also a hybrid of memoir and journalism. Hence, the experiences relayed as well as the articles and testimony included in the Appendix are those of the author. Some material in this book also appears in *The Moron's Guide to Global Collapse* or *Writer Wannabe Seeks Brush with Death.* If any reader should encounter it in more than one venue, I apologize but far more vigorously, I salute you.

# Morning

*Tues. 11 Sept. 11:50 am: If any of you hears news of how the kids at Stuyvesant are doing subsequent to this morning's attacks on the World Trade Center, please phone or email me by any of the methods below.[ii]*

Thus the Stuyvesant High School Parents' Association website read, although I certainly wasn't reading it on September 11. Back then, I had nothing to do with the Stuy PA or anything else downtown. My son Alex (some names and identifying details of private people have been changed) was a student at Stuyvesant but the school hummed along superbly on its own steam which was fine by me.

I was also, at the time, innocent of websites. I'd learned the computer to write a novel and had just added email to my list of cyber-achievements. But, incredible as it may sound in this era of online connection 24/7, the idea of looking for the Stuy PA website that morning didn't cross my mind.

At a quarter to nine on September 11, I was on my way to the gym when in the distance, something exploded. There had been a thunderstorm the night before. The skies were glistening now but I thought, in that wacky way which is a precursor to actual thinking, "Is the storm in New Jersey?" There had also once been an oil fire across the water, silent from our vantage point but impressive. Another one? Con Ed? So went my blasé train of thought at that last moment of the innocence of the world. I shrugged off what I couldn't explain and went on my way.

My neighbor Gary breached the usual distance of New York apartment building dwelling to say, "Did you hear about the World Trade Center? A plane flew into it. They think it's terrorists."

5

I looked out the window at two skyscrapers at the tip of Lower Manhattan.

Nothing going on there. A few blocks up, however, on the other side of town, an evil cloud of smoke trailed across the vibrant autumn sky.

"So that's where it is," I thought, still not fully awake. I'd only been there once and didn't pay attention to directions anyway since, growing up in New York, I'd never learned to drive.

"What'll that do to Alex' school?" I asked idiotically, but didn't wait for an answer.

I thanked Gary and ran back inside to call Stuyvesant. Busy, of course. So I called my ex-husband who worked in Lower Manhattan. The receptionist picked up.

"Kevin U., please."

"He's busy."

"A plane just flew into the World Trade Center."

"We know. Is there anything else?"

"Can he get Alex?"

"Hold on."

Kevin got on and I repeated the question.

"Alex! Holy shit... I can't go now. Listen, I can't talk. I just saw a guy jump out a ninety-storey window."

"My God," I cried.

"I'm sorry. I'll try to get to Stuyvesant as soon as I can."

Not too promising.

A call from my cousin asking if Alex was O.K. She'd heard on the radio that Stuyvesant had been evacuated. (It hadn't.)

I went to pick up Alex, still not taking in the ramifications of this thing but thinking it prudent for him not to stay around a disaster area.

The trains weren't running. You couldn't even walk across the Brooklyn Bridge; they'd just closed that too. Someone said something about the second building's being hit so I returned home and switched on CNN and the computer where my friend Jill popped up in the top left hand corner of the screen.

"The first building's down."

Still busy at the school so I called Kevin again. The receptionist sounded agitated, as one might expect from someone fielding the calls of a law firm in downtown Manhattan after the collapse of its neighboring world-reknowned skyscraper. In the background, a woman cried hysterically. Probably Laura, Kevin's wife and colleague. Well, he wasn't leaving now.

Finally Alex called, using his teacher's cellphone. (For anyone who's too young to remember, it was 9/11 that occasioned that spontaneous mutation whereby the cellphone became a human appendage.) The kids were heading up West Street.

"Where are you going?"

"I don't know, Mom. Maybe to the next place they're going to bomb."

"This is no time for jokes," I shot back with anxiety compressed into rage.

"I know," he replied in an appeasing tone. "I gotta go."

*Tues. 11 Sept. 12:05 pm: I've just heard by phone from my son. The school and the kids are OK. They were told at some point (perhaps before the WTC buildings collapsed) to evacuate. They started walking in groups away from the problems. No panic in the group my son was with.[iii]*

When the World Trade Center was hit, we were later told, an FBI agent showed up at the school. Principal Stanley Teitel asked him, "Is it possible those buildings could come down?"

"Not a chance," the guy replied.

Since the subways weren't running, most of the kids wouldn't be able to go home even if they were released from school. In addition, Assistant Principal of Student Services Eugene Blaufarb explained, "The federal officials were talking around me, saying they didn't know whether the planes were part of an overall plot.  It could have been a larger plot, with people on the ground, coming out of covert places."[iv]  (For the same reason, some parents who lived in Manhattan and were therefore able to get to the school, were not allowed in to pick up their children, since there was no way of telling whether or not they were terrorists.)  The safest option seemed to be to keep everyone inside.

Soon, however, one of the FBI agents told the school administration that the north building was in danger of falling and hitting Stuyvesant.  This was inaccurate but he also said that the shock wave could bring the school building down.[v]

When the first tower fell, the school was evacuated, the students quieter than Teitel had ever heard them.[vi] Administrator Renee Levine told them as they streamed past, "Grab somebody's hand.  It doesn't matter if you know them or not.  Stay in pairs and go north."

"It was great 'run for your life' weather," Alex later wrote in an essay for English class, "except for the cloud of dust coming towards us."

He had been in Physics class when the first plane hit. Students rushed to the window, in response to which the teacher simply closed the blinds and continued with the lesson.  One of my own students of English as a Second Language later mused that perhaps the teacher had been using the occasion to illustrate that paradox of quantum physics:  The plane was both there and not there at the same time.

Some students had witnessed people jumping.

"[T]hey looked like debris," Maris Ip, sophomore, recalled in a special issue of the Stuyvesant newspaper The Spectator, which would arrive inserted into the New York Times one Sunday.[vii]

8

In "Diary of a Mad Senior" from the same issue, Dylan Tatz described watching from the ninth floor chemistry lab:

*...men and women in expensive clothes glancing back into what was once their office, before throwing themselves toward the chaotic sidewalk hundreds of feet below. Some appeared to have had a running start while others stood at the edge until the flames licked their skin and pushed them off into the endless cloud of smoke...*

*At one point, two teachers noticed us in the vacant lab, and began to reprimand us for being in an unsupervised room. Without a word, we pointed to the window, and the teachers' authority disappeared as each burst into hysterical tears...*

*As we marched north, the Orpheus in me periodically glanced back over my shoulder to behold the smoky void where ninety minutes prior the Twin Towers had soared invincibly. Likewise, the Israelite in me prayed that someone would step out from the fleeing mass of people, part the Hudson, and lead us away from that chaotic hell and into the promised land of New Jersey.*

*Dylan Tatz, senior[viii]*

*...We heard this screeching noise and then a real loud boom. It was so loud it shook all the desks, and our desks are fastened to the floor; it was a lab room...*

*We think the debris has just become immense, until we look closer and realize that it's actually people jumping from the WTC... A few minutes later, we see the second building crumble. They eventually evacuate us and we're running outside. And then people are just screaming that the other building had crumbled as well, so they rush us back in the building, but most of us are already out, and the police push us out, but then we hear gunshots, and there's chaos everywhere. People start firing guns, and*

*the police tell us to stay low and run for our lives, so five miles later, we look back, and see everything in smoke.*
                                        *Jeng Tyng Hong, junior*[ix]

Some kids reacted initially with detachment:

*I was talking to my friend who was talking about the logistics of the whole thing and what he would have done with the Pentagon instead.*
                                        *Hamilton Davis, sophomore*[x]

*[P]eople were like "cool" and stuff.*
                                        *Lindsay Kim, sophomore*[xi]

*It was a feeling of great excitement... as if it was a Die Hard 4 or Godzilla of something.*
                                        *Paul Banec, freshman*[xii]

Other reflections were more personal:

*For the first time since I found out my mom was sick, I cried.*
                                        *Laurence Wooster, senior*[xiii]

*I am no stranger to grief, as my mother died when I was eleven. Yet each day I think "OK, I've passed that stage where it upsets me so much. I won't cry anymore." And each day I'm wrong. Each day I have cried just a little bit more.*
                                        *Jessica Copperman, senior*[xiv]

An insert in the magazine read:

*Found in a notebook at school on September 11:*
*If I die here today, who knows what can happen. I believe still, that people are inherently good.*[xv]

The quotation evokes the sentiment wrested from the *Diary of Ann Frank* by screenwriters Albert Hackett (my stepfather) and his first wife, Frances Goodrich, which proved the pivot for their dramatization of the iconic work: "Still I believe, in spite of everything, that people are really good at heart."

It is not the only appeal to hope in the issue which, in the hard copy edition, is bookended by statements from Jane Goodall. In her forward, entitled, "Concentrate on the Wonderful Things," she reminded the kids of the "wonderfully brave dogs who worked among the debris, burning their feet on the red hot concrete and steel" and the message of support "not only [from] America's usual allies but from countries like Iran and Syria and Libya. It is amazing and wonderful and... it could lead to a new global network of countries determined to stamp out terrorism."[xvi] The sentiments seem idealistic now and from her TED talks, it may appear that Goodall, like so many others, has tempered her optimism.

Unable to get into Manhattan, I went to the Red Cross to give blood. In a scene that would be repeated in Paris after the terrorist attacks of 2015, the line snaked around the block, as though to the gates of Purgatory after an earthquake. Ahead stood a couple of construction workers, a mother with a baby in a pram and a cluster of Swedish tourists. If you couldn't get into Manhattan, this was the next best way to help out.

"My niece is on the 80th floor," said a woman in front of me. She seemed worried but like me, hadn't yet taken in the scope of the situation. (The impact zone for Tower 2 was between the 77th and 85th floors.)

The Red Cross sent us away as they lacked the facilities to store that much blood.

*Tues. 11 Sept. 1:30 pm: I've now returned home from driving downtown to collect my son and four of his friends. They had walked about three miles, from Stuy to 42nd St. and 10th Avenue, which is where I collected them, by arrangement. They had seen the fireballs of the hits on the World Trade Center. Around 10:30 (they were rather vague, might have been half an hour earlier or later) all the students were told to leave and to walk uptown. There was excitement or nervousness but no panic, nothing scary happening.[xvii]*

Alex went with three other kids to the house of a classmate where my friend Miriam picked him up. He would have been able to get to her house on his own but as Miriam later explained, "I couldn't *not* do it. He sounded a little dazed and I didn't want him wandering around anymore." He'd walked five miles carrying twenty-six pounds of books. (When he came to my house a week later, I weighed them.) Like me, he has his vague side and hadn't gotten around to nabbing a locker. The previous year, he'd just carried his books all year long, a matter of some squabbling between us. ("They're not heavy, Mom.")

Miriam took him to lunch at Pete's.

"As we were walking there, we passed a woman crying," she recounted afterwards. "Alex said, 'Did you hear what that woman was crying about? She said she'd missed her bus. Otherwise she would have been in there.' He seemed fine but we had to wait an hour for a table. All the restaurants were filled with refugees from Lower Manhattan. We sat at the bar and watched TV. A baby came on the screen. That seemed to get to him a little.

'It took another hour to get served. He fell asleep at the table."

CNN played footage of the cloud that engulfed the plaza, then all of Lower Manhattan, after the first building collapsed. A woman next to the camera cried, "My God," and everyone started running. "It looked like a scene out of a Godzilla movie," resident Wendy Tabb later described. Although Alex adamantly maintains he escaped the cloud, I wondered how that might be possible; no one could outrun it.

*Tues. 11 Sept 4:15 pm: I've received a number of calls from parents who've seen this web page. Some parents still haven't heard from their children but I know that that is because they're walking long distances, trying to get public transport, etc. I just spoke with a girl in Grade 9 who just got home to Brooklyn. She said that a Stuy teacher, Danny Jaye, walked a large number of students to and across one of the bridges to Brooklyn and then made sure to get them safely onto subway lines that were working. Another parent who lives in Queens called 20 minutes ago very concerned because he had not heard from his son, and then called back just now to say his son had safely reached their home in Queens.*

*I also spoke to the mother (see below) who works in the WTC. She said she was in the North WTC building on a floor in the 80s when the plane hit, very close to her. It took her about 90 minutes to get out of the building and it collapsed only five minutes after she got out. She went to the hospital to have glass shards removed from her leg but is OK now.*

*Tues. 11 Sept. 5:45 pm: I've just heard from Marilena Christodoulou, President of the PA. She says she went to the school as soon as she heard the news, arriving there at 11:00. She met the principal and some assistant principals who told her that they had been requested by emergency officials to evacuate the school so it could be used as an emergency base for providing medical help. The children had been told to start by heading north, keeping on the West side of the street, so that they would be exposed to as little as possible of the smoke. (After a certain distance, clearly many headed in other directions.)*

*Marilena was assured by the school that no child or teacher was hurt in any way. Most who live in Manhattan are now home. Many who live in other boroughs are staying with friends or waiting until they can use the subways. (I understand that nearly all subway lines are now working, at least out of Manhattan.) However, some children are having difficulty phoning home because certain lines are over-busy or out of action.*

*THERE WILL BE NO SCHOOL TOMORROW, WEDNESDAY. No decision has been made about the rest of the week. Please pass the word on this to others.*[xviii]

Emails arrived from college friends in England and India. The British one, Celia, was a reserved woman I hadn't heard from in ten years. For the first time, she signed off, "Love, Celia."

"Alex is with a friend of mine," I answered her solicitous questions. "I don't know if he or Kevin will be able to get home tonight..."

Kevin picked up Alex on his way back to Flatbush – a trip which took two hours – where they spent the next week. In hindsight, it was better for him to be there than at my apartment in downtown Brooklyn where the plume of smoke headed upon leaving Manhattan.

*Weds 12 Sept. 4:00 pm: The mayor just announced that schools South of 14th St. (i.e. including Stuy) will NOT be open tomorrow, Thursday. Other schools will be open but starting 2 hours late. If anyone hears news regarding Friday, let me know and I'll post it.*

*....As students were leaving the building thru the North doors, the second tower collapsed. The wind was blowing lightly from the northwest and our wide and tall school shielded the students, staff and hundreds of refugees from the towers from the choking cloud of dust.*[xix]

In an interview conducted several years later, Stuyvesant Parents' Association President Marilena Christodoulou told a different story:

*The radio was saying the kids wouldn't be allowed out unless their parents came to pick them up so Aris [her husband] and I went down. We almost didn't have the car. Aris drove Peter [their son] down that morning because it was the day for the class picture and Peter didn't want to take his suit on the subway. But Aris couldn't find a parking space so he took the car home.*

*The amazing thing is that they allowed us to go down West Street. I told the police I was on the Stuyvesant Emergency Action team which was true but I had no proof. All I had was the PA President ID. That was after both buildings fell. It was like a snowstorm where the snow is grey. Everything was quiet. We couldn't breathe. We stopped at a firehouse. The firemen said, "Take whatever you need." We took respirators but we didn't know how to use them. I put a wet towel over my mouth.*

*I think all the kids must have been in the cloud for fifteen minutes or half an hour, depending. The kids who walked to Brooklyn were in it much longer, of course.*

*I told Teitel, "Talk to the press so they'll stop announcing that [about the kids not being allowed out unless their parents picked them up] over the radio."*

*Then [an overweight administrator who would retire at the end of the year] comes out with that Greek cook – what's his name? – and starts eating a huge sandwich.*

*September 13*

Miriam wanted to get out of town so we went to her friend Lee's upstate. Rudely but urgently, I ignored the conversation to focus on googling for a boarding school for Alex. The news had been speculating about another attack, especially downtown. (Other parents had similar concerns, though for different reasons: "After the attack, [Himanshu] Suri's mother and father each begged him to stay in the house. 'They didn't think it was a safe time to go out,' he recalled. 'They'd say, 'Hey, be careful, they're killing those Indian kids out there.'"[xx] Suri was the Stuyvesant High School Student Union Vice-President.)

Also, Miriam had hit on another problem:

The day before, she had met a friend for lunch in the Village, several miles from Ground Zero.

"I couldn't breathe," she said. "The air was yellow and the smell was unbelievable. I shouldn't have gone. I'm the canary in the mine," (Miriam has multiple chemical sensitivities) "but the air is what's going to be the problem." A double Ph.D., Miriam also has a habit of penetrating to the heart of a matter.

Lee, whose son was the same age as Alex, helped with the cyber-search for a boarding school. But as the year was already underway, the schools were all filled.

On the way home, when we got within sight of Manhattan, I cried: *My city's still there.*

My apartment was situated in the heart of Brooklyn's court district. That week there were three bomb threats as well as two evacuations – including one at the subway station – within a four block radius of the building. Across the street, a terrorist wannabe set a car on fire which no one bothered to put out, the fire department being otherwise engaged at Ground Zero.

The city – the whole world, it seemed – dropped everything else in the days following September 11. Like thousands of others, I bought food for the rescue workers (when he heard why I was cleaning him out of Danish, the deli guy wouldn't accept payment) and headed to Ground Zero, or as close as you could get, to leave the bag at a relief center.

*Fri. 14 Sept 12:15 pm: The following items are lifted from www.stuynet.com, a website maintained and used by Stuy students:*

*I was able to go to school today through the American Red Cross. They have turned Stuy into a medical center. I had the opportunity to talk to Mr. Lopa (the head custodian.) The school has no structural damage but the surrounding area is a hectic disaster zone. There is debris and dust everywhere. We won't be going back to school any time soon but we will stick together...*

*Jukay Hsu and Himanshu Suri, Student Union President and Student Union Vice President[xxi]*

After graduating from Harvard, Hsu would go on to serve in Afghanistan. Suri became a rap artist with the "pan-brown" group, Das Racist.[xxii] Benjy Sarlin, the reporter of the story from which this information is drawn, was also a Stuyvesant student on 9/11.[xxiii]

*...As for princeton review classes offered at stuy, that will be dealt with shortly, but Teitel's [the principal's] main concerns right now are to get us back into classes and to figure out a way to work out the issue with the college early action due date of October 1st...*

*Gary He[xxiv]*

Every few days I returned to Ground Zero although there was no longer a need for food – the public response had been so abundant, the site was being overrun with rats.

Each time, the barriers receded another half block or so, but with the exception of a solitary cop on the corner, the streets remained deserted, like a movie set for a city following a nuclear explosion.

On Sunday, a mosque on Manhattan's Upper East Side held what was no doubt a supplementary service, (the Islamic Sabbath being Friday,) followed by a press conference, to which they invited the non-Muslim community.

Hundreds of men knelt in the middle of the hall while a few women, mostly from the Columbia School of Journalism, sat roped in behind a red velvet barrier such as they have in museums to keep tourists from sullying the exhibits. A secretary handed out scarves to any who had come unprepared.

A spokesman for the mosque warned the men not to buy illegal guns and to watch what they said on the phone; they could fall prey to set-ups to catch Muslims.

Following the service, the press conference began in silence until the Imam asked, "There is a problem with the cameras?"

"No," answered a reporter. "We thought you were praying."

Relieved laughter broke the tension.

The Imam spoke of Arabs who had been harassed since September 11, particularly the women who, with their head scarves and abayas, stood out more prominently. One woman had been hit by a car.

"They spit at us in the street," said a woman now. "And one man stopped me from getting on the bus."

That afternoon at five, peace marchers congregated at the Moroccan Star restaurant on Atlantic Avenue before heading for the Promenade, facing the smoking remains of the Twin Towers. Arabs carried signs that read, "Not in My Name," while a short Yemeni man held up a sign that read, "America Stand Tall."

"Fifty thousand troops can't do diddly," observed Rabbi Bob Greenblatt from the Park Slope Jewish Center, referring to the US invasion of Afghanistan. A self-identified activist from the sixties, he described himself also as a Holocaust survivor who didn't want to see another Holocaust.

"What should America do if Afghanistan can't or won't hand over Bin Laden?" someone asked him.

"Don't bomb them. Spy; use bribery," he advised, as a woman handed out Shabbat candles.

On the way to the Promenade, the marchers sang *We Shall Overcome* and the *Star-Spangled Banner.*

"God bless America!" shouted an Arab man.

"God bless America!" everyone took up the rallying cry.

"Allah bless America!" shouted Rabbi Greenblatt.

"Allah bless America," the marchers echoed, a little more faintly.

At the Promenade, clergy from local mosques, churches and synagogues spoke, followed by four young women from Sakhi for South Asian women. Their colleague, Swarna Chalasani, who worked on the 94th floor of Tower 2, was still missing. (It would later be learned that she had not escaped.[xxv]) One of the women said, "Two of us are Indian; one is Pakistani; one is Afghan and I'm sure you can't tell which is which."

The vigil took place next to the playground where Alex and I had spent hours each day for six years. Butterflies flew around while across the river, two planes passed serenely over the bomb site. Further away, a sky-writer streaked towards White Plains. The vigil ended with a Muslim prayer and a blow on the shofer. The same Arab man as before started up the chant once more, "God bless America!" Someone answered with, "God bless all people."

It was a beautiful night with not a cloud in the sky – except for the one across the river rising from where the World Trade Center used to be.

Tuesday I had a doctor's appointment after which I walked downtown to a discussion group I'd belonged to for two years.

On the Upper East Side, a faint logo had appeared on the corners of the sidewalks like a religious apparition in red, white and blue: W.T.C. – R.I.P.

The walk was four miles long, each block reminding me of some fragment from the past:

Central Park, where my father had taught me how to throw a baseball. The highlight of these excursions came one morning when a boy of around eleven (i.e. awe-inspiringly big) missed a ball which rolled towards us. I threw it back to him. "Good arm," he observed before jogging back to his game. For him, a casual remark; for me, a moment whose glory trailed for years. Later, I brought Alex to a nearby field for pickup games.

The coffee shop where my grandmother and I had hot chocolate after seeing Camelot.

Carnegie Hall where I went to concerts with composer Louise Talma. I even sang there once, in the chorus of the music school I attended as a child.

The street where Michael R., a gentle boy with long eyelashes, lived after his father wrote a Broadway hit. At Michael's seventh birthday party, we were taken to Coney Island and let loose, each with a purse stuffed with dimes, the cost of a ride at that time.

In the wake of 9/11, the past, which had somehow remained alive for decades, had become history.

# IN THE BEGINNING

My father's line, "Mistakes are made in the beginning," has echoed through the years since 9/11, for it operates on several levels.  In a series of statements starting September 13, Environmental Protection Agency Administrator Christie Todd Whitman announced, "The air is safe to breathe."  This assertion proved a point of no return for if EPA had later said, "Wait a second; the data coming in show otherwise," not only would they have been legally liable to anyone who'd relied on the initial statements, but also, they would have lost credibility.  The fact that the illnesses and deaths of Ground Zero workers do far more to undermine that credibility doesn't change their thinking since it takes decades for the full impact of the disaster to reveal itself, by which time the officials involved have moved on.  Besides, since they are the agency of last resort, they can apparently get away with whatever they want.

Secondly, from EPA's announcement flowed the actions of state and local agencies – not to mention citizens who were placated or compelled by lack of options to return to a toxic environment.

But most importantly, it was in the beginning that the fires raged and smoldered and that exposure was therefore the most damaging.

Much soul-searching, and even more rationalizing, has gone on since then but at the time, the official message was uniform and dutifully parroted by a compliant media, most prominent among them, the New York Times:

*"The persistent pall of smoke wafting from the remains of the World Trade Center poses a very small, and steadily diminishing, risk to the public, environmental officials and doctors said yesterday...*[xxvi]

21

Buried in the article is a line which might easily be overlooked in the general din of good news: "Some government scientists, speaking only on the condition of anonymity, said they were concerned that city health officials had not done more to encourage those people who were caked in the dust as the disaster unfolded to avoid spreading it around once they were safe at home."[xxvii]

*'[T]ests of air and the dust coating parts of Lower Manhattan appeared to support the official view expressed by city, state and federal health and environmental officials: that health problems from pollution would not be one of the legacies of the attacks. Tests of air samples taken downwind of the smoldering rubble...disclosed no harmful levels of asbestos, lead or toxic organic compounds, officials of the federal Environmental Protection Agency said yesterday."[xxviii]*

As suggested in the above excerpts, crucial among the experts who did not protect the public interest at this critical juncture were doctors, including some of those who later became prominent advocates for sick and dying Ground Zero workers.

*Experts feared serious air-quality problems, but they now say the general public can breathe easy – there is little threat of any lingering health hazards.*
*"We anticipated a big problem," said Dr. Gillian Shepherd, an allergy-immunology specialist at Weill Cornell Medical Center-New York Presbyterian Hospital. "But thank heavens, it didn't happen...*
*[T]he city's Board of Health said its readings showed there was very little asbestos in the air.*
*Besides, said Dr. Murray Rogers, chief of pulmonology at Lenox Hill Hospital, "with asbestos, you need a lot of exposure over a long period of time before you suffer any*

22

*adverse effect. This didn't happen. The area was evacuated and those large particles fell to the ground. Then the rain washed the air."*

*Rogers said a bigger threat was posed by hot fumes that may have harmed victims' lungs and tracheae.*

*"Certainly, older people, people with chronic lung disease and young children [who have immature lungs] were more susceptible on Tuesday to whatever particulates were in the air. But the danger now has passed."*

*Still, many people were left choking and gasping for air. The best remedy, said the experts, is to drink lots of water..."*[xxix]

("So in other words," said State Senator Richard Brodkey to a government witness at one State Assembly hearing on the disaster, "what you're saying is, 'Take two aspirin and call me in the morning.'")

Dr. Mark D. Siegel, director of the intensive care unit at Yale-New Haven Hospital, echoed Dr. Rogers' assessment of the danger from asbestos with what would become a recurrent refrain: "Even in a worst-case scenario... most people with asbestos-related lung disease usually had long-term occupational exposure."[xxx]

In 2011, Dr. Joan Reibman, Director of the World Trade Center Environmental Health Center at Bellevue, reflected, "We didn't ask right off the bat, 'Is there a potential for harm?'"[xxxi]

And when almost 70 percent of examined patients developed new or worsened respiratory symptoms during or after their exposure, Dr. Philip Landrigan, who directed studies of Ground Zero workers,[xxxii] said, "We had no idea the number would be so high."[xxxiii]

Landrigan also told New York Times journalist, Anthony de Palma, author of *City of Dust: Illness, Arrogance and 9/11,* that the problems had persisted longer than expected.[xxxiv]

In a document entitled, "COMPLAINT AND ADDITIONAL EVIDENCE OF pH FRAUD BY: USGS, OSHA, ATSDR, NYC, EPA, and EPA-funded scientists — 1. Falsification of corrosive pH data for WTC dust — 2. Historical fraud by EPA of hazardous pH levels since 1980," Dr. Cate Jenkins, a chemist at EPA, wrote of Dr. Landrigan:

*In 2004, a large group of EPA/NIEHS-funded and EPA staff researches [sic] published additional findings on the human health consequences of the WTC collapse in the journal Environmental Health Perspectives (EHP)... This paper included a summary of the results from the earlier published EPA funded research. The lead author was Dr. Philip Landrigan, Mt. Sinai School of Medicine. Landrigan et al. falsely claimed that McGee et al. reported that the smallest PM 2.5 particles in WTC dust were neutral, non-alkaline. The McGee 2003 article said just the opposite...*

*... The third false claim in the Landrigan et al. publication was that bulk samples of WTC dust only had a pH level as high [sic] 11.0. Again, the same 2 studies (McGee et al. and Lioy et al.) were cited as a basis for this claim. Because the McGee et al. study only reported a maximum pH level of 10.0, the Lioy et al. study would need to be the source for the... claim that the highest pH was only 11. This also was a deliberate misrepresentation. The Lioy Study... found a pH level as high as 11.5 for one sample, which is over 3 times as alkaline as a pH of 11.0. Claiming that the pH was only 11.0 conveniently gets the pH level under the universally accepted trigger level for corrosivity to human tissues (pH 11.5). It would have been hard to overlook the pH level of 11.5 in the Lioy et al. publication, because it appeared in bold-faced type in the abstract, as well as being in the text of the article and*

*also a table as well. This third falsification makes it clear that the other falsification of the pH levels for the smallest particles was no casual error in the Landrigan et al. paper.*[xxxv]

Dr. Landrigan, who did not speak out early on about the particular risks to children, (my own memory is that he specifically downplayed them) became a stronger advocate later, testifying:

> *Children are particularly vulnerable to environmental toxins such as those released into the air of lower Manhattan on September 11. Several factors act together to increase children's risk.*
> *Children live closer to the ground than adults and thus are more like to inhale any materials stirred up from dust.*
> *Children breathe more air per pound of body weight per day and thus take into their bodies proportionately larger quantities of any toxic materials suspended in the air.*
> *Children's developing lungs and other organ systems are more sensitive than those of adults.*
> *Children have more years of future life in which to develop delayed diseases that may result from exposures to dust, asbestos or other toxic materials.*[xxxvi]

But it was in the early days that doctors and probing journalists could have made the most difference. They have argued that the data were not available yet but that is in the nature of the meaning of "early days." Besides, it didn't take an advanced degree to recognize that ten million tons of debris,[xxxvii] much of it in pulverized form, all burning and smoldering for months, is not an environment for unprotected people to move back to. But the media did not interview people with common sense; they interviewed experts.

Given EPA's sunny reports about the fumes downtown, to express doubts about this orthodoxy was tantamount to questioning the existence of God during the Middle Ages.[2] Thus neither Alex nor my ex-husband was buying my skepticism and since we shared custody, the hope of changing schools was off the table.

In an interview conducted several years after the attacks, Parents' Association President Marilena Christodoulou provided some insight into what was going on behind the scenes at Stuyvesant where attention was focused on the logistics of running the school.

*There were many emergency meetings of the Executive Board, the Principal, the Board of Ed. There was talk of splitting the kids between Martin Luther King and La Guardia [High Schools.] Danny Jaye [head of the Stuyvesant Math department] was talking to City College. Also the Julia Richman building [a former high school] was vacant. And there was talk of sharing the Brooklyn Tech building but with* no overlapping classes.

*[Parents' Association Vice President] Sheldon [Stachel] and I met with the Superintendent of High Schools who kept us waiting for hours. Then he came out and said, 'The decision's been made but I can't tell you what it is; it's confidential."*

---

2 These days, the "necessity" to accept the party line is even more stark: In England, "Young people who question Government or media may be extremists; officials tell parents;" Jon Stone; 1 December 2015; http://www.independent.co.uk/news/uk/politics/young-people-who-question-government-policy-or-the-media-may-be-extremists-officials-tell-parents-a6756086.html

*Statement to Stuyvesant Parents by the Executive Board of the Stuyvesant Parents' Association*

*Monday September 17, 2001, 11:00 pm*

*1) On Friday September 14, the Stuyvesant PA President was informed by the Deputy Chancellor, David Klasfeld, that:*

*(a) Until the Stuyvesant building is available, Stuyvesant will share space with Brooklyn Technical High School (BTHS), starting on September 20th.*

*(b) Class schedules at BTHS for BTHS students and Stuyvesant students will not overlap.*

*2) Over the weekend, the PA organized a phone tree to call 3,000 Stuyvesant families and inform them that school will resume, at BTHS, on September 20th.*

*3) Today, the PA Board learned the following facts, which conflict with what we were informed on Friday:*

*(a) Each day, BTHS students will attend from 7:15 am to 1:47 pm,* [they didn't want to give up their afternoon clubs] *and Stuy students will attend from 10:55 am to 6:11 pm.*

*(b) Each day there will be four "overlap periods," during which both student bodies are sharing the BTHS building. During each of those four periods, between 50% and 95% of Stuy students will not have classrooms – unless large numbers of BTHS students are to go without classrooms.*

*(c) Current plans for one of the "overlap periods" are for 2,000 Stuy students to have lunch in the cafeteria simultaneously. During others, up to forty classes will be*

*conducted simultaneously in the large auditorium, possibly using portable chalkboards.*

*(d) These arrangements might have to continue for up to six weeks, i.e. until about November 1st.*

*4) The PA Board held an emergency meeting this evening to discuss the situation. The Board was unanimously of the opinion that:*

*(a) The conditions at BTHS during the "overlap periods" raise serious safety and educational concerns for both the Stuy and the BTHS student bodies.*

*(b) It is essential, for the sake of both student bodies, that Stuy students return to the Stuyvesant building as soon as possible, and certainly much sooner than November 1st.*

*5) If parents share these views, they are encouraged to phone the Chancellor of the Board of Education, Harold O. Levy, at (718) 935-2000, or to fax him at (718) 935-3463, or to mail him at 110 Livingston St., Brooklyn, NY 11201. Please don't email him. [Note: This para amended 19 September 12:45 pm]*xxxviii

However, the Parents' Association did initially encourage like-minded parents to email the Chancelor.

*"We didn't tell them what to say," Christodoulou said. "We wanted the parents to say how they felt. We gave the facts and our concerns, and if the parents felt the same way, we gave the Chancellor's e-mail.*
*'By Wednesday morning, the Chancellor had received hundreds of e-mails asking for the immediate return of kids to Stuy..."*xxxix

From Christodoulou's in-person interview:

*September 18, I get a call from Klasfeld who says, "I have the Chancellor here."*

*The Chancellor gets on. He doesn't say, "Hello, how are you?" He says, "How dare you? You're filling up my mailbox with emails. This is irresponsible. Shame on you."*

*I said, "You're irresponsible. Shame on you." But I was civil; he was shouting.*

*I told him our complaints and he backed off immediately. He pretended not to know all this.*

*Teitel called and said, "You won." We got the staggered schedule.*

*When school opened at Brooklyn Tech, I said, "I want to be there." Teitel said, "You can't." He made some excuse about how the Principal of Brooklyn Tech didn't want the PA there. Then he backed down.*

*Klasfeld gave a speech thanking the teachers and everyone else but forgetting to thank the parents.*

*Gary He had a wonderful piece on his website saying everything is due to the parents. The Spectator picked up on it.*

*Fri. 21 Sept. 1:00 am: The following has appeared at Stuy. www.Stuynet.com, [the website founded by Gary He] an unofficial web site accessed by numerous Stuy students. "I once again must commend the Parents Association, and especially Marilena Christodoulou, on their efforts on trying to end the overlap, getting the building back under Board of Education control by October 1st, and now their current fight to get us back INTO the building by October 1st, not just switch control so cleaning crews can come in... They also played their role in the coalition by phoning hundreds of parents and getting the word out so parents could individually complain to Harold Levy. At the assembly, they received little to no thanks. In fact, the illusion was made that other parties had made it possible, not the PA. I am telling you that is not true. Thank goodness there is a PA, otherwise we'd be sitting in overlapped 40-minute periods for the rest of this term."*[xl]

*September 25, 2001*

The PA meeting that month was held at Brooklyn Tech, a vast, gallantly decaying art deco building whose mammoth auditorium was packed. Kids handed out the words to, *Oh Beautiful for Spacious Skies*, which we sang wholeheartedly, cynicism not yet on the horizon.

Then Deputy Chancellor of the Board of Education David Klasfeld spoke.

"The building is undergoing a million dollar cleanup," he announced. "We expect to be back in it by October 1st."

The room erupted in cheers and applause.

*Oh shit*, I thought. My worst fears realized. Ra ra patriotism and the kids are back in an unhealthy, unsafe environment. But if anyone points this out, especially if she has no data to back up her assertions, she'll be looked on as a spoiler, if not a hysteric.

"Any questions?"

"Classes are only twenty-six minutes here. How do you expect the kids to learn anything?"

The forty classes taking place simultaneously in the auditorium were particularly hard hit, especially if the subject required a laboratory. No one was learning anything, Alex reported, but it wasn't a complaint. He liked school mostly because of his friends anyway, a common enough attitude among teenagers, even at Stuy.

The gist of Klasfeld's response was, "This is hard on everyone. We're making the best of a bad situation. And this is why we want to get the Stuy building open for business ASAP." More applause.

"My son says some of the Brooklyn Tech kids spat at him."

Stuy and Brooklyn Tech are competitive. Techies thought Stuykids snooty, earning snooty responses from Stuykids.

"What about the air?" asked a woman with what sounded like an Israeli accent. Such is one's interpretation at Stuyvesant where a large percentage of the population is Jewish. Like me, she was not sharing in the communal exuberance. "I live downtown and the smell is terrible. It's going to be months before the kids should go back there."

"Bravo!" I shouted. At least let them know there's some dissent from the general charge into the valley of death.

"We're cognizant of the problem," responded Klasfeld with an earnest frown. "And we want to assure you we're doing everything we can to protect the kids' health."

*Uh huh.*

"Whatever you're doing to clean up," said a man on the other side of the auditorium, "don't forget about the ventilation system."

In the months to follow, I thought about that man often, prophet that he was. Did he sign our petitions, carry a sign at our demonstrations? (A few years later, a comment by Stuy father and State Senator Martin Connor during a discussion about the school's ventilation system – "I warned them about that"– indicated it may have been he.)

Bernard Orlan, Director of School Environmental Health and Safety, said the heating and ventilation system would be scrubbed and air filters replaced while the air would be continuously monitored.

And what would they do if, after the kids were back in the building, said monitoring showed hazardous levels?

"Then we'll pull them out again," said Klasfeld.

*Sure you will.*

The whole plan smacked of a, "Marry in haste; repent at leisure," mindset.  Just get the kids back in the building at all costs.

After the meeting, I buttonholed Klasfeld, grabbing the "Israeli" woman along the way.

"You work for the Board of Ed?"

"I'm the Deputy Chancellor," he replied, visibly puffing out his chest.

"You know, regardless of what it looked like in there, not everyone is anxious to go back to Stuyvesant."

"Yes, that's the impression I'm getting."

"A lot of people are talking about the air.  That has to be checked out first."

"I know."

Since the data were being suppressed, there wasn't much else to say.  At least, if he was inclined towards keeping the kids out longer, (a scenario which in hindsight evokes a hollow laugh,) he knew he wouldn't be left twisting in the wind.

Back home, I got on email and wrote to everyone I could think of in a position of power in relation to Stuyvesant – School Chancellor Harold Levy, David Klasfeld and the roster of the Executive Board of the Parents' Association.  Most were no more than names and emails. No matter.  I wrote about the air, the fires and environmental disasters of the past.

Eventually one of the Executive Board responded:

"You're using last year's PA list; many of these people are no longer on the board and some are no longer at Stuyvesant." *So there.*

But the board member didn't say which ones so I kept writing and whoever it was gave up complaining.

A card in the mail:  The kids are going back to the Stuy building the day after Columbus Day, Tuesday, October 9!  Stuy is open for business!

At least it's a week later than the original plan.

Marilena Christodoulou later provided the context:

*It was hard to find an independent expert [to assess the safety of the environment] because they all had conflicts of interest. We eventually found Howard Bader, an industrial hygienist. The weekend before Columbus Day we had to get out the PA bulletin.*

*We sent a letter to the Chancellor saying what we required before we'd go back. We asked for certification from the city that the building was fit for occupancy. We asked for removal of the [waste transfer barge which was positioned directly next to the school] although Bernard Orlan at the Board of Ed had told us about a chemical spray that could make the stuff at the barge not fly away. As you know, we never even got that.*

*And we asked for a complete abatement. Assuming that was done, we wanted to go back. At that time there was consensus on the Executive Board. We didn't even bother to take a vote.*

*On the Thursday before we went back, [PA Executive Board member] Charles Morrow, Sheldon and I had a meeting with Klasfeld. We told him we wouldn't move back until the pool was cleaned and Bader had the test results. Charles and I took the subway uptown together. He lives further up than I do. When I got home there were three messages from [a board member] screaming bloody murder. I knew Charles couldn't have told him what went on in the meeting because he was still on the subway. Sheldon swore it wasn't him. The only solution was that [the board member] was in kahoots with the Board of Ed which subsequently proved correct. But because of this, we made the letter to the parents even stronger. We said something like, "We question the Board of Education's good faith."*

*The sides were drawn. The letter was signed only by me and Sheldon.*

*It was homecoming weekend which is a major event so I distributed the letter there. Rochelle Kalish's daughter was a "big sib" so she helped. But [an opposing board member's] daughter was also a big sib so she found out.*

*Teitel was sitting with his wife. No one else went over so I sat with him*

*On Friday, the Board of Ed asked me, Dorothy Suecoff [head of the Stuyvesant chapter of the United Federation of Teachers] and Jukay Hsu [President of the Student Union] to check over the school. I called Dorothy and Jukay and told them not to go. So of all three constituencies, no one complied.*

*The same day, Bader calls and says, "I just got two big telephone books of data. I can't possibly go through them in time to tell you the building is safe."*

*I ask that guy, what's his name, a two-faced guy ending in [suffix] – I ask him to request a delay to enable us to look at the results. And he does.*

*About that, we were on the same page as the UFT. [United Federation of Teachers.]*

*Klasfeld refused. He said, "If they're bad, we'll move out." We subsequently found out they'd already moved files and everything else back to the building.*

As Marilena later wrote in the PA's October Bulletin:

*This decision [to return to the Stuy building] was made without prior consultation with the Stuyvesant PA... The PA's expert received the post-cleanup test sampling results and other extensive documentation from the Board of Education on Friday October 5 in the afternoon, an insufficient time for him to thoroughly review them and advise the PA that afternoon...*

*On Monday, October 8, the PA Board was informed of its expert's opinion that the indoor test results are acceptable. However, there are several important items that need to be addressed to ensure the continued safety inside the school building...*

*(a) the continued monitoring of the water quality and air quality (both inside and outside the school) after the students relocate, (b) the effects of continued demolition and recovery operations for impact within and outside the*

*school... and (d) safe access and transportation issues. The Board of Education had agreed to the PA's request that its Director of School Environmental Health and Safety write a detailed explanatory letter addressing these issues. To date, the Board of Education has not provided us with such a letter...*

*The PA Executive Board is concerned with the carting and disposal of debris from the WTC site onto barges located near the school. At its Special Meeting of October 5, the PA Executive Board passed a resolution that the barge operations, and the related truck traffic and noise pollution present a potential danger to the students and staff of our school and to the surrounding community.*

*Therefore, the Executive Board believes that the barges should be moved to another location as soon as possible. The Board plans to enlist the support of the community and of neighboring schools to achieve this goal.[xli]*

In the left hand column of the same Bulletin appeared a notice with a cheerier slant:

*PHONATHON RESULTS*

*Thanks to the commitment and generosity of the Stuyvesant community, the May 2001 Phonathon raised $289,000. Contributions are still coming in. We are grateful to the parent volunteers and members of the school's administration who manned the phones for three evenings supporting this important event.*

*The Phonathon is the Stuyvesant PA's only fund-raising event. The money raised is used to support the school in many ways: upgrading computer facilities, maintaining networks and PC's, purchasing non-traditional textbooks, funding the Speech & Debate and the Math teams, supporting math and science research projects, supplying uniforms for the sports teams and much more.*

*Because of the World Trade Center disaster, Stuyvesant will be facing many unanticipated expenses. As a result,*

*your contribution now is even more critical to the school. If*
*you have not already done so – or would like to add to*
*your earlier gift – please consider writing a check today.*
*Please send your donation to keep our school the*
*special place it is for our very talented kids. Checks*
*should be made payable to the SHS Parents' Association*
*and mailed to: Stuyvesant High School Parents'*
*Association, P.O. Box 3531, Church Street Station, New*
*York, NY 10008-3531.*
*— Donovan Moore, Treasurer*[xlii]

In the tense calm that preceded the storm of returning
to the school building, I reflected on the past month:

## The Days Since

In Union Square, a shrine appears
and then another 'til the place
attracts reporters who report
its volunteers' hard work and grace.
A fireman with a haunted look
sits on the bench, his eyes rimmed red.
A woman asks him, "Coffee?  Bagel?"
Without a word, he shakes his head.
Around, a wall of Wanted posters,
"wanted" in that other sense;
the Missing, all so very young.
The pictures stay up on the fence
for weeks, for who will tear them down?
Who'd commit that sacrilege?
And yet one night, somebody does
when hope takes its last breath.  It was,
in retrospect, a far-fetched dream
that anybody would be found
and nursed to health when a million tons
of stuff had crumbled to the ground.

A fire truck, not red but beige

with dust in which someone has written,
"God bless the New York Fire Department." Someone else has drawn a heart.
Across the street, the rectory,
where Father Mychal combed his hair,
they said at his memorial,
and raced downtown, to die in prayer.

T-shirts needed! Dogfood! Boots!
AOL provides a list,
all obsolete; they're overwhelmed
downtown. The chance is sorely missed
by millions who want to help out
and be part of this aweful thing.
For nothing matters next to this.
"God Bless America" they sing
at services all over town,
at meetings of the PTA,
at school, in concert on TV,
they sing from sea to shining sea.

The weeks go on and still the fire
burns. At Fulton Street the smell
still greets whoever's on the train
and says, "Ascend and witness Hell."
Upstairs the crowd stands quietly
and takes it in. The tired cops
sigh, "All right, move it; that's enough,"
to tourists snapping photo ops.
For foreigners are less appalled,
they, never having known it when.
Its metal's bent like willow branches.
The church clock's stopped at five to ten.
W-T-C, those letters,
now a code for grief and fear;
when I was studying music they
stood for the Well-Tempered Clavier.
A few blocks down, at Trinity,

the ancient graveyard's buried, itself,
in dust.  Another wrenching sign:
Its clock is stopped at five to nine.

Home is no relief, indeed
it fuels the burning energy
that drives us to consume more facts,
here, life is centered on TV.
The people falling upside down,
A man says he stayed in the room
by clinging to the doorknob which
saved him from the fierce vacuum.
A man and woman holding hands
fall - lovers?  strangers?  who cares, now? -
willing, finally, to greet
Death, just to get out of the heat.

The cast of characters comes on:
Rumsfeld, grim, tightlipped, thank God,
Powell and Fleischer, jauntier
as they joust with the press.  It's odd
how recent enemies are heroes,
Giuliani, for example
and former wits are reverent
towards our formerly witless President.
No one ridicules him now.
Indeed, he's less ridiculous.
If he said, "Pakistanians" now
no one would make such a fuss.
He gears us up for what's in store
This is a whole new kind of war.
The women, Paula Zahn, Queen Noor,
at one a.m. her time, Amanpour
reporting from Islamabad
in khaki, like a Sabra, say.
"She has a son, you know,"
"She does?  But where is she from, anyway?"
"Eat dinner out!  Go spend your money!"

they tell us. "See a play!  A game!"
"Don't let the bastards get you down!"
(And don't buy Middle Eastern honey.)
"Be careful of suspicious mail!
Don't touch it, move it; leave the room!
It could contain an anthrax powder!
Call 911!" You can't assume
the world's a friendly place these days.
Despite the work of CIA,
the FBI's half million tips,
we're speeding towards Apocalypse.

New Yorkers soon are introduced
to war and its accoutrements:
Gas masks, filters, body suits;
an unaccustomed vigilance.
We acquire expertise
in germs and chemicals right quick:
Sarin, hemorrhagic virus;
meanwhile, a little Arabic.
A money system based on trust
that leaves no trace, the East's hawala;
schools that feed while they instill
a willingness to die for Allah.
We're not so loved as we had thought.
The world prepares for years of war
as oppressed people rise protesting,
"We won't take it anymore!"
In China, the disaster footage
is seen as just another thriller
interspersed with scenes from films
found on the shelf, next to Godzilla.
In Pakistan, the angry mob
protests American arrogance.
From Malaysia to Nigeria
many think we've had our recompense.
Especially the Taliban
who escort foreign journalists

to show them what the angry mob'll
avenge:  The mile miss outside Kabul.

Tuesday morning:  To the doctor.
After all, life must go on.
"Oh by the way, could I have Cipro?"
The doctor, adamantly con,
however, thinks I am in error
to give in to those guys whose aim
is not just to destroy and kill
but also to instill in us, terror.

The city's quieter, subdued.
Where did everybody go?
Will we be quarantined?  Cut off?
Do they know something we don't know?
I walk down to the water's edge.
A child places a bouquet
at a shrine outside the park
where I used to bring my son to play.
A picture rests against the fence
to show the viewer where the World
Trade Center stood before that day
when we all lost our innocence.

## ONE BIG THING

"Please don't go to school tomorrow," I pleaded with Alex on Monday in the first of many such role-reversing conversations.

Alex shrugged. Sure, what the hell? Skip school and not get flak for it? Pay dirt.

The morning of October 9, according to the news reports that broadcast later that day, was an excited one. The much touted "return to normalcy" [sic] was on. Sound the trumpets.

A week before, Borough of Manhattan Community College, located katty corner to Stuyvesant, had reopened with barely a nod from the press. This contrast with the attention bestowed on the trophy school would become the source of some tension between the two institutions before they joined forces against the mightier enemies confronting both of them.

In fact, the triumphal focus on Stuy came at the expense of the kids who were used as mascots for the environment downtown. Indeed, ironically, the kids of BMCC may have gotten a marginally better deal: While their filtration system was said to be 80% effective, Stuyvesant's was only 10% effective until the end of January, which coincided with the period during which the fires burned. (At that point, it was reported to have been upgraded to 40% effectiveness.)[xliii]

The media, those lean and hungry watchdogs, lulled into the docility of lapdogs, ate out of the government's hand, interviewing the intrepid high-schoolers, symbols of New York's renewal. Most people swallowed the sugar-coated poison. As one parent put it, "I don't think they'd let the kids back in if it was unhealthy."

For the next several months, adolescent rebellion took an unusual turn as Alex and I re-enacted the following conversation:

41

*Me (begging): Please don't go to school.*
*Alex: I will go to school.*

The tug of war ratcheted up another notch after an extracurricular teacher had a talk with him that was half threat, half wink and a nod. "My doctor doesn't think I should be in the building either," the teacher explained, "but I'm here. My sister says she saw a news report in California about the air and told me not to go back too."

These conversations did not seem to me persuasive arguments for the teacher to be prodding or cajoling the students to attend her practice sessions in a toxic environment.

But if Alex hadn't done his homework, I was in luck.

This unholy mother-son alliance, which I kept from Kevin until Alex finally left Stuyvesant, caused some tsk-tsking among my amateur shrink friends.

But it wasn't just Ground Zero that was the problem; the school also had the World Trade Center site on its north doorstep. In violation of state law as well as the federal Racketeering Influenced and Corrupt Practices Act, the Office of Emergency Management had deemed Stuyvesant's "backyard" an appropriate site for the barge where much of the World Trade Center debris was brought before being hauled to its final resting place in Staten Island or beyond.

As if that wasn't egregious enough, the barge operation also precluded evacuation of the building to the north. If there was another terrorist attack downtown, the kids would be obliged to run towards it, rather than away.

"It's just temporary," agency representatives assured parents and residents who objected.

"Everyone has to make sacrifices," scolded Giuliani grimly, his sleeves rolled up as though he'd been digging through the rubble.  He did not spell out what those sacrifices might entail for developing kids.

But the word of the day was "emergency," an oft-cited term whose meaning was hazy.  For what sort of emergency could it have been after the first two to three weeks, when the hope of finding survivors was itself laid to rest?  However, in the shock and awe of those early days, anything goes, especially when you have the whole world cheering you on as Mr. Giuliani, soon to be knighted and anointed Time Magazine's Man of the Year, did.

The umbrella term "emergency" provided a sort of sovereign immunity that allowed the government to override such "speculative" considerations as long term health consequences, just as these days, it is being used to trump civil liberties or the long-term economic consequences of quantitative easing.

With the barge parked on our doorstep came an entourage of diesel vehicles: a crane and trucks that made hundreds of trips per day.

I made my own maiden voyage – onto environmental websites, to research diesel:

*Diesel has 40 toxic air contaminants, ranging in alphabetical order from acetaldehyde to xylene isomers:[xliv]3*

*Toluene, lead and cadmium are known to cause cancer, reproductive toxicity or birth defects.[xlv]*

*Benzene leads to disorders of the blood and blood forming tissues.*

*Dioxins are toxic to the immune and reproductive systems as well as being highly carcinogenic.*

*Formaldeyde causes asthma.*

---

3 The links provided in this list, as elsewhere, are current rather than the original ones of 2001.

*Sulfur dioxide causes permanent pulmonary impairment.*

*[D]iesel emissions account for almost 80% of the estimated lifetime cancer risk associated with outdoor hazardous air pollutant exposures.*[xlvi]

The playing fields of Stuyvesant had become a toxic dump.

I sent these findings on to the Parents' Association Executive Board as well as to other potentially sympathetic parents and media outlets that might be inclined to pay attention. After all, news anchor Kaity Tong was rumored to be a Stuy parent.[xlvii] (Oddly, that rumor seems to have become reality only several years later.)[xlviii] The updates may have paid off; a friend said she heard mention on the news of "concern" at the school.

To "prove" the safety of the building's environment, Schools Chancellor Harold Levy, with some fanfare, temporarily moved his office onto the premises. One freshwoman took advantage of the opportunity to tell the Chancellor she didn't feel safe inhaling the air downtown.

"If you leave now," he responded, "you can't come back."

She stayed.

By the end of the week, the Chancellor himself was gone.

In February of 2002, that freshwoman got headaches which she attributed to the need for new glasses. She was diagnosed with pseudotumor cerebrii and required a spinal tap to reduce the buildup of fluid in her brain. Her mother learned that the condition may have resulted from elevated levels of lead at the school.[xlix]

As for the Board of Ed's stand vis à vis the barge, when the Parents' Association wrote a report mentioning the possible effects of exposure to diesel, Deputy Schools Chancellor David Klasfeld responded, "I can only conclude, from the report's use of sensationalistic language, (e.g. "Diesel fumes are carcinogenic") that the intent of this report is not to provide parents with useful information but rather, to cause further stress and divisiveness to the Stuyvesant community and to damage the school's missions for educational excellence... nor does the report present any evidence or exposure data to support these specious claims."[1]

I hadn't given up on boarding schools since a prime target for future attacks was thought to be the subway. I would ask my mother to pay for the school. She'd been saving all her life for a rainy day, not only for herself but also for my brother and me. Surely the aftermath of September 11 qualified.

The schools were sympathetic, heartbreakingly so. I made an appointment to take Alex to the most likely candidate, Northfield Mount Herman, for their Open House on October 27.


Meanwhile, some residents in the area had become skeptical of the EPA's assurances and hired independent contractors to test for asbestos.

*One sample taken from the rooftop of a building near City Hall, about 10 blocks from the World Trade Center site, contained 4.5% asbestos, according to Eastern Analytical Services Inc., a laboratory in Elmsford, N.Y. Samples taken from a windowsill of the same building showed 2.5% asbestos. [1% is the threshold level considered dangerous, and that's for intact materials rather than dust.] The laboratory conducted the tests for a New York real-estate company that didn't want to be named...*

*Community Board 1, representing several neighborhoods in southern Manhattan, including Battery Park City, brought in two industrial-chemical consultants,*

*Eric Chatfield and John Kominski, last week to collect dust and air samples...*

*[T]he two consultants and [Community Board 1 Chairwoman Madelyn] Wils sneaked into an apartment in Battery Park City and one on Warren Street, some 10 blocks north of the site of the twin towers, to take samples...[li]*

*...They found high levels of asbestos in many of the samples, and recommended that all WTC dust be treated as asbestos-contaminated unless tested and shown to be asbestos-free.[lii]*

Executive Director of the New York Environmental Law and Justice Project Joel Kupferman had just finished working on the West Nile virus case in which Mayor Rudy Giuliani had decreed the spraying of the insecticide Malathion around town to combat what was touted as that year's potential scourge. Cops assigned to keep people out of the parks had wondered, "If it's not safe for the public, how come it's ok for us?" After they got sick, they came to know Joel. A week after 9/11, they called him again.

"You know that yellow tape they had at Chambers Street?" Joel says. "These cops were three or four blocks further away than that, supposedly past the danger zone. Some of them were coughing up blood. Their sergeant complained on their behalf. The police department transferred him over a hundred times, in retaliation.

'But the government did the same thing in the anthrax case at the Post Office. They put yellow tape around the contaminated machine. Then they put everyone back to work next to it.

'Of course, that's not what they did with the anthrax at the Senate. There, they evacuated the building.

'The cops got me onto Ground Zero. At the relief stations, they were handing out cigarettes. Obviously, health experts weren't running the show here.

'There was tufted material all over, like wild brush out West. We sent samples to the lab in Virginia that ATC [one of the main companies taking samples downtown] used. They were over 5% asbestos. The asbestos guy at the EPA said it wasn't his department because it wasn't a demolition or construction site; it was a new phenomenon.

'Anyway, asbestos wouldn't explain the coughing. So we tested for fiberglass and found 90%. I took the results to [Daily News reporter] Juan Gonzalez and we FOIA'ed [demanded under the Freedom of Information Act] EPA for their results. That's where [Gonzalez'] article *Toxic Zone* came from.

'When [NYELJP Policy Analyst Kimberly Flynn] and I FOIA'ed the City Department of Environmental Protection, we got a message that the information was unavailable, 'due to ongoing criminal investigation.'

'Fiberglass is considered to be 'likely to be carcinogenic' by the National Toxicology Program to which EPA and OSHA belong. When I asked EPA about the fiberglass we found, they said, 'Well, it's just *likely*.

'There was lots of fiberglass at [a particular building] but the landlord told the contractor not to test for it. And things went on in other buildings that will never come out because the tenants signed a gag order.

'Everyone wanted to know what we found. I had six detectives from the Detectives' Endowment Association asking me questions. They were upset the FBI were getting better equipment than they were. One of the detectives was pregnant and working at Fresh Kills. Do you believe it? The detectives had to inspect the dust up close.

'I asked them if anyone had told them not to take their clothes home. That upset them the most; not that they were in danger but that they'd put their families in danger. A welder's mother washed his clothes every night and ended up going to the hospital.

'No one trusted the government. Federal marshalls outside the Federal Court House were asking me what was in the air. Judges were thinking about suing because they weren't allowed to wear masks in court. Even low level workers at EPA were coming to us."

On October 23, the Law Project sent out a press release concerning EPA's response to their Freedom of Information Act request:

[Sulfur dioxide levels included] ...*a spectacular 0.9 ppm [parts per million] reading which is considered outright 'hazardous... Under EPA's own guidelines, levels of sulfur dioxide as high as these trigger public announcements warning asthmatics and people with heart problems to stay indoors. Yet we did not hear EPA or the media warning people working or living in the areas near where these readings were obtained about this dangerous gas...*

*Benzene was found in amounts over the occupational (OSHA) limit of 1 ppm on several days... The EPA should explain that while the amounts of these toxic chemicals were usually measured at levels below OSHA standards, these standards are set for the eight-hour work day. People who work longer than eight hours on the pile or who live near ground zero are exposed for much longer periods. And those individuals who both live and work in the area are exposed continuously.*

*More importantly, the OSHA standards are set to protect healthy adults. They are not intended for protection of children or people with certain health problems.*

*PCBs & DIOXINS EPA's data on PCBs and dioxins appears to contain errors or omissions. For example, there were days on which PCBs were not found in the air and water while, on the same day, very high levels of some PBs [sic] were found in water run-off the area [sic.]*

*FIBER GLASS. The EPA did not test for fiberglass at all. Yet the dust samples we took ranged from 10 to 75 percent fiber glass...the fibers are usually coated with a thin layer of formaldehyde-containing resin. In addition, the National Toxicology Program lists respirably size glass fibers as "reasonably anticipated" to cause cancer.[liii]*

"Juan and I were pretty surprised that everyone else wasn't doing the same thing. The media didn't FOIA. But after Bhopal, the public's right-to-know laws were expanded.

There are things you don't hear about. Like the World Trade Center had a shooting range [belonging to the Secret Service] with millions of rounds of ammunition.[liv] And you want to know about radioactive material? There's a rumor there were two Stinger missiles in there.[lv] Also, I found out how the chemicals at one chemical company were stored. You want to guess? Alphabetically. Think about it. You could have 'dynamite' next to 'detonator.'"[4]

On October 26, Gonzalez published a front page article under the headline TOXIC NIGHTMARE AT DISASTER SITE which explained the astronomical levels of contaminants downtown. Benzene had reached 40 times the occupational limit. Dust had been found to contain 5% asbestos, five times the amount that triggers an abatement. And surely 5% of a normal amount of

---

[4] Another little known fact is that "a US Customs lab had in its inventory thousands of pounds of arsenic, lead, mercury, chromium, and other toxic substances." http://www.historycommons.org/timeline.jsp?env_imp_gener al_topic_areas=env_imp_WTCworkers&timeline=enviromental _impact_911_attacks_tmln

dust is not equivalent to 5% of hundreds of thousands of tons of dust. (In her report of 2004, Suzanne Mattei of the Sierra Club quotes US Geological Survey scientist Greg Meeker's assessment: "[M]ost of the six million square feet of masonry, five million square feet of painted surfaces, seven million square feet of flooring, 600,000 square feet of window glass, 200 elevators, and everything inside came down as dust – leaving only the towers' 200,000 tons of structural steel."[lvi] In addition, it should be noted that the 1% standard for asbestos is for an intact material such as a pipe, on the assumption that the escape of even a couple of fibers poses a risk as they can be inhaled. But when the intact material has become pulverized, all of it potentially respirable, the same standard clearly doesn't obtain.)

After Gonzalez' article was published, Whitman called the paper to complain. They responded by affording her space to present her side of the story. For the next several years, Gonzalez' articles were subjected to greater scrutiny[lvii] while the metropolitan editor, Richard Pienciak, lost his position.[lviii] In 2007, The Daily News was awarded the Pulitzer Prize for its compassionate coverage of illness among Ground Zero workers, which was instrumental in the ultimate passage of the James Zadroga 9/11 Health and Compensation Act. Still overlooked, however, were Gonzalez' earlier warnings when they might have made a far more significant difference by preventing some of those same illnesses.

"Juan and I got a lot of flak," Joel Kupferman reflected later, "but no one ever said we were wrong. They just said we were alarmist."

I showed the article to Alex, who pushed it aside.

In the hierarchy of contaminants, asbestos reigned supreme, at least in the minds of the public and the EPA. The other contaminants were long words but with fewer clear associations for a lay audience.

The World Trade Center was built with hundreds of tons of asbestos.[lix] There would have been more, but for a ban on the material by the New York City Council in 1971.[lx] For despite assertions about occupational exposure and safe per cents, "[a]vailable evidence supports the conclusion that there is no safe level of exposure to asbestos."[lxi] And "[t]he EPA's own experts as well as physicians at the CDC and private research centers have shown that a 'single burst, heavy dose' of asbestos could be enough to cause... lethal disease."[lxii]

In January, 2002, an article by Andrew Schneider in the St. Louis Post-Dispatch, Joseph Pulitzer's muckraking journal, would elaborate on the EPA's misleading dismissal of "trace amounts" of the contaminant. Schneider quotes Dr. Jerrold Abraham, director of environmental and occupational pathology at Upstate Medical University in Syracuse, who states that for "pure chrysotile asbestos, there are 10 billion or more fibers per gram, or about a fifth of a teaspoon."[lxiii]

The same day that Gonzalez' article was published, the Stuyvesant Parents' Association Environmental Health and Safety Committee wrote a letter to parents:

*....Despite promises... The Board of Education has not*

*[1.] met with the manufacturer of the ventilation system to determine if or how the system can be retrofitted to accommodate HEPA filters (High-Efficiency Particulate Arrestance filters, the only kind rated to protect against asbestos fibers.)*

*[2.] been unsuccessful [sic] in moving or improving the truck and barge operation.*

*[3.] notif[ied] the PA and more importantly... the parents or children that recent monitoring results inside Stuyvesant indicate levels of lead and particulate matter above regulatory levels on some occasions.*

*[4.] provided the PA with certification from any government agency that the building is safe for occupancy, nor has it provided various safety protocols or written procedures.*

*Despite promises,*

*"2. ...the pool was not drained or cleaned prior to students' return. [We would later learn that swimming in the pool had led to a trip to the emergency ward for a student who hadn't had a similar asthma attack in seven years.]*

*3. the bridge [leading to the school] is not being regularly cleaned to help prevent contaminants from being carried into the building...*

*8. We also learned that the EPA did not release to the public some monitoring results that appear to contradict or weaken its assertions of environmental safety. EPA data obtained by environmental activists using Freedom of Information Act requests appear to show more frequent and higher measurements of asbestos, heavy metals, PCBs, dioxin, benzene and other toxics in and around the World Trade Center area than were previously acknowledged."[lxiv]*

Also, after high readings of $CO_2$ in several classrooms, the Board of Ed had increased the amount of outside air entering the school.[lxv]

Under normal circumstances, an increase in "fresh" air would be standard operating procedure. But these were not normal circumstances and what should have been fresh air wasn't.

*October 27, 2001   Northfield Mount Herman,*
*Massachusetts*

Gold trees under a deep, autumn sky. Football, cookout. Bright kids, one of whom even breakdances, Alex's passion.

Nothing doing, Alex says. "I want to stay at Stuyvesant."

"I thought you meant he would go to boarding school next year," his father says. "No, I don't want him to leave home yet."

"But he shouldn't stay at Stuyvesant," I say.

"Well, where are you going to send him? To the local crap school? No, no. If you can find a school that has the same educational value as Stuyvesant, fine. Otherwise, he's staying at Stuyvesant."

Two against one. Alex is staying in the city. At least if anything terrible happens to him as a result, I will be able to tell myself I showed him the best of the alternatives.

I call public schools that my ex- might accept as Stuy-equivalent.

"I'm sorry, we don't accept transfers at this late date," they say.

What about the GED?

You have to be past high school age.

A friend asks why I have such a deep need to be in control. Is it because Alex will soon be going to college and I can't bear to let him go? But I am mindful of what my own therapist once said: If you overstep, Alex could resent it so much, he'll rebel in destructive ways.

Meanwhile, I take driving lessons in case we have to evacuate. Or move, which is looking like an increasingly good idea. Only a New Yorker could have gotten this far in life without having gone through that all-American rite of passage.

In the ranks of the Stuyvesant PA Executive Board, some members are unhappy with the results of the air tests performed at Stuy and consequently, with the Board of Ed, while others don't want to rock the boat.

There is also a widening rift over what to tell the general parent body. A powerful faction is of the, "Don't frighten the horses" school of thought. And in retaliation for the disclosures to parents about Board of Ed neglect, it is said, a well-connected member of the PA contacts the New York Times. In the next Sunday edition which includes the special 9/11 issue of the Stuyvesant newspaper, the Spectator, nestled among the searing accounts and photographs from that day is an article entitled, "An 'A' for Air Quality."[lxvi]

The article quotes the PA's independent contractor, Howard Bader, assuring the Stuy community, "The tests so far have really scientifically proven that everything is all right... It's good data. There really was minimal contamination of the school... No lead has been detected in the air at all, and... since lead paint and other products containing lead have been illegal since 1961 – well before the World Trade Center complex was built – none is expected to be found."[lxvii]

Tests of the school's ventilation system at the end of the year would find thirty times the legal limit of lead for floors. (There is no standard for lead in ventilation systems.)

"Bader suggested that many symptoms that members of the school community are experiencing may be psychosomatic or induced by the stress of returning to the building for the first time since the September 11 tragedy."[lxviii]

The article closes with a quote from Donovan Moore, Treasurer for the Parents' Association: "Sometimes the most dangerous thing in the air is hysteria. And [hysteria] has been happening at Stuy." (See Hystericalmothers.com, Appendix W.)

(Google is not helpful on the main reporter for the story, Laura Krug, who'd won a Gold key for a short story the previous year[lxix] and in her senior year, would work with the conservative Hoover Institution[lxx] whose media fellow, Paul Sperry, is the author of "Infiltration: How Muslim Spies and Subversives Have Penetrated Washington."[lxxi] The other reporter, Abigail Deutsch, would go on to graduate from Yale and become an award-winning poet.)[lxxii]

*November 6, 2001*
*Letter from PA in response to the Board of Ed's*
*November 5 letter*

*Mr. David Klasfeld...*

*I would like to review several of the items in your response as, unfortunately, there are still several issues that have not been addressed.*

*Certification:*
*To-date, we have not received certification by State and Federal air monitoring agencies confirming that the building is safe to resume classes in. In her October 5th letter to parents, Dr. Terry Marx had represented that such certification had been obtained. At our meeting of October 30th, Joe Nappi had told us that he would get back to us on this item.*

*Request to Modify Air Monitoring and Indoors Sampling:*
*We understand from Howard Bader that these items have been agreed upon with Mr. Orlan. However, Mr. Bader has only received a draft protocol. Please provide him with the final protocol as soon as possible.*

*HVAC System Operation and Filtration:*
*We are aware that pleated filters are being used for the main air-handling units. However, based on the levels of*

*particulate matter inside the school, they are not deemed to be adequate by Mr. Bader.*

*Regarding the 300 unit ventilators, at our meeting of October 30th, we were informed by Mr. Orlan that the ordering of pleated filters for such units "fell through the cracks" and was never put through. On October 30th, two unit ventilators (one on the South side and one on the North side of the school) were fitted with new 4-ply ring filters recommended by Mr. Bader on a test basis. It was agreed that they would be tested and evaluated for one week.*

*On November 2nd, at the completion of the test period, Mr. Bader informed us and Mr. Orlan that the 4-ply filters have demonstrated some improvement (approximately 20%) in reducing indoor airborne particulate levels when compared to existing filters used throughout the school. The mechanical performance of the unit ventilators does not appear to be negatively impacted by the new filters. This marginal improvement indicates there may be significant air by-pass around the filters in the unit ventilators.*

*Mr. Bader requested of Mr. Orlan that, as an interim measure, the BOE install 4-ply ring filters in all unit ventilators in the school as soon as possible. Based on Mr. Bader's discussions with the manufacturer, we understand that 300 such filters can be obtained within a week.*

*As Mr. Bader explained to you last evening, based on the particulate levels we are still getting even with the 4-ply filters, these filters clearly are not a satisfactory permanent solution. We wish to confirm our agreement of last evening that the BOE will immediately bring in an Engineering Consultant to evaluate a modification or upgrade of the HVAC system to enable utilization of HEPA filtration in order to reduce or eliminate the intrusion of outdoor contaminants into the school...*

*Further, on the HVAC system, as I had brought to your attention in my letter to you of October 19th, **the HVAC***

**air distribution duct system was never cleaned or tested after September 11, and prior to reoccupancy.**[lxxiii] *[emphasis mine.]*

*November 13, 2001*
*Parents' Association meeting*

This is the first time I've been in the Stuyvesant building since last year.

Posters, quilts, projects from art classes from around the country cover the walls with messages that are wrenching but cathartic to read. Alex and friends claim indifference but when a gift package of notebooks and pens arrives, they descend on the contents like jackals.

In the auditorium, an array of government officials and experts fan across the stage ready to answer questions and, more to the point, assuage our "concerns."

Among them, Dr. Stephen Levin of Mt. Sinai. The son of a cabinet maker, he devotes much of his practice to union workers. (The New York Times' Robin Finn describes his tie adorned with salamanders, a gift of the asbestos workers' union. You can't get it at Bloomingdale's, she says.) His research on the interaction between asbestos and smoking (described in Dr. Marjorie Clarke's testimony in the next chapter) is a virtually unique study of synergy, whose effects EPA entirely ignore.

He has undertaken a study of Ground Zero workers and volunteers but it will be months before his team learns that their symptoms, contrary to expectations, do not go away with treatment. Beyond Ground Zero, Levin and other experts thus still maintain – despite the opening sentence of his Daily News obituary in 2012, "He knew how bad it would be"[lxxiv] – short-term asbestos exposure is not likely to result in serious health problems.[lxxv]

Dr. Paolo Toniolo from the New York University School of Medicine[lxxvi] talks about a study he hopes to perform on the students and the amount of money he still needs, $100,000, to perform it.

"How would that benefit our children?" Marilena asks. She is an accomplished professional and must be furious to pose such a direct question.

Dr. Toniolo is unfased as one might expect from a man who has the sang-froid to show up at a meeting of justifiably anxious people and suggest he'd like to use their children as guinea pigs – oh, and by the way, would they be interested in giving him the money to do so? But at least he admits there could be problems.

David Klasfeld from the Board of Education is back: "My daughter went to Stuyvesant," he begins, as though that makes him one of us, before presenting a sober-sounding talk in his usual, "Don't worry your little heads," tone.

EPA Spokeswoman Bonnie Bellow opens her talk: "I'm a Stuyvesant parent who just went through the college application process and I'm living proof that you can get through it."

She pauses for chuckles of recognition. We are not amused.

To put our supposed hysteria in perspective, she assures us, "You take a risk every time you bite into an apple."

That sounds suspiciously biblical but I assume she's referring to a scare within living memory over the apple pesticide alar rather than to loss of innocence.

There are a couple of oases in an otherwise dismal landscape. Dave Newman, an industrial hygienist at the New York Committee for Occupational Safety and Health and father of a Stuyvesant freshwoman, speaks about the dangers of the contaminants in the air.

"I think it irresponsible to compare breathing the air downtown to biting an apple," he says in a deviation into dissent that is rare for that stage on that fateful evening.

Then there is lawyer Joel Kupferman, who will become one of our strongest allies. Lacking a trace of the slickness that many associate with his profession, he looks more like a New York version of Rumpole of the Bailey. I imagine his office crowded with four foot high piles of papers and old coffee cups. If he didn't specialize in environmental law, cigarette stubs would also figure in the picture.

"Mayor Giuliani has declared himself prince not only over the laws of the land but also over the laws of physics. He has decreed that no molecule of contamination shall go past the yellow crime tape at Chambers St."

He makes sense, anyway, this lefty lawyer. (One of Joel's many admirers describes their first meeting thus: "I was at a forum about the environment where everyone was lying, of course. Then there was this Hobbit on the stage. But he was the only one telling the truth." Joel says the last time he was in criminal court, the judge mistook him for the defendant. But since getting recognized by so many news organizations covering the environmental aftermath of 9/11, he's become more elegant.)

Time for audience questions.

"I have a healthy child," a woman says. "He's six feet and a football player. Since October 9, he's been diagnosed with chronic sinusitis. He takes Augmentin, uses three inhalers and he's on steroids that could damage his liver."

"While the air is safe," Klasfeld says, "there are some people who are particularly sensitive. We recommend that if your child is sick, you take him to the doctor."

"Particulate Matter 2.5 has been high," says someone else. "The kids shouldn't be breathing that day in, day out."

"P.M. 2.5 is just a complicated name for dust," counters Klasfeld.

Howard Bader, the Parents' Association's consultant, adds that P.M. 2.5 is nothing to worry about because, "God willing," it's so small, your body gets rid of it. He makes the stuff sound like neutrinos, those subatomic particles that sail right through you without ever encountering anything.

"And you don't have to worry about P.M. 10 because you cough it right out again."

That's if you cough. But even the sickest kids aren't coughing all day. They do, however, breathe all day.

No one contradicts him. Those of us who think his line of argument sounds a little Pollyanna-ish still don't have the data to back up our suspicions.

The overall message is that we parents are "traumatized," (read: "irrational.") Anyone of a mind to hold a protest, as a handful of us are, is stifled by the opposition while potential allies view us as loose cannons. Among the latter prevails the belief that playing nicely will get us somewhere.

The sages' responses downplay the question driving that evening: What are the long-term effects of this exposure? ("You can hide the fire," Stuydad Dr. Tariq Malek later quotes Uncle Remus, "but how you gonna hide the smoke?")

"What about if we want to move our child from Stuy temporarily?" someone else asks. "Can we put them back in when the air improves?"

Principal Stanley Teitel takes this one.

"No!" He leans forward prognathously, prepared for a fight.

"Why not?"

"Because they might not have covered the material." Teitel has a rasping voice at the best of times. Now he is barking.

"Do you mean to tell me," asks a man with a paunch the size of a small beachball, "that if I put my daughter in Trinity you won't take her back because you don't think Trinity's as good a school as Stuyvesant?"

Trinity is one of the highest rated schools in the country with numerous Ph.D's on the faculty.[lxxvii] Parent John McEnroe once coached the tennis team. I know, because Alex's team played against them in seventh grade and got creamed.

"Maybe," Teitel returns gamely.

Beachball shakes his head.

More tales of illness: new onset asthma, resurgence of asthma that had lain dormant for years and a freshly coined diagnosis, "chemical bronchitis."

"Never heard of it," asserts Klasfeld as he will continue to maintain whenever the subject comes up again over the course of the year.

I raise my hand.

"What about this?" I pan the audience with Juan Gonzalez' tower-high headline.

"Don't show that article," Dr. George Thurston winces. "That's yellow journalism. Those levels are spikes."

Like Dr. Toniuolo, Thurston is from New York University, the value of whose property in Manhattan, which included at least one Ground Zero school building, nearly tripled between 1992 and 2006, to half a billion dollars.[lxxviii] In February, 2002, Thurston would testify to the Senate Committee on Environment and Public Works:

*Only trace amounts of asbestos were found in our samples. The less than one percent that was as PM2.5, or the particles that would reach deepest in the lung, was found to have a neutral pH, [contrast with Dr. Cate Jenkins' "Complaint and Additional Evidence of pH Fraud..." referenced above] with no detectable asbestos or fiberglass. Thus, while our analyses are consistent with the government's conclusion that the WTC dust is not likely to have short or long-term serious health impacts on otherwise healthy local residents, we found that it is very*

61

*irritating and capable of causing the symptoms reported by many residents.*[lxxix]

"You think all these levels in here are just flukes?" I ask, incredulous.

Thurston's interpretation signals the debut of an argument the government will resort to at scientific conferences for the next several years. Indeed, variants of it will also be used to wave away concerns about other environmental disasters, such as BP in the Gulf of Mexico, and even about the economy. Known variously as "spikes" or "outliers," and managed by a technique known as "averaging," (aggregating with tests of unaffected areas)[5] inconvenient data can be made to dissipate to the point of vanishing. In certain contexts, exposures are averaged temporally, rather than spatially, over a lifetime.

"O.K. you've had your turn."[6]

---

[5] "The human body, however, doesn't average. When the lungs are exposed to too much water, you drown. When someone overdoses on drugs, the human body doesn't say, "I'll average this out over a lifetime." You die of an overdose." Appendix S

How Science Was Abused to Perpetrate Lies After 9/11: A Cautionary Tale for the Approaching Peak Oil Disaster

[6] In 2007, EPA chemist Dr. Cate Jenkins released an email exchange between herself and Dr. Thurston.

Cate Jenkins
08/26/2003 08:38 AM
To: thurston@env.med.nyu.edu
Subject: Hey, George ---------
- - - - - - - - - - - - - - - - - - - - - - - -
George, I saw your quote in Newsday, 8/23 or 8/24 where you claimed that you told people at the time that everything was too preliminary to make conclusions. See attached early statement of yours in the British Medical Journal where you

said conclusively that levels were not of concern. Notice that in my 7/4/03 report I quote your Br. Med. J. statement in Section B.

Am debating whether to circulate an email to everyone saying that your recent quote this week in Newsday really is inaccurate and does not reflect what you were telling citizens at the time.

Yours truly,

Cate

---

"George D. Thurston, Sc.D."
<thurston@env.med.nyu.edu>
08/26/2003 12:19 PM
To: Cate Jenkins/DC/USEPA/US@EPA
Subject: Re: Hey, George ---------
- - - - - - - - - - - - - - - - - - - - - - -

I always said that the declaration that the "Air was safe to breath" was premature. Check my statement at the Senate hearing for one, which is a much more public forum than the journal article, and earlier on.

---

Cate Jenkins
08/26/2003 12:38 PM
To: "George D. Thurston, Sc.D."
<thurston@env.med.nyu.edu>
Subject: Re: Hey, George ---------
- - - - - - - - - - - - - - - - - - - - - - -

Really, George? You are defending yourself by saying the British Medical Journal really wasn't read by many people, but what you said at a Senate hearing was more widely disseminated, and thus we should excuse the British Medical Journal piece? Then what do you say about these other quotations from you, below, which were all much more widely distributed than your testimony at the Senate hearing?

Cate

[abstracts of the various earlier press quotations of Dr. Thurston were attached to this email]

---

"George D. Thurston, Sc.D."

<thurston@env.med.nyu.edu>
08/27/2003 10:49 AM
To: Cate Jenkins/DC/USEPA/US@EPA
Subject: Re: Hey, George ---------
- - - - - - - - - - - - - - - - - - - - - - -
As I said, I never stated that the EPA pronouncement was
appropriate, and always said (WELL b4 the Senate hearing)
that it was NOT appropriate 4 her 2 do so at that time, when
the issue came up. George

---

Cate Jenkins
08/27/2003 10:55 AM
To: "George D. Thurston, Sc.D."
<thurston@env.med.nyu.edu>
Subject: Re: Hey, George ---------
- - - - - - - - - - - - - - - - - - - - - - -
George,
It is irrelevant whether you specifically addressed the EPA
pronouncement. It is your own statements on the record that
said that the air was within EPA benchmarks for health
concerns, and your statements that if you yourself felt that
there was anything wrong with the air that you would be
"shouting it from the rooftops" and that the only hazard was
for irritant effects.
Cate

---

"George D. Thurston, Sc.D."
<thurston@env.med.nyu.edu>
08/27/2003 11:10 AM
To: Cate Jenkins/DC/USEPA/US@EPA
Subject: Re: Hey, George ---------
- - - - - - - - - - - - - - - - - - - - - - -
No, that IS the issue discussed in the article that you wrote 2
me about, and that I responded to in my quote.
See below.
George
70
http://www.nynewsday.com/news/local/manhattan/nyc-
epa0823.story

Cate Jenkins
08/27/2003 12:30 PM
To: "George D. Thurston, Sc.D."
<thurston@env.med.nyu.edu>
Subject: Re: Hey, George ---------
- - - - - - - - - - - - - - - - - - - - - - - -
George,
Whatever you said in the 8/22/03 quote is entirely irrelevant
and revisionist, as you well know. You are on record saying
to the public after the 9/11 attacks that the air was below
EPA health benchmarks and that if there were anything
wrong with the air you would be shouting it on the rooftops.
You are on my list, and always have been.
Cate

---

"George D. Thurston, Sc.D."
<thurston@env.med.nyu.edu>
08/27/2003 04:28 PM
To: Cate Jenkins/DC/USEPA/US@EPA
Subject: Re: Hey, George ---------
- - - - - - - - - - - - - - - - - - - - - - - -
What list is that?

---

Cate Jenkins
08/27/2003 04:28 PM
To: "George D. Thurston, Sc.D."
<thurston@env.med.nyu.edu>
Subject: Re: Hey, George ---------
- - - - - - - - - - - - - - - - - - - - - - - -
Guess. [*I believe Cate was referring to her email list. JO*]

---

"George D. Thurston, Sc.D."
<thurston@env.med.nyu.edu>
08/27/2003 04:37 PM
To: Cate Jenkins/DC/USEPA/US@EPA- - - - - - - - - - - - - -
- - - - - - - - -
What do you mean, guess? Why can't you tell me the truth?
What are you hiding?
George
Cate Jenkins

"I don't think our children should be here until we're sure it's safe," says a woman with long, strawberry blond hair. "Unless the Board of Education provides HEPA filters, I think we should strike."

"We're finding that attendance is normal," says Klasfeld. "And there are no unusually high numbers of trips to the nurse."

"My child missed two classes to see the nurse and finally gave up," another woman offers an alternative explanation.

"My child has been ill but he doesn't want to go to the nurse because it isn't cool."

Marilena steps in: "Could we have a show of hands now to see how many parents have children who are showing symptoms?"

According to the PA Status Report:

*...[I]n a letter sent to the parents by the administration, it was indicated that, as of last week, approximately 90*

---

08/27/2003 05:46 PM
To: "George D. Thurston, Sc.D."
<thurston@env.med.nyu.edu>
Subject: Re: Hey, George ---------
- - - - - - - - - - - - - - - - - - - - - - - -

Boy, George, you are starting to sound pretty desperate there. Hiding things and all that.
[Thereafter Dr. Thurston declined to respond to my emails]

To: Senator Hillary Rodham Clinton, Chair, Subcommittee on Superfund and Environmental Health; Congressman Jerrold Nadler; Congresswoman Carolyn Maloney and entitled, COMPLAINT AND ADDITIONAL EVIDENCE OF pH FRAUD BY: USGS, OSHA, ATSDR, NYC, EPA, and EPA-funded scientists; — 1. Falsification of corrosive pH data for WTC dust; — 2. Historical fraud by EPA of hazardous pH levels since 1980. By Dr. Cate Jenkins; EPA; May 6, 2007; http://www.journalof911studies.com/volume/200704/DrJenkinsRequestsSenateInvestigationOnWTCdust.pdf

*students and teachers reported to the physician's office at
Stuyvesant manifesting a variety of symptoms. At our
last PA meeting a show of hands indicated that more than
twice this number was probably more accurate.* "[lxxx]

That's out of only a few hundred parents from a
potential pool of over 6000. And the number of illnesses
would climb as the year progressed. When the PA
conducted their own survey, they found that two thirds
of the hundreds of respondents reported children with
incidences of illness attributable to the World Trade
Center.[lxxxi]

After the meeting, I go up to the strawberry blond
woman and get her email as well as those of other
restless-native types including the "Israeli" woman.

In retrospect, that PA meeting represents the turning-
point that might have been. Monona Rossel, a chemist
who'd acted as advisor to Joel Kupferman and is lauded
by Juan Gonzalez in his book *Fallout: The Environmental
Consequences of the World Trade Center Attack*, had
offered to speak on the panel, an offer I'd
enthusiastically supported. She was knowledgable
enough to have been able to counteract the bromides of
the conflict-of-interest-ridden experts but in the end, for
whatever reason, she was not there.

Thus any fledgling rebels, potential allies whom, from
their pointed questions, I've noted in the crowd, retreat
from the prospect of protest, feeling our numbers lack
sufficient heft. The better part of valor, goes the
reasoning, is to play along with the Board of Education
to stave off a fit of pique in which they might deny us
the crucially needed HEPA filters.

Since EPA has renounced jurisdiction over indoor air,
the Board of Education hires ATC Associates to test
inside the school for a variety of contaminants.

Most levels are deemed acceptable including those for
asbestos, even on November 28, when EPA makes a

special call to Marilena to tell her that the outdoor measurement is 123 – 53 higher than the limit for schools. ATC has a monitor right next to EPA's but they don't register the surge, which raises questions about their other measurements. (Later, residents testify that ATC employees entered their highly contaminated apartments – as determined by independent testing – and said, "I don't see any dust.")

However, isocyanates and tetrachloroethane come back with high readings while elevated lead is found in the cafeteria, where it can be ingested, as well as in the gym, where it can be deeply inhaled. Klasfeld writes to parents: "Lead is only dangerous in occupational-type exposures or when children consume it in lead-based paint."[lxxxii] So lead on rye is fine. And studying isn't an occupation because you don't get paid. As for the occupations of teaching and school maintenance, the Deputy Chancellor is silent.

One day, lead is found in two classrooms. Does the Board of Ed test other classrooms? Do they think that the findings might represent a warning of lead elsewhere in the building as well?

No. They clean the two classrooms. The PA protests until they do more widespread cleaning.

On the subject of the kids' illnesses, Klasfeld opines, "We believe the events of September 11 and its emotional aftermath have contributed to these incidents."

He does not say who is included in the word "we" but one may reasonably assume it isn't the kids' doctors.

However, most troubling is the result for **Particulate Matter 2.5, which is often higher than at Ground Zero.**[lxxxiii]

PM 2.5 is one twentieth the width of a human hair. Thus it's able to bypass the body's defense systems and penetrate to the deep part of the lungs and alveoli where it may cause respiratory damage or cancer. The number of lung cancer deaths from PM 2.5 increases

8% for every ten micrograms.[lxxxiv] And, as with asbestos and other toxics, there's evidence that contrary to what some experts assert, it's the smaller fibers that do the most damage.[lxxxv][7] In addition, its smaller size provides a relatively high surface area to volume ratio, allowing it to adsorb onto its surface more of the toxic chemicals in the debris at the barge.

However, Stuyvesant's filtration system was not built to handle such small PM. In fact, it wasn't built to handle threats to people at all. It filters out only the particulates that would injure the ventilation system itself.

I dream of dust gathering on the walls, as in a Hitchcock film, threatening to choke us all.

Back home, I write to the PA about Klasfeld. "Why do all these people think that just because their kids went to Stuyvesant, they identify with us?"

A reply! From Marilena, forwarding an email from one Rachel Lidov:

"Why does Bonnie Bellow think she can get away with exposing our children to contamination because her child went to Stuyvesant?"

---

[7]   *A new review of research on nanoscale materials suggests that tiny particles are often toxic because of their size and are likely to pose health hazards.*

*Dr. Vyvyan Howard, a pathology specialist at the University of Liverpool who examined results from 27 studies published since 1984, said that the type of material a particle is made of appears to be much less related to how hazardous it is than its size at such small scales.   ETC Group Occasional Paper entitled, "Size Matters! The Case for a Global Moratorium.)" April 14, 2003; Volume 7, No. 1; http://nwrage.org/content/nanotechnology-size-matters-case-global-moratorium*

Marilena is matchmaking.

I also get an email from PA Vice-President May Umeki, responding to my suggestion that the PA should inform the Chinese parents about what their kids are being exposed to. (May is Chinese but married to a Japanese man.) Many of them don't speak English well and so won't be on the internet searching.

"There's going to be a meeting of the PA Executive Board Tuesday," May replies, "and they're open to the community. BTW, what dialect of Chinese do you speak?"

I go to the meeting, calling the "Israeli" woman. (She is actually French but bemused at my mistake. What she most wants to be, it seems, is a New Yorker.) Instead, her husband shows up. He is New Yorker cartoonist Art Spiegelman, author of *Maus*, a Holocaust graphic memoir in which the good guys are depicted as mice and the Nazis, as cats. (His wife, Françoise Mouly, is the Art Director at the magazine.) All evening, he scribbles what might be notes but are more probably drawings of the participants. Will some attendees end up in an illustrated account of Stuy's travails? (The answer, a year later, is Yes, in the Jewish Forward.)

I introduce myself to May; her face falls. (Months later she jokes, "I was so excited; I thought another Chinese mother would be at the meetings. But look at her!")

Like many parents, until now I've ignored the PA Executive Board. Their war chest, amounting to several hundred thousand dollars a year, tends to go to the prestigious Intel competition, the major clubs. It's irrelevant to Alex who wants to be a comedy writer.

But now their power beckons.

When I enter Mount Olympus, the gods are squabbling. Some are outraged at the Board of Ed; others, mindful of the Board's power over their children's college record, remain deferential. As a result, there is discord over what to tell parents.

"My child was traumatized by being at Brooklyn Tech," one father says. "You all are preventing the return to normalcy."[sic]

"Where are the HEPA filters the Board of Ed promised?" asks someone from the other side.

"Give them time," answers one of the smoothe talkers. "This was an unprecedented attack. We have to be reasonable."

"All right, come to order," says Marilena, who commands the unruly pantheon with the authority of Hera. "I have written a letter..."

"You can't do that; it's against the Bylaws," interrupts a parent from the opposition.[8]

"No, it's not – it's right here," responds Marilena, citing Article and Roman numeral. A businesswoman with a Master's degree from the University of Pennsylvania who inspires as much hostility among the opposition as she does admiration among her allies, she has anticipated the argument and even when she hasn't, wields the Bylaws like a master swordswoman.

In her interview of a few years later, Marilena described her relationship to the opposition at that time:

*After [PA Vice-President] Sheldon [Stachel] and I sent the letter to parents [prior to returning to the Stuyvesant building,] the other side tried to establish an Editorial Board to approve any mailing going out. I take the position that it's in violation of the Bylaws. But they vote and the resolution passes. We have another Executive Board meeting. I hand out copies of the Bylaws to everyone and say, "Here's the section." I accuse [a fellow board member] of going behind my back. I take complete control. The revolution is crushed.*

*They continue to undercut me but now it's covert.*

---

[8]  As I didn't take notes for a book during this period, dialogue is reconstructed from memory.

Schools Chancellor Harold O. Levy is scheduled to appear at a breakfast forum at New York Law School. Four of us Stuyparents show up to impress upon him the need to address the conditions at the school.

Levy philosophizes about the "challenge" facing him. "Challenge" is the word *du jour.* Physically challenged. Mentally challenged. The New York Times post-September 11 section is entitled, "A Nation Challenged."

The Chancellor goes on to praise the heroism of the teachers at the elementary schools of Ground Zero, P.S.'s 234, 89 and 150, some of whom are only twenty-five themselves. (It was a child from P.S. 234 who said on September 11, "Teacher, the birds are on fire," while pointing at the people falling out of windows.) He asked them how they kept their charges from getting hysterical.

One replied, "I told them, 'More walking, less talking.'"

Question time. "What are you going to do about the barge at Stuyvesant?" asks Stuyfather Richard Roth.

"It's not dangerous unless the kids are standing next to it," Levy replies. "The debris is being watered down."

"We know," I interject. "They had a fire-drill; the kids *were* next to it. My son got watered down too."

The audience titters uneasily.

The watering down of the debris is an intermittent affair at best since the cleanup is proceeding at record breaking speed. The same day that Stuyvesant reopened, Governor George Pataki issued an Executive Order to suspend:

*...regulations regarding the transportation and handling of certain solid waste resulting from the WTC disaster. The order applied to persons working at the site under the supervision of New York State or the New York City government officials and* **suspended requirements to**:
*- obtain permits for collection, transportation and delivery of regulated waste...*

*- **Comply with hazardous waste management standards**...[lxxxvi]* [emphasis mine.]

At worst, during the winter, the debris isn't watered down at all because the water freezes, making removal more difficult. We welcome rain that winter.

Sabereh Malek takes a conciliatory approach.

"Chancellor Levy, I was impressed by your quotation that a society must be judged by how it treats its weakest members. Our children are its weakest members and right now, we need the Board of Education to protect them."

"This isn't fair," says Levy, gesturing impatiently to signal the end of the meeting.

As he passes her on his way out, Sabereh apologizes for having offended him. He doesn't acknowledge her but parts the milling crowd wearing a slick, rictus smile, like a shark through the waters.

One evening not long after, a mother recounts seeing Levy being interviewed on TV about the contamination downtown. Parents, he suggests, should worry instead about whether their children are wearing seat belts or having safe sex. (At the same time?)

Alex' history teacher has offered the kids five points on their semester grade if they bring a plant to class. Inspired by this innovative idea, on Parents' Night, I bring a plant to each of Alex' other teachers and suggest they practise shameless plagiarism of their colleague. Some are touched by the gift. Others, I suspect, put the plant on the windowsill and forget about it.

Later, a florist donates $1500 worth of plants, a generous and thoughtful gift. However, there are well over a hundred classrooms.

Psychologist Bruno Bettelheim wrote that lunatics did surprisingly well in concentration camps: The surroundings matched their inner world.

Analogously, 9/11 is the fulfilment of my worst nightmare: the one where your child is in danger, you're calling out for help and everyone drifts by, oblivious.

I stop attending my Tuesday discussion group. Social life recedes into the past in favor of research into the contaminants mentioned online or at meetings, and sending the results to a growing email list.

Others are similarly caught up emailing the PA Executive Board until Marilena summons the writers to a meeting.

Now that millions of people update their Facebook status several times a day and entire revolutions are organized on social media, it may seem laughable how we communicated back in the Stone Age of the internet. But not even Moveon.org had yet ignited the global (if futile) protests on the eve of the invasion of Iraq, so our intense emailing signified urgency. In fact, so heightened was that period of sustained emergency that even after months of meetings, some of us still didn't know each other's names.

We are a motley crew of government and office workers, academics, doctors, housewives, Bohemians and one bus driver. Some of us are immigrants. (At the end of the school year, taking a deep breath, psychologically speaking, for the first time since 9/11, Marilena tells us of growing up in Greece and watching the tanks roll in when she was sixteen. "I was happy because I didn't have to go to school." But then she had to live under the military coup. "I didn't think anything like that could happen in America," she says. The Shmuelis, from Israel, nod.)

Some of us have children who are sick; others, children with conditions that might predispose them to getting sick. The dilemma for the latter group arises because their kids love the school and the parents have to weigh potential regrets: Exposing their children to dangerous contamination or depriving them of joy in what could turn out to be a curtailed life anyway.

Some parents are worried that whether sick or not, our kids will be uninsurable because of their exposure to the World Trade Center disaster.

A number of us come from the ranks of the recently downsized. For once, two wrongs do make a right: The newly unemployed help the rest of us with the technology to get information out.

Despite being ahead of the curve on the environmental issue, these allies find ways to tell themselves their child will escape its most feared effects:

"My daughter's a Senior. The younger kids are more vulnerable."

"The smokers are the ones who're going to be hit the hardest."

"Scott has asthma so he wears a respirator on the way to school."

A father who is a doctor tells us of the risks of the endocrine disruptors to girls' reproductive systems. All the parents turn ashen.

The opposition have members fighting equally hard for a variety of reasons including maintaining a connection to a child following a divorce. Most, however, to coin terms of venery if not of veneration, are a suit of corporate types and a psychobabble of shrinks. They speak in oh-so-reasonable tones about stress and combat our pleas for the EPA to test indoor air by bringing in their friends to conduct mental health studies with questionnaires that seem to have been culled from the pages of Cosmopolitan Magazine.

The fault line between parents falls roughly along party lines. We are lefty types. The opposition are well-heeled guys or gals in suits, Republican types, regardless of whether or not that is their literal affiliation. Over the course of the year, we garner the reputation of being angry complainers while they cultivate an image of suave rationality. They have a large following among the parent body, many of whom do not want to antagonize the Board of Education or the teachers whose union, according to one member, is "in bed with the Board of Ed,"[9] and thereby jeopardize their children's chances of getting into Harvard or the equivalent.

Our opponents have critical mass while we, who are more critical, are far less massive as a percentage of the parent population. In addition, the majority have the party line to back them up starting with Christie's ringing words, party animal that she is.

The opposition make a good impression, in their suits. Like the fox in the fable, they know many things: The Board of Ed assures us... The EPA says...

We, on the other hand, are more like the hedgehog that knows one big thing: We're getting fucked. This is the one fact our nemeses refuse to face, like children who can't imagine their parents having sex.

Our anxiety focuses on the barge. But we are optimistic. Senator Charles Schumer's kid is a Stuy senior; she's even hung out at Marilena's house. Schumer can get the barge out of our backyard.

---

[9] Unions as "instruments of the national security state:" The CIA in National and International Labor Movements; Herbert Hill; International Journal of Politics, Culture and Society Vol. 6, No. 3, 1993; https://www.jstor.org/stable/20007098?seq=1#page_scan_t ab_contents
Victor Reuther's Revelations About U.S. Labor and the CIA; Charles Walker; April 2003 • Vol 3, No. 4; http://www.socialistviewpoint.org/apr_03/apr_03_36.html

Schumer is not interested in getting the barge out of our backyard.[10]  His wife, who oversaw the construction of Giuliani's bunker at World Trade Center 7,[lxxxvii] is Commissioner of the Department of Transportation which put the barge there in the first place.[lxxxviii]

For Plan B, we debate filing an injunction, using as evidence for its urgency the ever growing number of illnesses among the kids.

But unless there's a guy lying dead with a bullet through his heart, it's notoriously hard to prove cause and effect.  And no one is studying the kids who are neither unionized nor protected by Workers' Compensation.  All we have is what Deputy Chancellor Klasfeld refers to snootily as "anecdotal evidence."

"No judge would do anything right now to jeopardize the cleanup," say the environmental lawyers whom the PA consult.

They are probably right.  When I email a faculty member at the Harvard School of Public Health, asking

---

[10] Kristen Lombardi, a Village Voice reporter who brought to light Schumer's inaction vis à vis the post-9/11 environment, particularly compared to Hillary Clinton's involvement, was fired by the Voice which, ironically, later boasted of a prize she won for an article on sick Ground Zero Workers.  Fired Village Voice Writer Wins Top Investigative Journalism Prize At Alt Weekly Awards; 03/28/2008; Updated May 25, 2011; Rachel                                    Sklar; http://www.huffingtonpost.com/2007/06/18/fired-village-voice-write_n_52663.html  No stranger to injustice for her journalistic work, while at the *Boston Phoenix,* Lombardi had broken the story of sexual abuse in the Catholic church, only to see 100% of the credit go to the *Boston Globe.*  Out of the Spotlight: Does the Phoenix Deserve Credit for the Globe's Scoop?  Kyle  Scott  Clauss  October  30,  2015; http://www.bostonmagazine.com/news/blog/2015/10/30/phoenix-globe-spotlight/

for data that might support our cause, he responds, "I wouldn't want to interfere with the cleanup."

# ASBESTOS FACTORY, MOTHER OF ALL INCINERATORS, CREMATORIUM, VOLCANO

Around the same time as the first meeting of what will become the Stuyvesant Political Action Committee,[lxxxix] the only mother I know to have transferred her daughter to a different school calls to tell me of a State Assembly hearing on the air downtown. I race over.

A lumbering agency rep from the Office of Emergency Management is testifying. What a tragedy, says Greaseball, but OEM has risen to the occasion. To date, they've removed (however many) thousands of tons of debris.

More self-congratulatory testimony from the Department of Health, EPA and the City Department of Environmental Protection, all prancing before the State Assembly who nod respectfully. (Months later, when they figure out the con, they cross-examine these witnesses grandiloquently but nothing ever comes of it.)

At noon, the TV media rush out to edit their stories so what gets aired that night is all good news.

This is how most hearings will go since, if they're not allowed to speak first, the agencies often refuse to testify at all. (Further details on how the press is manipulated may be found in "Sins of Omission – Stories the Media Overlook," Appendix B.) The one hearing that does not follow this self-defeating protocol is the EPA Ombudsman's, which is perhaps why EPA declines to show up for it.

In the afternoon, those who stick it out hear a different story from Paul Bartlett of the Queens Center for the Biology of Natural Systems, who is an expert in the dispersion of contaminants. He looks the part, with hair that is half mad-scientist, half kid-who-just-got-up.

He speaks about the precautionary principal which underpins environmental policy in Europe, and warns of the health risks to residents of the dust that might have penetrated into their apartments.

"Buildings are known dust collectors," he says. "It doesn't rain in people's apartments. The wind doesn't blow contaminants away."

This observation is later corroborated in a January, 2002 article by Andrew Schneider in the St. Louis Post-Dispatch:

*To ignore the indoor environment for asbestos defies logic,' said [Hugh] Granger, the Virginia toxicologist. 'Outside, the normal air movement dilutes and dissipates asbestos concentration. Inside, the fibers are trapped by four walls. They constantly get resuspended just by occupants walking on carpets, closing the drapes or having the air conditioner or heat go on or off...[xc]*

And tenant representative Caroline Martin is told that if the dust in a particular building were to be made airborne, the air would violate Occupational Safety and Health Administration (OSHA) standards.

"What would it take to make the dust airborne?" Martin asks. "An earthquake?"

"A thunderclap could do it," the inspector replies. "Or a truck backfiring."

Finally, EPA itself says that fine particles, believed by many scientists to be more dangerous, were more likely than coarser particles to have penetrated indoors.[xci]

City Councilwoman Kathryn Freed[xcii] testifies, "If there's nothing wrong downtown, how come we're all getting sick?" She has been diagnosed with chronic bronchitis.[xciii] "The government is behaving like the Ford Motor Company when they did a cost benefit analysis and figured out that it would be cheaper to pay all the wrongful death suits that would result from a flaw than to prevent them."

Dr. Marjorie Clarke of Lehman College offers a version of testimony she will later submit to the US Senate

Environment Committee Hearing on Air Quality Issues Surrounding the World Trade Center Collapses and Fires:

*...[T]he WTC collapses and fires constituted a brand new, combination type of air pollution source with aspects of a 1) crematorium... 2) a solid waste incinerator of unprecedented proportion... 3) asbestos factory (but on a scale thousands of times the size and intensity of what would be found even in a badly operated factory) and 4) volcano (the initial cloud was similar to nuee ardente – hot gases and dust could – in some respects, depositing ash in a large area.)*

*...The emissions from the WTC fires were orders of magnitude more than any incinerator, many months have passed and we have heard very little about serious attempt to contain the emissions from the site. No attempt had been made to put out the fires (i.e. by cutting off the sources of oxygen from above and the tunnels below.) No procedures have been established to require or do this. Why wasn't there discussion to erect a temporary structure (dome) over the site, and install incinerator emissions controls to clean the air inside the dome so that the workers could do their work in safer conditions and the cleanup around downtown be finished, once and for all?...*

*Third, there has been a toxic and carcinogenic 'soup' of air pollutants in the downtown air, constantly being generated by fires, and worse, smoldering embers that incompletely combust thousands of tons of toxic precursors present in the form of fine particles and gases – the perfect recipe formation of dioxins, furans and similar products of incomplete combustion.*

*It's hard to imagine a more perfect machine for generating toxic and carcinogenic air pollution. First, there were thousands of tons of asbestos, fiberglass, silica, and very alkaline concrete which was pulverized into various size fractions, but much of which was extremely fine in size. Then there was a tremendous source of heavy metals, PCBs, and acids just from the building's contents (latex paints typically contain mercury – think of the number of gallons there was on the walls.) Lead came from volatilization of lead from car batteries, leaded glass in computer screens, lead solder, and lead pigments among other sources. Mercury would have come from batteries, fluorescent lighting, paints, thermostats and thermometers, mercury light switches and other sources. The same is true of cadmium, chromium, arsenic and other heavy metals. Most of this was initially pulverized; much of that was then in a form easy to volatilize given a high enough temperature.*

*In addition there were combustible products and packaging all over the buildings--everything from products and packaging made of paper, cardboard, wood and plastic, including furniture, floor coverings, textile partitions just to name a very few. Fire is easier to start when the combustible matter is a very fine size because the temperature and oxygen can get to all surfaces quickly (try to start a log burning vs. small scraps of paper). The source of heat in the WTC came not only from burning of the jet fuel, but also from the cars underground, as well as from the combustible materials in the building (paper and plastic are highly combustible).*

*The paper and plastics are not only important because they fed the fires, which volatilized metals and other toxic gases, but also because under conditions of a few hundred degrees to 1800 degrees Fahrenheit, dioxins, furans, and similar compounds form, de novo, when paper and plastic smolder where insufficient oxygen and temperature is present to burn them thoroughly. In the 1970s, before it was known that municipal solid waste incinerators needed to be designed and operated very carefully to combust the waste thoroughly, some incinerators created tens of thousands of nanograms/cubic meter of dioxin emissions. The stack size of one of these incinerators was a tiny fraction of the equivalent stack size of the World Trade Center air pollution source. In the pile, there was certainly little oxygen, there was a great deal of dioxin precursors (paper and plastics), and the temperatures were perfect for incomplete combustion, so the smoldering would have permitted the generation of an enormous quantity of toxic and carcinogenic organics.*

**Dioxin is a family of 210 discrete man-made chemicals that are some of the most carcinogenic and toxic chemicals known. Dioxin is the contaminant of Agent Orange that was responsible for birth defects across Vietnam after that war ended. Dioxin adheres very tightly to particulate matter in incinerators, and is stored in fatty tissues in human beings for long periods of time.** *[emphasis mine.] Dioxins are created in large quantities in poorly designed, uncontrolled incinerators, when products such as paper, cardboard, wood are incompletely burned with such substances as PVC plastic, benzene, and other chlorinated ring structures. The Trade Center was full of fuel for such incomplete combustion. The optimal temperatures for formation of dioxin are roughly between 400 to 1800 degrees Fahrenheit. European dioxin emission standards from an incinerator with a small stack (as compared with the area of Ground Zero) are 0.1 nanograms (billionths of a gram) Toxic Equivalents per cubic meter of emission.*

*The finer the size of the particulate matter, the greater that amount of volatilized heavy metals, dioxins/furans, and acid gases that can condense from the air and adsorb onto the particulate surfaces (because the surface area of the particulate is so much greater). Also, the finer sizes of particulate matter, laden with toxic and carcinogenic substances, can evade the body's coughing mechanism--the cilia--all the way down to the alveoli (air sacs) where they can reside for the long-term.[11] The longer the fires burned, the greater was the source of volatilized metals, organics, and acids. The fires burned and smoldered for at least 100 days; a decision was made on some level not to attempt to suffocate them (i.e., blocking off all the sources of air from above and below). Because the decision was made not to contain the site, every time we have a heavy wind, the dust that is still all over Lower Manhattan is kicked up and spread around more.[xciv]*

Dr. Clarke also warns not only of the additive effects of the toxic soup ("It's common sense that elevated levels of five pollutants is worse than one,") but also of their interactive effects:

*"When 1 + 1 + 1 does not equal three but equals 30, this is called synergy. The Mt. Sinai Environmental Sciences Laboratory, which pioneered research into the health effects of asbestos, has found that **those exposed to asbestos and who smoke, have not twice but 80 to 90 times the probability of suffering from asbestos-related diseases such as lung cancer, mesothelioma and asbestosis.**"[xcv] [emphasis mine.]*

She speaks of the violations in transporting the debris:

---

[11]    This phenomenon is reiterated by Hugh Granger, a scientist at HP Environmental: "I don't even know whether EPA knows the very small fibers are there, but to say that small fibers and [sic] not dangerous defies logic...In most of the autopsies on asbestos victims, the predominance of fibers we see are small, are under five microns..." NYC under an asbestos cloud; ANDREW SCHNEIDER, ©2002 ST. LOUIS POST-DISPATCH;         January         13,         2002; http://www.seattlepi.com/news/article/NYC-under-an-asbestos-cloud-1077322.php

*"There are standards for reducing entrainment of incinerator ash. These involve spraying water and containment in leak-proof, covered trucks.[12] Why aren't we enforcing those standards? Is it because this is not an incinerator?... We heard that 'guys with guns' enforce covering of trucks – now. But I had heard from people who lived in the area, that the military had been enforcing the opposite in the first weeks, when pollutant levels were highest, so that they could check the trucks' contents.[xcvi]*

Dr. Clarke seems like a down-to-earth prophet. I get her card, as well as Paul Bartlett's, and once home, share their findings with an email list that now includes parents at the other Ground Zero schools as well as residents, activists, workers, more members of the press and political staffers.

There is no significant follow-up to the hearing. As with its confrères in the City Council and even the federal government, independent scientists or members of the public present explosive testimony which either doesn't find its way into the media or gets buried so deep in the article and couched in so many qualifiers that the message is lost in translation, its original sound and fury ultimately signifying nothing for the victims. Occasionally out of one of the hearings, a report is issued and the press sounds the alarums. But then it retires to a shelf for posterity.

---

12 For at least three weeks following the attacks, the trucks were equipped with the wrong filters. WTC TRUCKS HAD WRONG DUST FILTERS; Kenneth R. Bazinet; August 15, 2002 http://www.nydailynews.com/archives/news/wtc-trucks-wrong-dust-filters-article-1.502058

I call Hillary Clinton's office, as does the Parents' Association, to ask them to use their influence to move the barge.

"That's a local problem," responds aide Gabrielle Tenzer.

The country gets bombed but the fallout is a local problem.

This stance epitomizes the problem of choosing the right time to strike, in every sense of that word. Dr. Margaret Mead famously said, "Never doubt that a small group of thoughtful, committed citizens can change the world; indeed, it's the only thing that ever has." The nuclear energy activist Dr. Helen Caldicott, nominated for the Nobel Peace Prize by Nobel laureate Linus Pauling, went one step further when, a few years after 9/11, I told her about the difficulty of moving the government towards meaningful action in Lower Manhattan.

"*You* must do it," she said.

"We are," I replied, referring to the small but valiant coalition of downtown activists that worked tirelessly for years.

"No – *You* must do it," she emphasized again and this time, I understood her to mean a belief I'd always held: that a movement can, in fact, start with isolated individuals.

These are inspiring thoughts and correct, as witnessed by revolutions in scientific thinking. But chapter two of any such narrative involves a band of people getting on board with the idea. In order for real change to take place, such a core group must then expand to a point of critical mass as in the story of the hundredth monkey. According to this phenomenon, which seems to have sprung from the realm of fable rather than science, when one monkey finds a new way to wash sweet potatoes, the monkeys near him or her pick it up from watching. The monkeys around those disciples then in turn learn the new method. But there comes a tipping point when the paradigm shifts and all the monkeys "spontaneously" adopt the new technique which gets absorbed into the monkeys' "culture" in perpetuity.

Similarly, while no activist or even politician can accomplish much as a solo operator, someone has to make the first move. But it's also crucial to make it at the right time, which is to say, where it will reach at least one set of open ears. Too soon, and you alienate possible allies.

Clinton would not have been perceived as a kook if she had spoken out more forthrightly in the early days, as Congressman Jerrold Nadler did; her office alone carried more than the weight of a respectable coalition. However, in a system that is corrupt at its core, politicians first check whether the winds are favorable, all the while telling themselves that the end justifies the means. But in most cases, those winds only become favorable when the problem can no longer be concealed – in other words, when it's too late.

*****

For decades to come, there will be debate on why the EPA did not take the reins in the early days of the disaster. The National Contingency Plan, which went into effect when President Bush declared a state of emergency, put EPA in charge of the environmental cleanup. However, according to popular wisdom, Mayor Giuliani told EPA, "Thanks, but we can handle this on our own," and the agency readily obliged. Certainly, Christie Todd Whitman places the blame in Giuiliani's court,[xcvii] a rare instance in which she is supported by lawyer Joel Kupferman who says, "He's the one who told OSHA [Occupational Safety and Health Administration] to leave. He was pretty much in charge." (Joel, of course, differs from EPA's position on whether this absolves them.)

Thus, in the tradition of Werner Von Braun, *("What goes up must also come down, 'That's not my department,' said Werner Von Braun,"[xcviii])* EPA maintained that indoor air lay outside their jurisdiction and that under the NCP, they had the right to delegate the matter to the city.

The city, however, was not up to the task. Its Department of Health:

*...had trouble testing the heavy concentration of thick particles in the air after the towers fell. With Passage of the Clean Air Act, it had been decades since such heavy amounts of contamination had tainted the air over any American city. Testing equipment had long since been recalibrated to detect much finer particles of pollution.* **The heavy dust from the trade center had quickly overloaded the monitors. Instead of resetting the instruments and repeating the tests, the city's health department had simply listed those test results as 'ND,' which stand for 'No Detect.'**[xcix] *[emphasis mine.]*

The buck then got passed to entities that were even less well equipped to handle the problem: First, to landlords. However, there was little follow-up to ensure compliance.

For cleanup of apartments, the New York City Department of Health advised residents to do it themselves using a wet mop or wet rag and where the dust was really bad, to wear long pants.[c] (Apparently, the DOH was unaware that some buildings had no water.[ci]) They also suggested lowering curtains slowly so as not to dislodge any dust, while also trying to avoid inhaling it. However, children and pregnant women did not need to take any special precautions.[cii] Inevitably, women who were pregnant at the time and exposed to the dust gave birth to babies who were twice as likely to be below average weight by several ounces.[ciii]

Residents whose apartments were visibly wrecked applied to their insurance companies. But because the EPA had said there was no problem, those companies often refused to pay for cleanup.

At a hearing held by Senators Hillary Clinton and Joe Lieberman in February, 2002, Community Board 1 member Elizabeth Berger described the results of these policies:

*We reluctantly made our own rules, divined from press reports, high school science as we remembered it and the advice of friends and neighbors. But even that was mixed. One scientist friend had his apartment tested and declared safe for his family; the managing agent of his building, however, reported high levels of asbestos and lead. In the end, 248 stuffed animals, 8 handmade baby quilts, 5 mattresses, a trousseau's worth of sheets and towels, a kitchenful of food and 13 leaf-and-lawn bags of toys went into our trash but not our books, draperies and upholstered furniture or our clothes, though the bill to dry-clean them industrially was $16,500... We washed the walls but didn't repaint. Some people we know repainted but kept their mattresses. Some people kept their stuffed animals but threw away their furniture. Some people kept what they couldn't bear to lose and got rid of the rest. We have still not decided what to do about our floors: Will stripping, sanding and resealing them contain the toxic mix of asbestos, fiberglass, concrete, human remains, heavy metals and the vague 'particulates' or just release more of it into our indoor air?*[civ]

Berger would die in 2013, at age 53, of pancreatic cancer. (As she'd been diagnosed only shortly after 9/11 and the quiescent period may be ten to fifteen years,[cv cvi] no cause and effect relationship to the attacks should be inferred.)

At 125 Cedar Street, there was no electricity, so residents climbed the stairs as many times as was necessary to remove tons of debris. Some, such as videographer Mary Perillo, have experienced respiratory symptoms as a result.[cvii]

At the same time that they were telling residents to deal with their apartments themselves, EPA had a different attitude towards their own building at 290 Broadway. Although it lay six blocks northeast of the World Trade Center site, outside the "zone of contamination," so called because according to EPA's own assessment, there was no asbestos over 1% at that distance, they hired an industrial hygienist to test the lobby for asbestos. Some of the settled dust samples were collected with a micro-vac and analyzed using transmission electron microscopy which can reveal the presence of chrysotile asbestos (a form which they were telling residents was not dangerous.) These tests came up positive[cviii] while analysis via the less sensitive method of light microscopy did not.[cix]

In the words of EPA scientist Dr. Cate Jenkins, **the agency then "had its own offices cleaned by certified asbestos abatement contractors.** [emphasis mine.] At taxpayer expense."[cx] To add insult to injury, they would later state that micro-vac collection of dust samples and TEM testing were not necessary for schools and residences in Lower Manhattan. And at 105 Duane Street, they would even *discount* results obtained and tested using these methods when they contradicted the agency's own results.[cxi]

To combat EPA's blowing toxic smoke in residents' faces, the World Trade Center Environmental Coalition was founded by Maureen Silverman, a diminutive redhead who advocated for the New York City Coalition to End Lead Poisoning;[cxii] legal aide attorney Foster Maer and Vice President of the Independence Plaza Tenants' Association, Diane Lapson.

Diane Lapson
*Interview conducted c. 2003*

*That morning, I was in the street. It was Election Day. I was with [former City Councilwoman] Kathryn Freed*[cxiii] *at P.S. 234. She was running for office. The first plane came over our heads on Greenwich Street. Instantly I knew that something really terrible was about to happen. I felt so helpless and stunned. I believed the plane was in trouble and was trying to make an emergency landing in the Hudson. IPN is a tall building and I thought it was in the way. I thought the plane was going to hit 310 Greenwich [one of IPN's buildings.]*

*Everything became like a cartoon. My brain reduced it down.*

*Alan Gerson was running for City Council and Kathryn was running for Public Advocate. Gloria from IPN ran up and said we have to evacuate P.S. 234. The Principal said, "We're O.K. We're O.K. The parents are coming to pick up their kids."*

*I remember looking at Kathryn. She said, "We're under attack." I didn't believe her.*

*We thought we'd better start pushing people uptown. Then the second plane hit.*

*Kathryn said, "Now do you believe me?"*

*She said we should go to the precinct to try to get help. Things were going on in the street. There was a Jamaican woman whose legs were buckling. She said, "My daughter's in one building; my son is in the other." They were on the top floors. My hope is that her daughter who was in the second building got out. I asked her if she lived here. She said No. I called out, "Does anyone know this woman?" A woman answered, "I'll stay with her."*

*Then I heard the Pentagon was hit. In my head I was saying,*

91

*"This is the end of the world." I called my daughter. I said, "Something happened. Close all the windows and turn all the air conditioning off." We were lucky. She did.*

*There were no police at the precinct except one officer. He seemed shaken. Kathryn had a badge so they let us through. Kathyrn said, "I was hoping to get a car. I'm afraid the buildings will fall."*

*My father was the electrical engineer on the World Trade Center and I thought it was the rock of Gibraltar.*

*The policeman said, "There's nothing we can do for you. Do what you have to do."*

*We went back to Greenwich Street and yelled at people to move uptown. Some people listened to us. One man ran toward the Trade Center shouting, "No!" It was scary when he did that. Then the first building came down. Everyone started running.*

*I couldn't find my daughter. I didn't know where she was. Someone said they saw her with her dog.*

*Then the second building came down.*

Q:  Did you feel the vibrations?

*I don't remember. It was rumbling. It wasn't the noise I thought the Trade Center would make. It was too silent for what it was. It melted down like the wicked witch of the east in the Wizard of Oz. A year later I was walking in Florida and I remembered what I had seen earlier which was people jumping out the windows. I had heard about it and I knew it from the news but I didn't remember seeing it until I went to Florida.*

*We found my daughter. She couldn't wake her friend who lives a block and a half from the Trade Center. They went to the roof of his building. To this day I can't get straight what they did but it's a good thing I didn't know it then; I would've had a heart attack.*

*We thought IPN would be evacuated. I told tenants to pack a bag. I thought more buildings would be attacked: the Empire State and the Statue of Liberty. And our building is tall. A lot of people left and weren't allowed back in. I thought they might be killed.*

*I was in Kathryn's apartment. We were trying to figure out where we could stay. We all had cats and animals so there were a lot of people with a lot of cases. I couldn't reach John Scott who's the Vice President of another building. I didn't realize they'd lost power.*

*In the lobby were a bunch of seniors clutching together. They had no place to go. I said to Kathryn, "We're not going anywhere." She said, "I know."[13]*

*We put everything back. I said, "I'm Vice President of this building. I don't know anything about emergencies but I'm in charge. We're going to use the intercoms." We sent everyone upstairs. The smoke was terrible.*

*WTC 7 fell at five and we lost our phone system.*

*We have floor captains and they understood they were part of this.*

*We didn't have hot water. Home care attendants hadn't been allowed to come. It was before nine when the first plane hit and they hadn't gotten to work yet. So we had disabled people with no attendants."*

Q: What did you do about people who had run out of medicine?

*Food came first. The Red Cross had set up tables for volunteers at Harrison Street. We asked if we could get thirty meals for the people who were the most in need. They said No. Understandably, they were focussing on rescuing people at the Trade Center.*

---

[13] Months later, when someone unsympathetic to residents' complaints of illness asked Kathryn, "Why don't you leave?" she replied, "I started to leave on September 11, but we were cut off downtown and there were old and disabled people in my building who had run out of their medications. I stayed then and I'm staying now."

*But we noticed that in the evening they threw stuff out. No one was dealing with our building.*

*One of our tenants is a therapist and she asked if she could open a trauma center. So management gave her an empty apartment and other therapists joined her. One woman said, "I don't know what to tell my children. My son said, 'I saw people jump out the window.' Should I tell him they had parachutes?"*

*The Red Cross approached us. We asked them to check on tenants. They checked on seniors and disabled people.*

*We weren't sleeping much and we were breathing that stuff.*

Q: Did you get the thirty meals?

*You know what happened? A man appeared with sixty meals saying, "I don't want to discuss this." I don't even know his name. I asked him but he just kept walking.*

*Someone else said, "I just took my last heart pill." Forty people were waiting for medicine in the mail but there was no mail.*

*Alan Gerson showed up with a car from the Borough President's office to get Kathryn to the mayor. Once she was there, I was able to get through on my cell. She tried to get a doctor from Chinatown to take empty pillboxes from tenants and fill them. The doctor never made it.*

*Kathryn smuggled in a guy who owned a drugstore. I said, "Do you need people to run the drugstore?" He said, "Yes."*

*I said to the tenants, "I have good news and bad news. The bad news is the doctor hasn't arrived. The good news is, Steve is in the drugstore."*

*We'd been told if we left the neighborhood we couldn't come back.*

Q: What about if people worked uptown?

*They couldn't come back. From Tuesday 'til that weekend. The Red Cross had evacuated 310 Greenwich because it had lost all power and phones. They were afraid if people got sick from the smoke, they wouldn't be able to get them down in the elevator.*

*There was a shelter at Irving Plaza. Other people had nieces or nephews pick them up. But some people refused to leave. John Scott communicated by email.*

*The building manager was very helpful. We'd never had a great relationship but we became like a team.*

Q: Are you still on good terms?

*That connection created a bond. But a year and a day after September 11, we were told the building was being sold and taken out of Mitchell-Lama [affordable housing for moderate- and middle-income families] so if we don't fight, we could lose our homes.*

*After the weekend, they allowed home care attendants to come in and they opened Canal Street – just when we'd told people to go to the hospital.*

*So many things were donated that there was enough for everybody. A minister from a shelter showed up with a truck with food, the sort of stuff you'd get at a shelter: tremendous containers of powdered milk...*

*People were cooking for their entire floors. There were people who went into cardiac arrest. The Red Cross took one person to the hospital.*

*On the third day, I took a break. Maureen said she wanted to have an environmental meeting. I felt guilty. I'd almost stopped smoking but when the buildings came down, I started again. I thought, "I'm going to be on an environmental committee and I'm smoking." But we got Foster Maer and a bunch of people and that's how the World Trade Center Environmental Coalition started.*

*The Department of Health told us to just take wet towels to clean our apartments. It was hot on September 11 and some people's windows had been left wide open. They just swept with brooms.*

Q:  Have they gotten sick?

*A lot of people at IPN have had asthma, skin conditions, nose-bleeds.  Some of them still do.  I had five eye infections I couldn't get rid of.*
*But we didn't know if it was worse to tell people how bad we thought it was; they were so traumatized.*
*One woman was pregnant.  She kept asking if she should stay.  I told her, "Look, if I was in your position I'd leave."  She did.*
*Leaving made people more traumatized.*
*I didn't open my windows for a year and a half.  I didn't turn on the air-conditioning 'til I bought special filters for allergies.  I used the a.c. during the winter.  FEMA told us the a.c. probably had organic parts, body parts which would disintegrate the coils so we should replace the unit."*

Diane told her story in a sing-song as people may do when they need to distance themselves from a seismic event.  But the recitation enhanced the lyrical quality of the memory so I wrote a second version of her narrative in verse:

Diane's Song
*(In the triple meter of "'T Was the Night Before Christmas")*

When the plane passed right over our heads I thought it was
In trouble and trying to land in the water.
It hit the first building.  Then Kathryn said,
"We're under attack."  I thought, "Where is my daughter?"

I thought that an awful mistake had been made.
In the street all the people were running uptown
Except for one man who, holding his head,
Shouted, "No!" while running not up, but down.

And people were jumping from windows, a sight
I forgot for a year – Did my eyes deceive me?
The second plane hit.  Then Kathryn turned
And said, "All right, now do you believe me?"

In the street a Jamaican woman stopped
As her legs buckled under her.  That mother
Clasped her hands together and cried,
"My son's in one building; my daughter's in the other."

A woman stayed with her as Kathryn and I
Ran home and told our neighbors to leave.
We gathered our work, our clothes but that's
Not all for it seemed everyone had cats.

We met downstairs, the neighbors with all
Of their carrying cases, when there before us
Stood forty-two seniors with no place to go.
"We can't leave," I said.  Kathryn said, "I know."

So we put back our stuff and we stayed as the cloud
Engulfed our homes and insidiously
Set up house in our lungs; as hour passed hour
We lost water, phones, then the rest of our power.

Someone said that they'd seen my missing kid
She'd gone to a friend's house a block from the Center.
Thank God that I didn't know then where she was.
To this day I can't get straight just what she did.

For the next several days we drank powdered milk
Courtesy of a curate who came in a truck.
Things seemed to be going O.K. until

Someone said, "I just took my last heart pill."

We found medication; we manned the drugstore.
A mysterious stranger brought by sixty meals.
Over time we got back some power, the water
And phones. The toxics came too, more and more.

The government told us the air was O.K.
So we didn't think twice; we started to clean
While a mile up Broadway some scientists found
The most toxic small particles they'd ever seen.[14]

Now the neighbors have come down with asthma and
rashes,
With Trade Center cough and severe sinusitis.
I've had five infections; the cat has had three
And Kathryn and her cat have chronic bronchitis.

The rest of the world has moved on. People think
In the war against terror, the U.S. is winning.
But we of downtown wonder if for us,
September 11th was just the beginning.

On December 18, the World Trade Center
Environmental Coaltion holds the first demonstration to
protest the EPA's failure to address the air quality
downtown. *New Yorker* cartoonist and Stuyvesant
parent Art Spiegelman designs a poster of two
elementary school kids wearing gas masks, their
pictures seeming to have been lifted from a first-grade
reader of the sixties such as Alice and Jerry or Dick and
Jane. "New York City to Kids: Don't Breathe," warns the

---

[14] Dr. Thomas Cahill of UC-Davis found the highest levels of
very- and ultrafine particles out of 7000 tests his team had
performed around the world, including at the burning
Kuwaiti oil fields.

accompanying slogan with a subscript for adults:
*Breathing May Be Hazardous to Your Health.*

Feeling the poster may frighten their children, some of
the elementary school parents remove their sponsorship
of the demonstration which, nevertheless, brings out
hundreds of supporters and, considering the blackout
in the media at that time, earns impressive coverage.

It is overly simple to assume that EPA abdicated its
responsibility merely in order to avoid paying to clean
up Lower Manhattan.  Although the cost of doing the job
properly would probably have been no more than about
$2 billion – a pittance in comparison to, say, one month
of the Iraq War – 9/11 served a larger purpose:  That of
overturning the long-standing precedent of testing in
concentric circles following a disaster and cleaning up
as indicated by the results.  The agency's new, "You're
on your own" policy would come in even more useful in
future disasters which were inevitable as riskier
methods became more common to drill for ever harder-
to-reach pockets of that ever-diminishing resource,
easy, sweet crude oil (as distinct from shale oil or the
stuff that is produced from tar sands.)  Had the agency
continued its established precedent with 9/11, there
would have been hell to pay when the Deepwater
Horizon exploded in the Gulf of Mexico, for instance,
resulting in the contamination of 1300 miles of
shoreline from Texas to Florida.[cxiv]

Because of the pollution, the kids at Stuyvesant aren't
being allowed out for lunch.  They are getting restless,
with gambling now the default pastime among the boys.

"Did you know about this?" I ask Alex.

"They only caught us once!" he exclaims.  "Since then
we've been playing on the stairs.  No one's seen us."

And I hadn't even been trying to smoke him out.

It must be my father's poker genes.

A corollary effect of the new lunch policy is a boom in the mouse population. The next PA meeting comes to a close with Marilena looking nervously behind her as the Recording Secretary announces early adjournment: "There's a motion on the floor and it's a mouse."

One day an email arrives from South Korea, in response to a delivery of steel from the World Trade Center. The writer wants to know whether or not it's contaminated.

"It probably is," I reply, "but don't feel discriminated against; they're exposing us to the same stuff."

This is the first indication that metal from Ground Zero is being sent to the other side of the world. In India:

*...[t]he scrap was unloaded, as any routine consignment would be, by port workers with absolutely no protection...*

*Similar shipments have reportedly reached China, where Baosteel Group purchased 50,000 tons of the potentially toxic scrap. Malaysia and South Korea are also reported to have received shipments. Eventually, most of the 1.5 millions tons of scrap from the cleanup may end up dirtying Asian ports and threatening Asian workers.*[cxv]

I do not keep this email as I might today. With Alex still at Stuyvesant, I remain in emergency mode, focusing only on amassing evidence that can convince my ex-husband that our son should not remain at the school. Any thought of a book later, which is always at the back of a writer's mind, vaporizes in the white heat of sharing research, punctuated by meetings and hearings.

So it comes to pass on Christmas night that I pursue a way-out idea: Love Canal? Could we really be in such bad straits?

On Google, the parallels leap out and grab you by the throat: The official denials that there is a problem, the

100

popular blind belief in benevolent beings in charge; the sacrifice of a school.

With a frisson of horror, I email the Love Canal website.

"We've been worried about you," they respond.

There is bittersweet solace in empathy from veterans of the most notorious environmental disaster of its time.

We are getting a new Mayor!

This is both good news and bad: Good that Giuliani's out; bad that we have to start all over again, educating the new arrival, a Sisyphean task to add to our others.

"We have to give him a chance," someone says to general nods of agreement.

"We must tell him, 'We welcome you,'" says an ally who's worked in government. Then, as she remembers Giuliani, "Oh, how we welcome you! It'll be a while before we can get aggressive."

We hold back, writing polite letters to him, to the daughter who is said to be one of his closest consultants, to his staff. (One of his deputies, Mark Shaw, is also a Stuyparent! More luck!)

To no avail. When Marilena and President of the World Trade Center Residents' Coalition Sudhir Jain meet with Deputy Mayor Daniel Doctoroff, he says that the problem with the cleanup lies in "communication." In other words, there's nothing objectively wrong with the environment; only with our perception.

*January 14, 2002*

Andrew Schneider of the St. Louis Post-Dispatch publishes a lengthy exposée of the environmental disaster of 9/11, revealing how the EPA managed to conceal damning data by, for example, using twenty-year-old methods for collecting and measuring asbestos. **For every fiber detected by the agency,** he quotes

EPA scientist Dr. Cate Jenkins as saying, **independent scientists found nine. The risk of cancer from the asbestos alone could reach one person in ten.**[cxvi] [emphasis mine.]

We would later learn that **EPA Region 8, which encompassed the Superfund site of Libby, Montana, offered state-of-the-art equipment to Region 2 in New York. The latter refused with the words: "We don't want you fucking cowboys here**. [emphasis mine.] The best thing they could do is transfer you to Alaska."[cxvii]

The article also mentions what will later become a sticking point in activists' and independent scientists' arguments with EPA about their proposed clean-up protocols: They are overlooking the critical area of heating and ventilation systems.

Schneider quotes Dr. Jenkins comparing the dust inside homes around Ground Zero to that in Libby and highlights the disconnect between EPA's off-hand advice to residents and landlords – who hired day laborers with dustpans, brooms, mops, buckets and normal household vacuum cleaners – with the way cleanup of the same material was being conducted out in the street, using micro-filter vacuums while wearing regulation protective clothing and respirators.

More than 1,800 volunteers from the Southern Baptist Church, the Salvation Army and other groups wore cloth or paper masks when they cleaned hundreds of apartments, he reports, while only one of the 29 most available brands of masks on the market contained filters fine enough for asbestos...

*[EPA Spokeswoman Bonnie] Bellow admits that the EPA's website linked to incorrect guidance for office and apartment landlords and renters...*

*A check of EPA's website yesterday found the same links were being used...*[cxviii]

The Board of Ed is holding a hearing for parents from around the city.

Stuymother Linda Lam testifies powerfully about her daughter's asthma so I tell her about the meetings of the Parents' Association Executive Board which are open to everyone. Rochelle Kalish, Peggy Sarlin and Rachel Lidov testify about the barge, the high readings for particulate matter and asbestos; the illnesses.

"And the ducts were never cleaned," I add, my voice rising. Klasfeld holds up his hand in a shushing gesture, the wise father seated ever so slightly above us on the dais, calming the turbulent, metaphorically unwashed horde below. (See Hystericalmothers.com, Appendix W.) He's pinker and fatter than before, as though he were turning into a pig before our eyes.

It's hard to get a reading on the Board of Ed, which is said to be on the outs with Levy. On the other hand, they are bureaucrats accustomed to standoffs with parents.

Still in the audience when we testify are parents from PS 89, an elementary school across the street from Stuy. They have been doubled up with another school at some distance from Ground Zero but are scheduled to return to the area at the beginning of February.

Our testimony galvanizes them. The next day they initiate suit to enjoin the Board of Ed from sending their kids back to their home building.

In the mean time, they do their own tests which come back with high lead readings. Also, diesel keeps appearing on the windowsills after they've been wiped, as in a religious miracle.

One woman offers her son a puppy to change schools. He refuses.

The injunction works. The date for P.S. 89 to return to Ground Zero gets moved to the end of February.

*Stuyvesant PA General Meeting*

"I don't like to speak," says a Chinese mother haltingly. "My English not good. My daughter sick. Every night she cough. For two weeks, she don't go to school. Then she go back, she sick again."

The mother cries, which is becoming par for the course at PA meetings.

Another newcomer speaks up: Paul Edwards, who is angry.

"Forget negotiation," he says. "We should have a demonstration!"

A fellow lunatic, whom I make sure to intercept on our way out.

Paul is no stranger to battling big guns. He once published a newsletter about ways for consumers to save money and was sued by American Airlines. The settlement's confidential but the newsletter survived intact.

Now that there are two of us at the radical end of the spectrum, and more weeks have passed of being given the run around by the guys in suits, the downtown community takes the notion of protest more seriously.

Since the barge hasn't budged, it becomes the focus of our discontent. I bring Paul to the World Trade Center Environmental Coalition to propose that we hold a demonstration against it. One activist chastises us for daring to entertain such an idea before raising it with the group. What about the democratic process? We are being "inappropriate."

Like belching at the dinner table?

"This is about kids," I respond to mollify the activist, who is worried about his own two.

Our timing coincides with the arrival in town of the World Trade Organization with, in its wake, a circus of demonstrators. A few of them, with multiple arrests on their resumés, organize a training session on Civil Disobedience.

A cluster of Quakers, dressed thriftily, take off their shoes and sit crosslegged on the floor of the sparsely furnished Friends' meeting hall.

"Bring any medication you may be taking," says the trainer, a man of about thirty with the air of a latter-day hippy. "You may need it in jail. If you normally carry nail scissors, leave them home; they'll be confiscated and you may not see them again when you get out. Women should tie back their hair so the police can't pull it.

'Expect to stay in jail up to 72 hours.

'Now, suppose they let you off the hook *but*," the trainer spins 360 degrees on his heel, "they give you a sentence of Community Service anyway.

'You guys," he addresses the Quakers, "spend your whole lives in Community Service. Reminding people of this has worked in the past."

Barbara Zeluck, a life-long activist whose husband died of asbestos exposure from building ships during World War II, gives me the email addresses of the WTO protest organizers with the thought that they might be interested in sending over a few stringers.

They would all love to join us in a demonstration, they say; we would be the jewel in their crown.

We are thrilled but wary. Aren't these the people who threw rocks in Seattle? As protesters against government endangerment of our children, we cannot afford to do anything destructive.

What kind of demonstration were you thinking of? I inquire queasily.

They don't respond. (A month later, I get notification about a changed email address.) But their New York demonstration is a model of decorum and I regret doubting them.


From the *New Yorker*'s Talk of the Town column: Merchandise from Century 21, situated at the corner of the World Trade Center site, has found its way to a discount clothing store in Maine. Bargains galore! The dustier the clothes are, the cheaper.[cxix]

*February 8, 2002*

Joel Kupferman has invited everyone to his office for a press conference with the EPA Ombudsman. The usual suspects are there – Maureen Silverman, New York Environmental Law and Justice Project Policy Analyst Kimberly Flynn – as well as resident Ilona Kloupte who has brought the bucket that will become her trademark. Wrapped in plastic since it is contaminated, it features a red cross, having been a gift from the agency in the early days of the cleanup when the NYC Department of Health first told people to clean their own apartments. Ilona has had rashes and been diagnosed with several respiratory disorders. She is staying in a hotel but her grant from the Federal Emergency Management Agency is about to run out.

The Ombudsman, Robert Martin, and his Chief Investigator, Hugh Kaufman, stride in like two cowboys newly arrived to town. (Hugh even has on the boots.) But as Bob Martin is a Makaw Indian, that may not be the right image. However, several months later, he reflects on what his position at EPA has taught him: "I never realized the government treats *everyone* like Indians."

Resembling John Travolta playing an undercover cop, (though he is usually described as "the guy with the ponytail,") he has a soft-spoken manner which undoubtedly serves him well in delivering uncompromising assessments. Hugh is an imposing figure with a beard and a booming voice which surely aids in instilling the fear of God into what a left-wing version of George Bush might call "evil-doers." The son of a mathematician who worked in Federal Trade

Statistics until he was 86, (Florida Senator Claude Pepper had gotten rid of the mandatory retirement age requirement,) he has always been involved in public service and was a founding member of EPA back in the day when it actually protected the environment. His daughter attends the Washington equivalent of Stuy.

After listening to our stories, the Ombudsman and his Chief Investigator announce they will hold hearings to investigate EPA's probable criminal abrogation of its duties.

First order of business, however, is to write a letter advising that the Stuyvesant building should not be occupied. That, along with a picture in the Healthy Schools Network Newsletter of Stuyvesant's toxic backyard, finally convinces my ex- to let me transfer Alex to another school, whether college-friendly or not. When all is said and done, my ex- is a lawyer familiar with the lies government authorities tell to avoid liability.

The concession arrives just in time, for the Board of Ed Truant Office has called. (Their protocol, it's said, is to go into action after twenty absences in five months but Alex has racked up that number in three.) The automated call sounds gentle, the Truant Office perhaps figuring that anyone loopy enough to keep their kid home doesn't respond well to authority.

The gig is up. No more half-assed in-Stuy-but-not-showing-up stuff; I could lose joint custody. But my biggest fear is that the Board of Ed will send a van to transport Alex physically back to Stuyvesant.

I find a last-resort school that will accept applications midyear. An alternative high school, it caters to kids who don't fit the traditional mold or who've flunked out somewhere else. Instead of attending classes, (except for a mandatory course in Planned Parenthood,) students do internships, jobs for which they earn credit. The arrangement works for most: They graduate whereas in the past, such students tended to drop out. And for some, the outcome is the stuff of dreams: During one of our visits, the Principal gets a call from the school's first alumna doctor. However, when the list of schools is published in the Times at the end of the year in order of performance, this one shows up next to last.

A setback for the demonstration: A core group of residents has had a change of heart and Paul wants to wait until we can amass more support.

*February 11, 2002*

Hillary Clinton and Joe Lieberman of the Senate Committee on Environment and Public Works are holding field hearings in Lower Manhattan.

Marilena is up. Her testimony leads to an exchange with Bernard Orlan, the Board of Education's Director of Environmental Health and Safety, about Stuyvesant's ventilation system:

*Senator Clinton* Mr. Orlan, let me turn to you, because there are two specific issues that were raised, and I want your direct response to them. The first, with respect to Stuyvesant, were the ventilation systems and the ductwork cleaned, and who did that work, if it was done?

*Mr. Orlan* The air mixing chambers and the ventilation system were cleaned by an asbestos hazard abatement company prior to the reoccupancy of the school. Prior to that weekend, and there was a holiday weekend, to ensure that there was nothing lurking behind the ventilation system, the ventilation system was run, a number of air changes, after which air sampling was conducted throughout the school. The analysis was using the TM analysis, we were able to get down to the smallest level of particulate. Those results were shared prior to reoccupancy of the school with both the environmentalists with the UFT [United Federation of Teachers,] with the various regulatory agencies and with the parents' association consultant.

*Senator Clinton* Ms. Christodoulou, you just heard Mr. Orlan's response. What's your response to that?

*Ms. Christodoulou* I think it was not a direct response. Your question, Senator, was, were the ducts cleaned. Mr. Orlan responded that the intakes of the ducts were cleaned. It's a—

*Senator Clinton* Let me stop you. Were the ducts cleaned, Mr. Orlan?

*Mr. Orlan* The ducts themselves were not cleaned.[cxx]

The audience gasps.[15]

---

[15] The caught-with-his-pants-down interchange at the Clinton/Lieberman hearing does not stop Orlan from asserting at a later Parent's Association meeting that the ducts were cleaned by having air "vigorously blown" through them.

"What he means," explains PA consultant Howard Bader, "is that they turned the system on."

Dr. Marjorie Clarke is taping the proceedings, dressed in a make-do shirt and khakis. She should be on a panel but instead we get NYU's George Thurston and other EPA apologists.

My father's genes surge up in me. (One of his jobs was as a press agent.) I tell Ralph Penza of NBC that he could get a radically different view of the proceedings if he talked to Maggie. He's game and so, it turns out, is she.

Seeing the camera light up, four other media outlets turn to cash in on the interview. A star is born and a soundbite of truth, aired.

The first Ombudsman hearing takes place twelve days later on a Saturday. EPA doesn't deign to come, which Bob Martin says is unheard of for an agency being investigated. The Ombudsman lacks subpoena power but EPA knows he won't let them off the hook.

"Looks as though they have something to hide."

In the audience is a mother with a ten-month-old baby. (At the City Council hearing, Councilman Alan Gerson had introduced her and she stood with the baby, who was nursing, as some sort of symbol of the resurrection of Lower Manhattan.)

Unlike the other hearings up until that point, the Ombudsman hearings don't put agency reps on first. The first witness is Dr. Cahill of U.C. Davis who measured **very- and ultrafine particulates a mile north of Ground Zero during the week Stuyvesant reopened. The results came back higher than any of the 7000 samples his team had ever taken around the world, including at the burning Kuwaiti oil fields.**[cxxi]

Lieutenant Manuel Gomez testifies that workers at Ground Zero had been told not to wear respirators for fear of causing panic. He has brought along the mask they wore instead.

"Read the warning," Hugh says.

Gomez reads the bold red letters: "DOES NOT PROTECT LUNGS."

Heidi Mount testifies that her husband, a sanitation worker, had also been protected only by a paper mask and has since been diagnosed with hepatitis, among respiratory and other illnesses.

At 10:30 PM, the Stuy contingent gets its turn.

John Healy testifies about his son, a big guy, a football player.

"'Strong like bull,' as my grandmother would have said," observes Hugh.

"Right. 'Strong like bull.' Now every night he coughs himself to sleep for forty-five minutes."

Hugh proclaims the 9/11 case to be rife with conflict of interest. Christie's husband owned shares in Citigroup which insured much of Lower Manhattan.[cxxii] And Harold O. Levy, as Hugh elaborately calls him, making him sound like an Irish Jew, had left his job with Citigroup to become Schools Chancellor.[cxxiii]

The hearing goes on until eleven.

"Don't you all have something better to do?" grumbles the partner of one witness, who wants to go home.

"No, actually, we don't," replies the New York Environmental Law and Justice Project's Kimberly Flynn. "There's nowhere else we'd rather be right now."

Alex and I have an appointment at the alternative school to meet one Mike Salvatore and oh, how appropriate that name sounds now. If, in thirty years, I'm around and some of Alex' friends are sick and Alex isn't, I will look back on Mike and this school as our salvation.

The school has an internship at the Irish Rep Theater which sounds like a promising possibility for Alex. Mike says it's good if they have a show on; otherwise, it's a lot if filing.

"We had one student who went to Irish Rep and wound up marrying the daughter of [an acclaimed director.] Now he's not only got a wife; he's working for the guy."

I dare to have hope for this school.

Mike pushes over the papers to sign.

"He really belongs at Stuyvesant," he says as a last caveat before we take the plunge. Alex looks at me hard which causes me a moment's pause as I weigh the regrets on both sides. But why did we come here, after all? I sign.

Irish Rep does not have a show in the works and Alex spends six hours a day filing. He switches internships; Irish Rep is understanding. For the rest of the semester, he spends half the week filing papers at the Intrepid. Because the work is menial, he says, "people treat me as though I'm stupid."

When he asks his supervisor how a certain set of papers should be filed, she answers, "Alphabetically. You're familiar with the alphabet?"

"Well, I know the song," Alex replies, matching her sarcasm.

The other half of the week he spends doing equally menial work at, ironically, the office of Senator Charles Schumer. Towards the end of the semester, another Stuykid joins the office, his mother also trying to keep her child away from Ground Zero.

Now that he's out of Stuyvesant, I throw out all the clothes Alex wore there as well as his bedding, since the scientific consensus is that they cannot be adequately cleaned. This is why I buy bargains: Easy come, easy go.

But he pines to return so my involvement with Ground Zero continues unchecked. On top of that, an almost superstitious fear for his future health compels me to work on behalf of whatever may still be salvaged, as though then the fates may have mercy.

Paul Edwards has reached "go for broke" point.

"Forget it," he says. "I'll demonstrate even if there are only three of us." The third person he is alluding to is his wife, Marianne, an artist.

Since the first question the press ask is what organization you represent, we call ourselves the World Trade Center Environmental Organization, (not to be confused with Maureen Silverman's World Trade Center Environmental Coalition.)

When we propose the idea of a demonstration at the next meeting of the Stuyvesant Parents' Political Action Committee, father Richard Roth quashes talk of further delay by saying, "These people have jumped the gun on us and we can't afford to let them fail."

The barge demonstration takes place March 20 at the foot of the bridge leading into the school. Rochelle Kalish drapes an enormous banner and Marianne Edwards makes posters which appear prominently in the New York Times photo. The activist who'd been annoyed at our independence stands with us in the rain, bringing three neighbors who chant up a storm.

Literally, for the weather is awful. But it helps our cause, as it shows dedication in addition to accounting for why there aren't more people, in case any cynics are wondering. However, they're probably not. We are substantial enough to fill up a wide shot which is what counts most, as anyone who watched the supposed throngs cheering the downfall of Saddam Hussein's statue knows. (Pictures of that demonstration imply hundreds of people. But longer range footage reveals that the rest of the square was empty.)

"Take charge, move the barge," eighty-four protesters cry in unison from under their umbrellas. (Thanks to the efforts of the Stuyvesant PA Political Action Committee as well as other Lower Manhattan activists, over the course of the morning, an approximate two hundred come and go.)

After several minutes of this pounding spondee, Kimberly Flynn suggests an alternative: "Dust, dioxin, lead, asbestos/ We don't care if you arrest us."

"Uh-uh," I say, with regret that the wit will have to go unsung or rather, unshouted. "These people *do* care if they get arrested. Also, it's too complicated." We have already tried a more inventive chant, with sorry results. "They won't get the rhythm without a rehearsal."

"Act Up did more complex chants than this."

"That was a bunch of gay guys."

"You mean they all know showtunes?!" she exclaims, incredulous.

"Uh..." I stall, having painted myself into a politically incorrect corner, "yeah."

The press turnout is excellent for the same reason coverage of the school's reopening was so extensive five months earlier. Stuy is reknowned, with a record number of students winning Intel prizes and going on to first rate colleges every year. Former Stuyteacher Frank McCourt whose memoir, *Angela's Ashes*, is still showcased in the school library, won a Pulitzer Prize while four graduates have won the Nobel.[cxxiv]

However, in a city of overcrowded, failing schools, we avoid playing the elite card.

# I SUE YOU; YOU SUE ME;
# WE ALL SUE THE B.O.E.

Richard Ben-Veniste, special prosecutor at Watergate and a Stuyvesant graduate, calls the Alumni Association to ask if he can be of help. Sol Stern, author of *Breaking Free*, an account of the New York City public school system that defends vouchers and now a Stuydad, takes Marilena to see him. Thus begins the lawuit to force the Board of Education to clean the ventilation system.

This is not a universally popular move at the Parents' Association and several members of the Executive Board file grievances against Marilena for not following the Bylaws or for being imperious or something, while other parents jump on the bandwagon and file grievances against each other.

"You can't do that," protests one father about a particular grievance. An opposing father throws the book at him – literally: the book of Bylaws.[16]

The traffic of grievances thickens.

The Parents' Association's general membership is about to vote on whether to sue the Board of Ed. Speaking in favor are Richard Ben-Veniste and Hugh Kaufman; for the opposing side, testing company ATC.

After hearing the main arguments, parents line up in two queues, pro and con, to speak for one minute each. On behalf of the "cons," a Russian father says, "Education is more important than health," prompting Hugh to observe afterwards, "They're Stepford wives." (He should have been there the night Dr. Marjorie

---

[16] This conversation is approximate but the book throwing, real.

Clarke presented a version of her historic testimony to the PA and got heckled for her troubles.)

As a former parent, I'm allowed to speak at Marilena's discretion. I use my minute to ask Hugh the impression of ATC he gleaned from the Ombudsman hearings.

"I'd have some doubts about what they said," he replies.

The votes are counted by an equal number of people from both sides. To confirm that voters are parents, they are asked their children's birthdays.

"Mothers were pretty good," reports Richard Roth. "Fathers were O.K., except for one guy who didn't make any sense. He said he got confused because he had twins."

The PA votes two to one in favor of the suit.


Christie Whitman has moved the Ombudsman's office to that of the Inspector General. The Ombudsman will no longer be allowed to talk to the press, choose his staff or initiate cases. Instead, he will man the hotline.

The move, she maintains, is to fulfill his wish for greater independence. *("You want more independence, eh? Here.")*

Months later, Ombudsman Bob Martin tells me other reasons why the move to the I.G.'s office was so out of whack.

"The Ombdusman's office is about working things out. The I.G.'s office has two divisions, civil and criminal. They're about enforcement – with badges and guns."

"Guns?"

"Yeah. You know, black suits, white shirts. And some

of them carry guns."[17]

Marilena and I, along with other champions of the Ombudsman's office from around the country, go to Washington to support his appeal of EPA's decision. Towards the end of the hearing, Congressman Nadler asks EPA spokesman Joseph Martyak some pointed questions about the agency's lies following 9/11. Martyak answers minimally and as soon as the hearing adjourns, heads for the door.

There, however, he finds himself blocked by a woman in a neck brace.

"Tell these people the truth," she orders, referring to the New Yorkers who have leapt into the opening provided by Nadler.

Martyak is trapped.

"Who do you work for?" bellows Hugh from the back of the room, for the sake of anyone who might not know.

"EPA," says Martyak.

"I've never seen an agency where so many people are so dishonest," marvels Nadler.

Kaufman tells the Coeur d'Alène Press: "We're wounded but we're not dead and there's nothing more dangerous than a wounded tiger."

Shortly after this hearing, Bob Martin comes to New York to testify to the State Assembly on the aftermath of 9/11. The more immediate issue, however, is news about his appeal.

His phone rings: The Ombudsman has lost on a technicality. EPA is in Bob's office removing files while

---

[17] The trend for agents outside defense related departments to carry weapons is intensifying: "The number of non-Defense Department federal officers authorized to make arrests and carry firearms (200,000) now exceeds the number of U.S. Marines (182,000)." If The Public Shouldn't Have Them, Why Does The IRS Need AR-15s? Tyler Durden; Jun 24, 2016; http://www.zerohedge.com/news/2016-06-24/if-public-shouldnt-have-them-why-does-irs-need-ar-15s

Hugh salvages what he can before they change the locks.

Bob must fulfill his threat (or promise?) and quit.

He explains why he has fewer free speech rights than the janitor.

"If the janitor says, 'EPA's on the take,' he's protected. The Ombudsman isn't, because crticizing EPA is his job."

## IT'S ALWAYS THE FISH

"It's time to form a coalition of all the affected communities," says the New York Environmental Law and Justice Project's Kimberly Flynn. She has experience as an activist from working with the AIDS organization, Act Up, and experience with environmental struggles from advocating against the spraying of New York City with Malathion during the West Nile virus scare. But her affinity for coalitions may be traced back further still, to childhood, when she was one of four siblings on occasion uniting against parent authority figures.

In bygone years, she worked in the theater, most notably as dramaturge on *Angels in America*, starring Academy Award winner F. Murray Abraham on Broadway. A TV production featured Al Pacino as Roy Cohn and Meryl Streep playing four roles including Ethel Rosenberg and a male rabbi. Tony Kushner, the playwright, who'd been tutored by Kimberly's ideas on sadomasochism and environmental destruction,[cxxv] wrote a tribute to her as an afterword to part two of the play, *Perestroika*.

We arrange to hold a summit at Pace University on April 20th in which Hugh Kaufman, Congressman Nadler and Nadler's legislative aide, Lisette Morton, will lay out the National Contingency Plan. Representatives from downtown will then vote on whether or not to pursue the NCP in Lower Manhattan.

Some constituencies are leery of forging an alliance with us as the government's strategy of divide-and-conquer has sown discord between the east side of Lower Manhattan and the west. In a microcosmic reflection of global tensions, residents of Tribeca and Soho were 41 times more likely to have received post-9/11 aid than those from the less affluent neighborhoods of Chinatown and the Lower East Side.[cxxvi] They're also more likely to have health insurance.

Nevertheless, a total of sixty people attend, from an array of organizations ranging from Community Boards and schools to the Good Old Lower East Side which, at first, sounds like simply a quaint description of the neighborhood. Among the attendees is Sudhir Jain who represents over five thousand tenants.

We ask two Stuydads to check the list of invitees in order to keep agency representatives from gate-crashing the meeting.

Shortly after everyone has arrived and our security guard dads have determined it's safe to settle in to their seats, Dan Slippen from Pace slips in. Kimberly's eyebrows shoot up. He's provided us with several hundred dollars' worth of sandwiches, cookies and soft drinks but used to work for Chris Ward of the Port Authority, not an entity that's sympathetic to our agenda. We ask him to leave.

After Nadler's and Hugh's presentation on the National Contingency Plan and explanations from Lisette who, at twenty-six, is the most thorough NCP scholar of all, we vote unanimously to pursue the plan in Lower Manhattan. The sole "abstain" comes from a staffer from Clinton's office who has sat in the back row saying nothing, her presence becoming conspicuous only in the breach.

As part of our portfolio, we also agree to advocate for the re-opening of the Ombudsman's office. While the fox is minding the hencoop, he's the only dependable watchdog we've come across yet.

We decide on a name for ourselves – 9/11 Environmental Action – and break up into newly formed committees: One, to prepare for our first trip to Washington; another, to take on the health registry; a third, to set up a website; a fourth, to work with scientists on testing protocol.

There is to be no Chairperson or other designation of leadership. If press ask who the head of the organization is, as they routinely do, we are all entitled to identify ourselves as spokespersons. (The press are dubious about this arrangement but soon adapt and an analogous democratic structure will be used, nine years later, at Occupy Wall Street.)

I become the sole active member of the press committee whose first assignment is to write a press release about the meeting. The announcement ends with a quote from Hugh: "Even the fish in Alaska were treated better than the people of New York." He is referring to the Exxon Valdez case in which the plight of the fish prompted a better cleanup than we have received. (It was also fish that derailed the Westway highway project planned next to the Hudson River in Manhattan.[cxxvii]

But with the advent of the Bush administration, even the fish can't get a fair deal. The Army Corps of Engineers dumps 200,000 tons of "toxic sludge" into the Potomac River every year, in violation of the Clean Water and the Endangered Species Acts. This, they argue, is actually protective as it forces the fish to "flee the polluted area and escape fishermen."[cxxviii])

The coalition votes "aye" on the press release except for the line about the fish.

Among our missions is that of hounding Christie Whitman where- and whenever possible, thereby drawing attention to our cause. It happens that she went to my high school, a WASPy private school catering to Rockefellers and similar fellers. But as there's no reunion for a while, we can't figure out how to make use of this.

Soon enough, however, we learn from a well-placed ally that she is to speak at the Queens Hall of Science. So with twelve hours' notice, we plan a demonstration in the lobby.

Christie looks down at us from the balcony and asks with a thin veneer of concern that fails to mask her annoyance, what we are protesting about.

"National Contingency Plan!" we cry and, "EPA! MIA!" [Missing in Action]

"We're talking to FEMA," she says, in a show of appeasement.

A brief lull follows while she gives her talk inside. Then she exits out the back.

Our well-placed ally tells us the line about talking to FEMA is "code for, 'We're talking to the White House.'"

Brad Gair, FEMA's director of disaster relief for the World Trade Center, says he has funded all EPA's requests. They're the experts; he's just the bank.


Threatened with litigation, the Board of Ed has been testing the Stuyvesant ventilation system for lead. Paul Edwards reports that although the wipe samples are supposed to be collected under the watchful eye of Howard Bader, instead, the BOE has been collecting samples on their own from the spots that are least likely to harbor any dust. Howard has received a tip from a source that remains anonymous and steered the project back on course.[18]

Now the results are out but the BOE refuses to release them.

"We're waiting for the dioxin test results," they say, "so we can give them all to you at the same time."

"That's not necessary," says the PA.

PA Executive Board elections are approaching, critical for follow-through on the lawsuit and cleanup.

---

[18] Tests were taken over an extended period which has been collapsed here in the interest of simplicity.

Another day, another accolade for Christie. This time it is the "Gift of Breath" award which is being presented by a blameless – indeed, a worthy – children's organization.

Chanting, "Christie Whitman is no good! She won't clean our neighborhood!" we gather outside the Tribeca Rooftop as Christie and begowned, betuxxed Beautiful People arrive in limos and cabs, smiling vaguely as they float into the $350 a ticket gala.

"Give Christie the Gift of Breath award?" reads a sign by journalist Keith Crandell's daughter, Annie. "You must be choking."

We wanted to bring buckets and mops as props but Joel, our omnipresent Legal Observer, has said the mops could be seen as weapons.

Inside, a resident who's bought a ticket to the event tells the curious onlookers what the rabble outside is raving about. Later she reports that Christie devoted the last quarter of her speech to defending herself against our accusations.

"We should do something about Wall Street," proposes resident Nina Lavin during our next monthly meeting. "That's where the power is."

Since the cleanup of Ground Zero is about to end, after which the press will lose interest, a few days later, we hit the Stock Exchange and surrounding subway stations with fliers.

"They're not menus," resident Wayne Decker[cxxix] assures passers-by, thus getting rid of his stash in record time.

First lobbying trip: Where to stay? Church basement? Six of us in one room at the Holiday Inn?

"Can you imagine the morning with everyone needing the bathroom at the same time?" Marilena asks rhetorically.

Sudhir Jain and I end up at a B&B furnished with family portraits from the 1880's.

"Help yourself," says "Erin the Innkeeper," indicating the decanters of lemonade and sherry in the parlor.

The following morning, Marilena arrives after pulling an all-nighter at the heated Stuy PA election. One father shouted, prompting another to call the cops. And the results were a fiasco: We lost the presidency and a majority of the board. The only good news is that Linda Lam is Vice President.

Hugh lays out his advice for our efforts in Congress: With Congressmen Markey, Dingell and Pallone, we should emphasize transparent process. With a staffer for a Missouri Congressman, for instance, we should point out the volunteer firefighters from Missouri who are getting sick.

Hillary Clinton, he says, knows EPA is full of shit. We have to let her know that *we* know.

Two scientists, Paul Bartlett and Monona Rossol, have come with us as well as CBS reporter Paul Moniz.

In one Republican office, we are greeted with skepticism until fashion designer Pat Moore[cxxx] shows the aide pictures of her apartment at 125 Cedar Street, which looks like Pompeii. She and her husband shoveled out one and a half tons of debris.

The highlight of the day is a meeting with Hillary herself. Unlike the other Senators', her office exudes taste, with yellow silk arm chairs and elegant drapes as opposed to the grim, I-have-more-important-things-to-think-about furnishings of the men's quarters.

Hillary listens intently to Paul Bartlett's explanation of the precautionary principle which prevails in Europe. But she seems particularly captivated by Dorothy Suecoff, Stuyvesant's chapter leader to the United Federation of Teachers, whose voice is hoarse from the contamination she's been exposed to all year. This impression is confirmed when Hillary sends Dorothy a thank you note.

The rest of us fill in the gaps. I say that FEMA has not released billions of dollars, which could turn into a scandal along the lines of the one at the Red Cross where almost half the funds collected for victims of 9/11 were saved for future catastrophes;[cxxxi] an observation which Hillary has her aide, Gabrielle Tenzer, note. (Continuing in the same tradition, in 2011, the Red Cross raised $500,000,000 for Haiti with which they built a mere six homes.[cxxxii] Perhaps that is one of the reasons why, when Hurricane Matthew leveled homes in 2016, Haitians specifically asked for donations to bypass the Red Cross in favor of local charities.[cxxxiii])

"What do we do next?" someone asks as soon as we've completed our rounds.

"I learned from the Civil Rights movement," says Dorothy, who's African-American, "you turn the heat down but you don't turn it off."

Having held onto them for six weeks until the elections were over, (they never did like the current PA, particularly after it initiated the lawsuit,) the Board of Ed, under threat of litigation, now releases the results of the lead tests.[cxxxiv]

Some are over 1100, thirty times the legal standard for the floor. (There's no legal standard for ventilation systems.)[cxxxv]

*So what?* pronounces Klasfeld, a self-confessed non-expert. *The lead will stay in the walls.*

"He seems to think the Stuyvesant walls are a sort of Roach Motel," Paul Edwards remarks. "The lead gets in but it can't get out."

Paul speaks with Chris de Angelis of the Department of Health who says lead in the ducts doesn't count and the Board of Ed hasn't found lead in the air. Paul reminds him that that's because the Board of Ed hasn't *tested* for lead in the air.

Paul tells De Angelis that Howard Bader says the dust in the ventilators is a quarter of an inch thick. De

Angelis does a one-eighty and says that that should be cleaned up no matter what it's made of.


In a dramatic turnaround from its previous *noli me tangere* approach to indoor air, EPA announces that it's launching a cleanup of Lower Manhattan residences.[19]

Why not businesses and schools? Or Chinatown, where kids are coming down with new-onset asthma?

"This is a good place to start," explains Regional Deputy Administrator Kathleen Callahan, in what she surely knows is a futile attempt to mollify us. (For other shortcomings of the plan, see How Science Was Abused to Perpetrate Lies After 9/11: *A Cautionary Tale for the Approaching Peak Oil Disaster*, Appendix S.)

But the main flaw of the cleanup plan is that it abandons EPA's scientifically-based protocol of representative testing in concentric circles from the epicenter of the disaster, followed by cleanup as warranted. Instead, the agency couches their present plan in come-and-get-it terms, on top of which, their flier aims not at getting the job done but rather, at quelling residents' "concern."

"While scientific data does not point to any significant long-term health risks," it reads, "people should not have to live with uncertainty about the future." The accompanying photo looks like an Ikea ad, with kids playing on the carpet. The response among residents of Lower Manhattan is predictably, and perhaps intentionally on EPA's part, anemic.[cxxxvi][20]

---

[19]  As this account follows events on several fronts, there's inevitable overlap in the time periods of successive sections.

[20]  As usual when EPA has abrogated its responsibility, Joel Kupferman steps in, testing a downtown building at the request of a tenant who has found asbestos on the roof.

The cleanup proceeds as a game with idiosyncratic rules. If you "prefer," they will first test your apartment rather than clean it. But with the exception of 250 apartments,[cxxxvii] whose results won't be released until after the program is completed, they will only test for asbestos. If you have a high reading, you get a complete asbestos abatement. If not, you forfeit your chance for any cleanup at all, regardless of whether you have cadmium, lead, mercury, silica, traces of human remains or any of thousands of other contaminants. If you opt for a cleanup without testing first, it'll be less thorough than the abatement but presumably better than nothing.[cxxxviii] (That presumption would later be challenged by residents who reported reckless violations of protocol including fans, a key part of the post-cleanup test, either missing, facing the wall or not being turned on at all.) In addition, EPA won't be testing dust, just air, although air tests have been known to fail in comparable situations, such as in the Brookfield,

---

EPA accuses Joel of planting the asbestos.

"70% of New Yorkers don't trust you," Joel tells them. "I have a better track record than that."

He goes on to add that the Asbestos Hazard Emergency Response Act standard should apply at the daycare center housed in the building.

"That's only for schools that go from K-12," says EPA.

"So the littler kids shouldn't be protected?" Joel retorts.

EPA excuses itself by explaining they have only one investigator and he has a back problem.

Joel concludes: "So the health of Lower Manhattan depends on this guy's chiropractor."

He and environmental consultant Uday Singh also go down to the subway to collect dust samples when a cop stops them in the belief that they might be terrorists.

"Look," says Joel, "We're not leaving dust – we're taking it."

He finds out which precinct the cop is from and tells him the ways in which it's contaminated.

The cop takes his card.

127

Connecticut school system. And, as described earlier, in their own building they relied on dust samples to justify a full asbestos abatement.

They'll also clean if you have "visible dust." But what that means is not clear. One inspector tells tenant representative Caroline Martin she doesn't have World Trade Center dust because World Trade Center dust is "brown and gritty." Another asserts that a different tenant doesn't have World Trade Center dust because World Trade Center dust is "gray and fluffy." The visible dust criterion also ignores the fact that the most lethal dust may be *invisible*. (At one point, EPA even defines "visible dust" neighborhoods as those whose dust had been visible, in the aftermath of 9/11, from an airplane.)

The real sticking point is that the agency won't clean ventilation systems where, experience has shown, much of the contamination came to rest.

Finally, EPA is relying on a standard of contamination that's a hundred times higher than they have traditionally used at most Superfund sites where only one extra person per million would get cancer from a particular contaminant. In our case, the criterion is one in ten thousand – *per contaminant* – and there were over two thousand contaminants.

Why? Because when they shoot for a higher standard, their instruments clog. Eventually Bertram Price, a scientist who is otherwise hostile to our complaints, suggests, "Why not run several instruments side by side for a shorter time? Then they won't clog." EPA doesn't answer.

The other reason for their slipshod standards in this case is the importance of Lower Manhattan to the economy. (For the implications of that brave new policy, see The EPA and a Dirty Bomb, Appendix E.)

*Besides,* protests EPA, *the job is too big. This was an unprecedented attack.*

"It's not unprecedented!" Hugh explodes. "EPA has cleaned up all these contaminants before."

A newly hatched activist joins our ranks, fired with enthusiasm for ideas which she has no intention of carrying out herself, for she is to be the brains behind the operation.

The suggestions are familiar, having been proffered by other newly-hatched activists who have come and gone:

1) We should call our elected officials.
2) We should get ourselves a good lawyer, pro bono, and sue the government.
3) We should commit civil disobedience, preferably after securing the lawyer in 2) whose first job can be to get us out of jail.
4) We should get ourselves a celebrity.

Needless to say, we are regularly in touch with our elected officials, cherish Joel as our pro bono lawyer and have debated civil disobedience ad nauseam. I have also tried the celebrity route, sending emails to two former clients of my father as well as to Erin Brockovich at her law firm, run by the Albert Finney character in the movie that put them on the map; finally, to a connection at the *Daily Show*, because its host, Jon Stewart, lives in Tribeca.

Several members have also tried *Sixty Minutes*, the big brother you dream of bringing to school to show the bullies. As one insider puts it, "The last thing politicians want is for *Sixty Minutes* to interview someone who's sick, then cut to Congress voting the wrong way."

Dignified silence or "Decline"s on all sides. It will be several years before *Sixty Minutes* airs a report on sick Ground Zero workers, still more before Jon Stewart, working with John Feal and other Ground Zero heroes – in addition to 9/11 Environmental Action under Kimberly's directorship as well as other Lower Manhattan organizations – successfully browbeats

Congress into permanent passage of the James Zadroga 9/11 Health and Compensation Act.

What about forming an alliance with the victims' families? Marianne Edwards suggests. Horrific as are the reasons for it, they qualify, for the moment, as celebrities. Wouldn't it be great if they'd say something like, "We don't want to see any more victims?"

One Stuymom who lost her sister in the disaster is willing to speak so we plan an occasion. Then the workers find her sister's remains and the moment passes.

Complicating the situation is a growing rift between some of the families and residents over construction at Ground Zero, the families advocating for the site to be considered hallowed ground and left untouched. A few even petition for debris to be returned there from Fresh Kills, Staten Island, in the hope that their loved ones' remains will be at least represented, as this is "the only grave they will ever know." Eileen Horney, whose 26-year-old son died at the World Trade Center, protests that she'd like to stop "visiting him at a garbage dump."

But what families envision as a memorial of absence "from earth to infinity," residents see as "a big hole in the ground" that will prevent them from walking across the plaza to get home.

(After constructing a website for the newly "revived" World Trade Center Environmental Organization, which had been founded to instigate the barge demonstration, I would later co-ordinate with several families for a protest at the laying of the cornerstone at Ground Zero on July 4, 2004.[cxxxix] Family members would also lend their invaluable support to the passage of the James Zadroga 9/11 Health and Compensation Act.)

"This is driving me nuts," Kimberly complains one morning about an activist who might more accurately be described as a hyperactivist. "Asking why we don't slap signs on passing busses? Do you know what kind of fines you get for that? Plus jail time. I think he might be a plant. If he is, he's the most ingenious plant imaginable.

'And this taking us to task for failing to organize 'the masses.' Ah, the elusive masses. I feel like saying to him, 'O.K. See you at the demo, 5 o'clock – you bring the masses.'"

Then the activist signs an email, "Vladimir."

"This answers your question," I tell Kimberly. "He's not an EPA plant – he's a Russian spy."

9/11 Environmental Action is past its honeymoon phase, with too much on the agenda and too few hands to do it all.

EPA holds a press conference for which we receive no more than an hour's notice so that the only people available to counter their claims are Joel, Kimberly and me. The press, however, are more open to conflicting opinions than nine months earlier and we get soundbites into several reports.

Independence Plaza, the moderate-income housing complex where some of our core members live, faces a new lease which will effectively evict them. They hold a demonstration for which they need our support.

Our allies at BMCC, the college across the street from Stuyvesant, protest at City Hall against budget cuts.

Finally, Chinatown mobilizes against FEMA, the Federal Emergency Management Agency, to protest the "toxic air" downtown.

Theirs is a whole new order of magnitude of demonstration with hundreds of people marching in costume, playing drums, accompanied by a dragon and press in a variety of languages. Everyone leaflets everyone else about still other upcoming demonstrations.

Afterwards, one of our company heads to the Midwest where protesters have been getting death threats from the local mining community.

"An activist's work is never done," observes Kimberly.

Despite the aching need for participation, however, it's hard to maintain standards since everyone is working for free. Regardless of job title, the work ends up getting done by whoever decides to do it, a "method" – if it can even be called that – that results in some squabbling since, to keep the coalition cohesive, we have to reach consensus on all major actions. This means that any member who signs a letter or testimony in the name of the coalition has to run it by everyone else first, a process whose results can have the feel of a camel as in the definition: "A horse drawn by a committee."

Such a forced marriage/lifeboat/holding pen invites a fourth cliché: a ticking time bomb.

One disaffected member, upon hearing that Maggie Clarke, who cannot come to a hearing, will have her statement read aloud by Kimberly, says that's inappropriate since Kimberly is not, herself, a scientist.

"In response to your point that it is not a good idea for me to impersonate a scientist," Kimberly responds, "let me hasten to say: *Duh.*"

Then she gets raked over the coals for "doing outreach" we supposedly haven't authorized her to do.

"Why don't you take the Lower East Side and let her take Chinatown?" suggests a would-be mediator, as though Lower Manhattan were spoils to be divided.

"What is this?" Kimberly fumes later. "It's not as though we're in high school and I talked to her boyfriend in the hall."

Finally, an email we don't recognize infiltrates the listserve and uses it to broadcast complaints.

"Could this be XX...@yahoo.com?" Diane Dreyfus speculates, referring to an earlier mole. "Someone with Multiple Personalities, all of them unpleasant?"

"Your problem," observes Miriam, "is: Too many chiefs; no Indians."

If we didn't have immediate tasks, we'd fall apart.

FEMA announces that it is releasing $20 million for the Ground Zero schools to be cleaned over the course of the summer. The Board of Ed, however, holding true to its m.o. of passive aggression, balks at removing the carpet in the Stuyvesant auditorium even though the room had served as a command center for Ground Zero workers. Eventually, though, they back down, agreeing to change the carpet... for aesthetic reasons. It seems they never liked it anyway.

Having learned of ultrasonication, a test developed by EPA itself for soft surfaces, I forward several memos on the subject to those Stuyparents who are still active on the environmental front and who are now known as "Concerned Stuyvesant Community" (a *faux* tip of the hat to a member of the opposition who, like EPA, refers pseudo-solicitously to our "concern.") Where air tests failed to detect asbestos in the Brookfield Connecticut school system, ultrasonication uncovered levels that led to a thorough abatement.[cxl] Why not perform the test on a piece of the carpet? Concerned Stuy gives a green light to the idea.

PA engineer Howard Bader takes two samples, one of which comes back at 2.4 million structures per square centimeter. The standards for ultrasonication are not established but using the less sensitive microvac, the normal background level in a city is between five and ten thousand. The experts we consult strongly recommend a complete abatement in this case, more thorough than the currently planned cleanup.

True to form, Klasfeld maintains that the asbestos will stay in the carpet. Thus there's no need to test, much less replace, soft furnishings (more likely to harbor contamination) such as the auditorium seats. We counter that it's unlikely the asbestos eschewed the seats in favor only of the carpet.

We send out a press release entitled, "Stuy High Asbestos Sky High." Then Linda Lam, John Healy, Paul and I meet with Marla Diamond of CBS radio for her series called, "Rising from the Ashes," one segment of which is to be devoted to Stuyvesant. Two of the others will focus on firemen and residents; the fourth, to EPA. Can we recommend anyone for her to speak to there?

"She wants contacts at EPA?" Kimberly exclaims when I tell her. "Give her Cate."

"You're a genius."

"And what about our other friend?" she continues, meaning Hugh. "She wants EPA, we'll give her EPA."

Not long after the press publish the Stuy test results, in a report on the health benefits of the prospective smoking ban in restaurants, Mayor Bloomberg chooses a noteworthy analogy, to our ears: "For instance, if you found asbestos in the air, you'd close the building immediately."

One morning, two seats from the auditorium go missing. I look at Paul.

"Wasn't me," he shakes his head with a regret that suggests he's telling the truth. Like me, he's jealous. But Paul works in financial services and has several securities licenses which he can't afford to put at risk with an arrest.

The Board of Education swears it wasn't them either but not long after, they agree to test the seats for asbestos. However, they refuse to use ultrasonication on the grounds that the EPA-generated method is "controversial." Instead, they devise their own protocol which involves beating the seats with sticks, then testing the air.

This test is less controversial because no one's ever done it before.

If they must do such a test, advises one scientist, they have to beat the seats with baseball bats for four hours.

"What we need is a world class dominatrix," muses Paul, "and a couple of Sumo wrestlers. When they've finished beating the seats, they can sit on them. Then the Board of Ed'll *have* to replace them."

At a Parents' Association General Meeting on the issue of what to do about the seats, a member of the opposition scoffs at us for "sifting through the dust like amateur detectives."

She is the last speaker of the evening so we have no chance to point out that in our "amateur sifting," we have, in fact, *found* high levels of contamination.

One of the new members of the PA Executive Board explains that she was elected on a platform of moderation. Allowing tests recommended by scientists critical of the EPA would be kowtowing to the radical left.

She seems to think that in the choice between life and the risk of death, if you opt for life, you're being an extremist.

The PA votes to let the Board of Ed test the seats in whatever way they see fit.

The seats pass the Board of Ed's test.

Over the course of the summer cleanup, the Board of Ed which, under the stewardship of its new Chancellor, Joel Klein, has refashioned itself as the *Department* of Ed, does not use union labor. Local 78, the asbestos contractors' union who've placed an inflatable blue gorilla outside the school to advertise the violation, tells us that you can see asbestos on the workers' shirts.

*Ombudsman Hearing*

We get there early and stake out seats in the front row. Nadler and crew arrive with Lieutenant Manuel Gomez in his uniform adorned with medals. Senators take their places on the dais with their shadows, the staffers, standing against the wall behind them, ready to lean in with notes or whispered reminders.

I recognize Susan Shortz and her colleagues from the last Ombudsman hearing. They're from Pennsylvania where the EPA let acres full of lead from used batteries decay for years.[cxli] Susan says that a large number of kids in her neighborhood have learning disabilities. Also, people die off younger than average around there but when Susan has brought this up with the State Department of Health, they have replied, "No younger than anyone else in this part of Pennsylvania." Susan figures that's because companies are burying toxic material all over the area.

A woman comes in aided by two other people as she walks with heavy-duty metal canes and has difficulty sitting down. I figure her illness must be the result of an environmental disaster; she'll make an effective witness.

Since I have long since given up belief in the Inspector General as an actual person, I don't look for him. If indeed there is such a person, I imagine him a nondescript bureaucrat in a Kafkaesque nightmare. But as no one has ever referred to the Inspector General by name, I figure that while there may have been such a person once, the term now refers only to an office.

A panel of agency reps testify. Then it's Nadler's turn.

Four days before September 11, he testifies, in Libby, Montana, Christie said, "It would be immoral not to pay for remediation of homes." His final salvo, "An independent Ombudsman is intolerable only to an agency that has something to hide," meets with spontaneous applause. The only reason that more don't join in is that they know better. Senator Jeffords admonishes us to hold fire as though we were in a hospital. Kimberly says later that the chiding was pro forma and that covertly, if that's possible, Hugh was clapping too.

Hillary says she'll give Nadler's testimony to colleagues who helped create the agency to show them how it "has been eviscerated" and gives the Ombudsman credit for bringing to light facts which before their hearing had remained hidden.

Now Susan Shortz testifies that at the Pennsylvania site, there are enough lead battery casings buried to fill twelve football fields fifty feet deep. The company would pile the casings "as high as this room," (an august cavern with lofty ceilings,) bulldoze them and pile them up again. The EPA cleaned up people's backyards but still, some of those yards are within fifty feet of the site itself. When you vacuum the living-room, it pulls the lead up. Susan and her cohorts have been fighting since 1987.

Katherine Zanetti, a petite woman from Idaho, is next, introducing herself as a forty-nine-year-old grandmother four times over. Her beef with the EPA, unlike that of everyone else on the panel, is that they won't go away. She's glad to hear from the other witnesses that it is possible to get rid of them.

Hugh later tells us that's one of the reasons he decided to investigate the Idaho site: To point up the "arbitrary and capricious" nature of EPA involvement.

Idaho's Senator Mike Crapo is on the committee. Although a rightwing NRA sympathizer, when it comes to the EPA, he's on our side. The same seems to go for everyone on the Environment and Public Works committee. From right to left, politically speaking, they all understand that their constituencies have suffered at the hands of the EPA and they're all behind the reinstatement of the Ombudsman. The only exception is Carper from Delaware who doesn't have anything like a Superfund site in his state and to whom this is all news.

The other Senators, though savvy about EPA, don't have a clue what's been going on in New York. I decide that my written testimony, which I'd been planning to mould around S606,cxlii the Senate bill about what should be done with the Ombudsman's office, should focus instead on details of the last nine months in Lower Manhattan.

Now the woman with the metal canes gets up to the witness panel. Her name is Nikki Tinsley and she is, of course, the Inspector General. Her testimony would be innocuous enough, if it were true: The move to her office was to enhance the independence of the Ombudsman, as he had requested.

The trouble is that her testimony is not true.

Hillary asks to reverse the order of witnesses and bring up Ombudsman Bob Martin. Tinsley "has another appointment" but is prevailed on to cancel in order to sit side by side with her nemesis.

Pennsylvania Senator Arlen Specter grills her, saying he doesn't believe that what the EPA was doing was enhancing the Ombudsman's independence. After all, wouldn't the Ombudsman now have to report to Nikki Tinsley herself? Well, yes. And wouldn't she be the one to decide to act on his recommendations? Well, yes. Then, doesn't that, asks Crapo, make *you* the Ombudsman?

Martin testfies that there had been several attempts to seize his files while his temporary restraining order was in effect. When he was moved, the EPA finally came in and took his files under protest by the only person who was there from his staff at the time, a scientist by the name of Bell. Tinsley says her office called him in advance but Martin wouldn't talk to her. Her intention had only been to move the files to her office.

Martin says he was never called.

Hillary says she finds it suspicious that the Ombudsman was uncovering conflicts of interest, then suddenly, there was no more Ombudsman.

"Would you be willing to negotiate a mediated arrangement with Ms. Tinsley?" Specter asks Martin.

"Yes."

"What about you, Miss Tinsley?"

"I'm not sure I have the authority to agree to that," she equivocates. "I'll get back to you."

The upshot is, she's going to have to.

After the hearing, we talk to a sympathetic journalist who later describes us as New Yorkers who claim the Ombudsman was the only one to get things accomplished in Lower Manhattan.

*EPA's First Public Meeting*
*Community Board 1*

We show up at 5:30, only to settle in for half an hour of listening to Community Board 1 mull over liquor licenses. ("The bar downstairs will seat twenty; the upstairs one, ten. No – no band.") To pass the time, we read EPA's handout of FAQs from their website, which Kimberly refers to as EPA's "fack you" to residents. Finally, with licenses and warnings about noise, the hopeful restaurateurs file out.

First up from EPA is Ray Basso. He is at his most affable but we cannot be cajoled into good humor.

Spokeswoman Mary Mears says the reason EPA hasn't sent out brochures educating the public the way the city did for West Nile virus is that they lack the funds.

Like the Board of Ed or any other transparent liar, EPA toggles between excuses as though choosing one because the other is in the laundry.

Excuse #1: "There's no money."

When their opponent points out that there is indeed money, they switch to...

Excuse #2: "There's no problem." (At one point, a member of EPA even describes the dust in one building as consisting of "nutrients," as though if we could just remember to eat it instead of breathing it, WTC contamination would be nutritious.[cxliii])

They're going to publish the scopes for the cleanup, they assure us, once they've gone through peer review, to which Maggie Clarke responds, "I'm a peer and I'm telling you they aren't any good."

Mears seems on the verge of tears. We remain as unmoved as Mme. Lafarge knitting throughout the beheadings of the French revolution.

Although we've been told that EPA wants to meet separately with the coalition, an attitude which would give us the upper hand, a couple of our less experienced members are too impatient to wait for them to make the first move. We tell them Hugh Kaufman asks why we're meeting with EPA at all, the stronger stance being to expose them in the press. As a compromise, someone suggests that we present them with a list of bare minimum demands that have to be met before we'll talk to them again, as opposed to our wish list. The problem is, there is no wish list. All our demands are bare minimum.

A meeting is set up for which we debate how forceful to be.

"Bring *Awake* Magazine," says one resident, referring to the pamphlet published by the Jehovah's Witnesses. "That way they can't throw you out; it'll be a free speech issue."

We gather in the lobby of the EPA building where time-honored quotes from Martin Luther King and other inspirational figures have been etched into the marble floor of the building whose foundation rests on an African burial ground.[cxliv] Bush and Cheney look down from the wall, wearing the crooked smiles of used car salesmen. But, to paraphrase Tolstoy, each is crooked in its own way.

We're in a paradoxical position since EPA is failing on every front. Yet we need them to clean since they're the only agency with the resources to do the job properly;

it's not as though we can hire someone else.[21]

And with their present cleanup plan, even more dilemmas appear. On the one hand, the plan is fatally flawed; on the other, their outreach to promote it is self-defeating.

Region 2 Deputy Administrator Kathleen Callahan, as always, professes sympathy for our "concern." We respond that we're concerned EPA is treating the issue not so much as one of health, but as one of psychotherapy.

"I'm sorry you feel that way," says Callahan, in a classic tactic that appears to acknowledge a problem while simultaneously sidestepping blame. She might as well add, "Because I'm not going to do anything about it."

Not long after, EPA meets with independent scientists we have recommended.

"It was scary," reports Kimberly, "watching [architect and PS 89 parent] Amie Gross educate EPA on ductwork and hearing them say, 'Really? Wow! Could you, like, recommend some contractors?'"

---

[21] EPA feels differently, of course, and at every turn, will continue their tradition of shunning responsibility: "Regarding the eternal issue of EPA taking the lead on the demolitions: EPA has taken to using the phrase but that's far from doing the deed. 'Taking the lead' means... being the ultimately responsible party. What EPA means by it is that they're busy on the phone fobbing off responsibility onto other agencies. They've adopted an ever-so-polite stance of, "Department of Labor, you're such great experts in asbestos and you, Department of Health, are the authorities on lead; you must, of course, take the lead." Then when it's time for the lawsuits, we'll have a room full of agencies pointing fingers at each other." Appendix Q; Testimony to the World Trade Center Expert Technical Review Panel; February 23, 2005

Adding to the difficulty with ducts is that at one particular housing complex, they're not designed to be cleaned rigorously; as the linings are made of sheetrock, they'll simply fall apart.

To shut us up, EPA changes some of its protocols, now allowing whole buildings to apply to be cleaned. (The term "whole building" is misleading, however, as they still haven't budged on HVAC systems.)

We talk about mobilizing people downtown to choose that option. EPA Region 2's Administrator Jane Kenny says, "You're in a better position to do that than we are."

Why? Because we're a bunch of ragtag activists and they're a billion dollar federal agency? We point out that it's harder to mobilize people when they're busy pooh-poohing the risks.

"We're not a public health entity," Kenny says, "so it's not our job to declare a public health emergency."

"Then it also isn't your job to tell people there's *no* public health emergency," I respond.

Resident Barbara Einzig reports that one of her neighbors was told not to put her dog on the floor because there was mercury on it but it didn't need to be cleaned because mercury is not a problem on the floor (unless you're a dog or a baby.)

The cleanup scopes should be out Monday.

True to their word, EPA distributes to several members of 9/11EA its proposed scopes. But to make sure we don't go running to the press with the document, a watermark of the word "DRAFT" is stamped across every page.

(After we meet with them to protest the scopes' shortcomings, they make minimal changes, remove the watermark, then do an end run around us to hand them to the press themselves.)

There are to be two types of cleanup, Scope A and Scope B like those Dr. Seuss characters, Thing One and Thing Two.

Scope B is an asbestos abatement.

Scope A uses asbestos abatement contractors but not to do asbestos abatement. Scope A is a lick and a promise.

You get Scope B if you have too much asbestos, according to EPA's test. But EPA will still only do an air test. If your asbestos is in the dust or the furniture which is not currently being disturbed, it won't be found. Also, EPA will leave it to you whether or not to have "aggressive testing" done. Their misleadingly labeled "modified-aggressive" testing probably won't find asbestos. But if you want aggressive testing, EPA hands you a release with threatening-sounding consequences that you will be taking upon yourself. What the release does not say is the thing we worry about most which is the reason we hesitate to recommend that people go for that option: It could release WTC toxics that would otherwise remain latent.

We organize a press conference in which Dr. Majorie Clarke and Monona Rossol critique EPA's plan. NY1 airs its report repeatedly over the course of the weekend but as this is the dead of summer, no one's around to see it.

Having debated whether or not to advise tenants to apply for EPA's cleanup, we decide simply to inform them of how to make the most of the current offer.

Diane Dreyfus and a few other members download forms from the agency's website to sign up for a cleanup and hit the streets, getting a brisk response until EPA's Ben Barry claims that there's a risk of fraudulent contractors showing up.

"What kind of crazy contractor would clean apartments for free?" Diane retorts.

Barry then says he's afraid that in the process of signing people up, 9/11EA will criticize the cleanup.

"We couldn't get them interested if we were trashing the plan, now, could we?" Diane points out.

Finally, EPA says they won't accept the forms because they weren't electronic. The upshot: We could all be legally liable for people who took our advice and thought they would get a cleanup but now won't.

Once the cleanup gets underway, EPA follows hazardous waste protocols for removing debris but yet again, does not have the workers wear respirators, prompting one activist to observe, "What they're saying is, 'We treat you worse than dirt.'"

We organize a protest outside the agency's headquarters where resident Ilona Kloupte shows us the rashes that she acquired from putting on the clothes in her contaminated apartment. People should have two sets of clothing, someone remarks, "like keeping kosher." (When Ilona later holds a press conference with Nadler and Hugh Kaufman because despite her lab reports indicating contamination, EPA is giving her the low-key cleanup, the media have a field day with the CNN cameraman who refuses to enter the apartment.)


NY1 is holding a Town Hall, to be broadcast live nationwide on C-SPAN, concerning physical and mental health after September 11.

Maggie and Marilena were to have been on the panel but were replaced at the last minute by shrinks.

EPA doesn't show up, notes NY 1's John Schiumo with some irony.

When it comes time for audience comments, Maggie asserts that Bush and Co. rushed us all back downtown to save Wall Street, a claim which will be confirmed the following year by no less an authority than the EPA Inspector General's report.

Ilona Kloupe has brought pictures of workers on the pile with respirators while she, a hundred feet away, had no such protection.

"And what is the result?" she asks rhetorically. "This!" She pulls out a bag of medications.

High School for Leadership and Public Service mother Janis Jones says that when the school first reopened at its home building one block from Ground Zero, the kids complained about having to watch body parts being carted through the street. The Board of Ed bribed them with fifty-dollar gift certificates to Waldenbooks or the sporting goods store Modell's for one month's perfect attendance; a hundred for the whole semester.

Lest the public be put off by the recent environmental alarums in the media, the Lower Manhattan Development Corporation launches a campaign to quell their unease with grants worth up to $14,500 for a two year commitment to live downtown; **the closer to Ground Zero, the bigger the amount**.[cxlv]

Those who take the bait are the hardest sell on problems they might have signed up for. As one of them puts it: "Twelve thousand dollars buys an awful lot of beer."

Around the rest of the city, FEMA puts up notices on street lamps about a HEPA vacuum/air purifier/air conditioner giveaway, with phone numbers to rip off as though they were offering guitar lessons.

First you order whichever appliances you're interested in for up to $1600, then apply for reimbursement which you may or may not get. (A call to CleanAir, the company contracted for the project, is reassuring on this point: They say they'll wait for your order to be approved before shipping it.)

A deft PR move on the part of the federal government but no substitute for scientifically-mandated cleanup. HEPA vacuuming is, of course, effective for some

145

contaminants but others, such as mercury, may vaporize, rendering them inhalable.

On the media front of the government's campaign to silence criticism, an article appears by New York Times health columnist Jane Brody, asserting that people busy themselves with environmental toxics because they already have enough to eat and are looking for something to worry about.

To underscore her point, Ms. Brody consults a psychiatrist from Topeka, Kansas, who explains it all for us: "People are scared about environmental dangers. Being scared affects their ability to think realistically and use good judgment."[cxlvi] Moral: Don't listen to people who raise questions about environmental hazards, however justifiably. They can't think straight.

Underlying our fears are uncertainty, the psychiatrist continues; a tendency to overreact and seek scapegoats in stressful situations; guilt about our affluence; and an unspoken wish to return to a simpler and purer world.

"A cardinal rule in toxicology," Brody explains, "is 'the dose makes the poison.' You can eat a dozen carrots at once with no ill effect but 400 carrots could kill you."[cxlvii] Whether from Vitamin A poisoning or burst stomach, she doesn't say. But the analogy does evoke the memory of EPA Spokeswoman Bonnie Bellow's asserting from the stage of Stuyvesant that you take a risk every time you bite into an apple.

The question is: How much dioxin, mercury, cadmium, PCBs, lead, tetrachhloroethane, isocyanates, PAHs, diesel, asbestos and thousands of other contaminants does it take to equal 400 carrots?

The U.S. Department of Labor has just found that Hugh Kaufman suffered retaliation from EPA for "performing too effective a job" in his capacity as lead investigator with the Ombudsman's office.

The result is that he is immediately reinstated – a move that Hugh says makes him, in effect, the Ombudsman – and is to continue investigating all twenty-six open cases. Unfortunately, the ruling does not affect Bob Martin's status, except in so far as it draws further attention to the EPA's recent absorption of the Ombudsman's investigatory functions into the Inspector General's Office.

EPA has five days in which to appeal, an opportunity Hugh assures us they will not miss.

This news promises to shift the context for Tuesday's Energy and Commerce Committee hearing on the Ombudsman's office when Congressman Nadler hopes to question witnesses, possibly including Whitman herself.

Surely not coincidentally, a few days later, the EPA Inspector General clears Christie Todd Whitman of alleged financial conflicts of interest.[cxlviii]

Five of us go to Washington to lobby for the reinstatement of the Ombudsman: Artist Miriam Songster, photographer and author Carla Breeze[cxlix] and I serve in supporting roles to two stars from the army: Lieutenant Manuel Gomez who worked on the pile 26 days for the New York Police Department and Sergeant David Abreu who worked as a fireman for about six days. However, both are lobbying as civilians which is confusing since Manny is in uniform. Still, with him around, we're less easily written off as envirokooks.

First stop: Office of Senator Inhofe from Oklahoma. His environmental staffer, Donna Michalek, is polite but hard to read. (The more we learn more about Inhofe's climate change denial in the years that follow, the better we understand her reticence.)

Carla lays out why we're there and introduces Manny who talks about the masks that could've and should've been worn by the recovery workers – there were thousands in storage – but weren't. Hugh has given us a copy of Juan Gonzalez' book, *Fallout*, which I place so that Donna can't miss the cover showing Giuliani in a paper mask.

Manny pulls such a mask out of his briefcase as he did at the Ombudsman hearing – the one with the legend, "Does Not Protect Lungs." The point is not lost on Donna.

Manny asks David to talk about the masks available to the firemen. How long were they good for? Forty-five minutes, David says. Manny says when he worked on the pile, masks were worn by the people in charge but not by the people doing the hard labor. One day, Manny brought along his own mask but was **told not to wear it for fear of creating panic.**

He also says that in the April before September 11, he submitted a report about how to respond to terrorist attacks. The report was based on the Oklahoma City bombing (and look whose office we're in!) but its warnings went unheeded after September 11. He also has what he calls a "hooked on phonics" kit to detect chemicals in the air. You break open an ampule and the chemicals turn different colors; the chart's on the back.

Donna reacts sympathetically and says that as a scientist, she specializes in particulate matter. I make sure to tell her about the P.M. 2.5 at Stuyvesant.

Miriam says she has worked in government and this is the first time she's felt betrayed.

Afterwards in the hall, we agree that she has stumbled on a great tack. She expands on her background: She used to work as an economist at all levels of government: State, city and federal. I think she should play this up in case they get the idea we're left-wing Bohemian New Yorkers.

"But I *am* a left-wing Bohemian New Yorker," Miriam points out. Still, she agrees to go along with the conservative approach.

148

On to John Stoody in Young's office. We saw him on our last lobbying trip so now he treats us like old buddies.

"I'm with you," he says, "but you've got to watch out about allying yourselves too closely with the Ombudsman. This Ombudsman has quite an ego. He was poking his nose into all sorts of things he wasn't supposed to."

Ego doesn't sound like Bob Martin. More likely, he means Hugh, who once began some advice, "In my humble opinion, not that I've ever had a humble opinion in my life..." As for Stoody's other complaint, isn't the whole point of the Ombudsman's office to look into things people don't want him to look into?

"Well then, why didn't Christie just fire him?" I ask provocatively, though feeling treacherous. "Why do away with the whole office?"

Stoody doesn't answer.

Next stop, Graham's office from Florida whose staffer tells us that our issues are "a New York problem."

The guys are hungry so for lunch we go to the Senate cafeteria where there's an all-you-can-eat buffet for $10.95.

Manny tells us how he got to know Nadler: He was back from the army on leave when he got stopped on the subway because he looked like a suspect in a robbery. They called him in for questioning. He showed his bus ticket that proved he was nowhere near the scene of the crime. Didn't matter. "You go the nice way or you go the hard way," he tells us, "but you go anyway."

At the precinct, he was let go. But three years later when he applied for a job, he was rejected on the grounds that the incident was still on his record. Everyone understood he was innocent. The judge said he was sorry but there was no law to wipe Manny's name from the books. He even wrote Manny a letter attesting to his innocence but that was all he could do.

Manny was furious but didn't know where to turn. Then one night at three a.m., he was up listening to Martin Luther King give a speech. Inspired, he went to the law library, read laws to see how they're constructed and drafted his own called the "Clear Your Good Name Act."

It took 47 drafts before he was satisfied. (Manny tells us that Nadler has dubbed him, "the soldier who won't go away.") He took the Clear Your Good Name Act to Nadler's office.cl Nadler invited him in for "five minutes" which turned into two hours at the end of which, he agreed to push the bill. The ultimate compliment was that he introduced it as Manny had written it, almost verbatim.

Manny says, "What I like about Congressman Nadler is that he knows he puts his pants on one leg at a time, like everybody else."

(The next day after the Ombudsman hearing, Hugh and the Ombudsman cheering section – Kimberly, resident Ann Arlen, journalist and activist Keith Crandell and I – run into Manny and David in the cafeteria. Manny tells this story again to the mostly new audience. After he and David leave, the rest of us discuss where Manny should go to law school and whether he knows how smart he is. Hugh thinks he knows he's street smart but doesn't realize he's also "smart smart." Anyway, it doesn't matter as he has the courage of his convictions. We decide on Yale rather than Harvard.)

For an hour, we make our way down the halls, leaving folders of information in the offices of Senators who might be receptive or who are on environmental committees, and sometimes managing a meeting with a relevant staffer. Then we split until 3:30 when we have an appointment with the environmental aide for the day's heavyweight, California Senator Barbara Boxer.

I walk around checking out the sights:

– In the office of a Senator from Montana, a picture of the boss with snow on his eyebrows;
– The office of Energy and Natural Resources with a poster of Eisenhower and the legend, "Your work is vital to victory. Our ships... Our planes... our tanks MUST have oil!"
– In the office of Senator Jerry Lewis from California, a hatrack with two sombreros, one black, the other red, both encrusted with cheap jewels. I imagine the only Jerry Lewis I know running around in a red sombrero.
– In a window looking out onto the courtyard that houses an enormous black Calder-like mobile, a sign that reads: Radioactive Roads Ahead.
– On the wall of the office of Don Young from Alaska, a nine foot polar bear.

*3:30 p.m: Senator Barbara Boxer's office*

We're led into the conference room by Boxer aide Bettina Poiret.

"I'm with you," she says. "We're investigating EPA for a series of violations.[22] In the interest of full disclosure, we had anthrax here." We shift uncomfortably in our seats.

---

[22] August 1, 2002: Boxer investigates EPA's neglect of Superfund sites which has led to mutant alligators in Florida and green rabbits at a plant that produced Agent Orange. S. Hrg. 107-1007; SUPERFUND PROGRAM: REVIEW OF THE EPA INSPECTOR GENERAL'S REPORT; HEARING BEFORE THE SUBCOMMITTEE ON SUPERFUND, TOXICS, RISK, AND WASTE MANAGEMENT OF THE COMMITTEE ON ENVIRONMENT AND PUBLIC WORKS; UNITED STATES SENATE; ONE HUNDRED SEVENTH CONGRESS; SECOND SESSION ON JULY 31, 2002; https://www.gpo.gov/fdsys/pkg/CHRG-107shrg83719/html/CHRG-107shrg83719.htm

"We called EPA but Dupont warned us that the chlorine they were using to clean the office could cause an explosion. When we confronted EPA, they just stopped circulating their cleanup procedures.

'One of our staff members had a recurrence of asthma and had to work from home for several weeks. We no longer accept hand-delivered packages."

After debriefing in Nadler's office, Manny and David go back to their hotel and I head over to the Senate gallery where they're discussing legislation all evening.

Along the way, the hall is lined with photographs:

– Senators playing football on the Capitol grounds, ties flying.
– Senator Robert Griffin bowling, tie flying.
– Senator Milton Young (R-ND) practicing karate.
– Nixon petting a lion's nose.
  (I will be reminded of this after the Iraq war when pictures are found of Uday Hussein posing stiffly with his pet lions. *What macho guys these politicians are!* is the not-so-subliminal message.)
– Senator Muskie giving a commendation award to Lassie who holds it in her mouth.
– Senators George Murphy (R-Ca) and Thruston Morton (R-Ky) walking a frog on a string.
– President Truman holding a birthday cake.
  (*And they're funloving too!*)

Two women mingle with the guys on the wall: A Senator campaigning from a plane, wind blowing her hair (female equivalent of tie flying.) And Rita Hayworth on a ladder in front of the Capitol, wind blowing her hair.

The debate on the Senate floor is about the imminent demise of Amtrak. This is followed by an update on wildfires raging in several Western states.

Court reporters spell each other every half hour, walking from one Senator to the next with their

152

stenographic machines tied around their necks, making them look like cigarette girls.

My notes end here because the usher chastises me that there's "no writing in this room."

I return to the B&B where, in the tranquility of recollection, an image returns of Nadler leaping into his pants two legs at a time.


It is the month leading up to the first anniversary. The press, particularly the French and the Japanese who, with their own history of mercury poisoning and radiation, have followed our story from the beginning, go into high gear. A Canadian newspaper, La Presse, comes out with an article called, "*Le cocktail chimique de Ground Zero*" ("*The chemical cocktail of Ground Zero*") and Patrick Bourat does an extended report for French TV. He will later be killed by an American tank in Iraq when he leaps to push a cameraman out of the way.[cli]

Univision calls for an interview. They have been unable to find a native Spanish speaker (we have not yet met the cleanup workers who have fallen ill) and without one, can't proceed with a report.

"Do you speak Spanish?"

I took French and Latin in school and I used to make up Spanish with the woman downstairs. Also, I have a Spanish dictionary.

"A little."

They come over an hour before airtime.

After some hurried corrections from the reporter, I say the three lines I have cobbled together from the dictionary and Univision leaves with a soundbite.

However, the press are most keen on talking to sick people. No one wants to be the poster child for World Trade Center illness. On the one hand, our members have had to endure their diagnoses' being dismissed as negligible; on the other, even when their symptoms have been acknowledged, they nevertheless justifiably believe they deserve to be seen as activists rather than as mere victims. But recognizing the importance of publicizing the issue, Nina Lavin and a couple of others agree.

Tomorrow is the first day of school. New Schools Chancellor Joel Klein meets Concerned Stuy and Joel Kupferman at the Tweed Courthouse, which is to be the site for the offices of the Department of Education. Klasfeld who, as a member of the previous administration, is on his way out, greets us affably, inviting us into a room which has yet to undergo its makeover; it looks like the set for a production of an Ionesco play, stripped of all furniture but for office chairs.

Paul Edwards explains that we feel betrayed by Klein's predecessor.

"I hope you'll never feel that way about me," Klein replies.

We tell Klein the scientific protocols that we've learned are necessary to ensure safety (two ceiling tiles per floor taken from places with high air flow; testing of upholstered furniture) and suggest that he meet with scientists not from EPA.

Klein, who takes diligent notes, says he is interested in meeting the scientists we have in mind and we leave feeling hopeful. But what do we do about the demonstration we've planned for the first day of school?

Don't call it off, we decide. Nothing's in writing and besides, it's a week before the first anniversary of 9/11.

We arrive at the demonstration the next day with esoteric slogans ("Air tests are for the birds") transformed into agitprop art.

Paul and Marianne Edwards' son Brian has made a sign that reads:

S. tuyvesant
A. sbestos
T. est

Stuyvesant SAT: 2.4 million

The opposition is quoted as saying, "The only toxins in the air are the fear that these people are instilling in our children."

Alex does not return to Stuyvesant as a scientist has told me that the tests performed following the summer cleanup were inadequate. At his new high school, he signs up for three college classes, the maximum allowed. But his advisor, who's only been on the job a week, misses a deadline so Alex only gets into one.

A Stuyvesant mother suggests I try to get him into Murrow.

"I tried them last year," I tell her.

"Don't go through the guidance office," she says. "Call Sol Bruckner, the Principal. He's very unusual."

Although school is three weeks into the semester, Bruckner takes Alex.

"Have him sign up for as many AP [Advanced Placement] classes as possible," he says on his way out of the interview.

At this off-hand suggestion that life may be returning to normal, I cry.


Meanwhile, Stuydad John X. is watching NY1 when they run a story about PS 65, an elementary school in Queens that's built on the site of an old airplane parts manufacturing plant. Toxic chemicals have been leaching into the ground water and kids have been getting sick. The Board of Ed says everything's fine.

John pursues the story, calling the parents who've been interviewed and finding out about a meeting they're holding. But then John has a family emergency so I go instead.

By way of preparation, John has given me the numbers of the parents who are at the forefront of the battle. I manage to reach Joe R. who groans when I tell him John can't come. There's been some major bonding going on, I gather, the solidarity of the trenches.

I tell Joe that his situation sounds like Love Canal. He's too young to have heard about that disaster so I tell him the story: Abandoned chemical plant; contaminated land; elementary school; illness. What turned the situation around was that the locals kidnapped an EPA official. That got the attention of the President at the time who was Carter. (One reason we haven't tried similar tactics this time is they wouldn't work so well with the current administration.)

Before meeting with the P.S. 65 parents, I google "toxic waste" and "elementary school" which yields more than ten thousand hits (as of September, 2016, that number has risen to 65,500) and take along printouts from the Center for Health, Environment and Justice which was founded by Lois Gibbs, the grassroots organizer at Love Canal.

The neighborhood is dilapidated, consisting mostly of unmarked buildings no longer officially in use. (Later on in the evening, a father tells me that behind some of the blank walls are illegal auto body repair shops. They have minimal electricity and no sewage system so on a good day, the smell downwind is revolting. He points to the wall across the street.

"There used to be a sign there, although it was a different one every month. But since all this stuff," he waves around P.S. 65, "they took 'em down. Probably there's someone inside there watching us now.")

Over a hundred people are standing outside the school: kids with their parents, cops, cameras and press with notepads.

"They're not letting everyone in," someone says. "The auditorium can only fit half the school at a time. Is that ridiculous for a school or what?"

I meet Joe and the leader in the struggle, Katie Acton. I explain I'm from Stuyvesant and 9/11 Environmental Action and we believe we have much in common with P.S. 65.

"Really?" asks one man. "And what might that be?"

"The Department of Education is allowing the kids to go to contaminated schools," I answer.

"I see," he responds. "By the way, I'm from the Department of Education."

I ask him why the press aren't allowed in. He says, "You know what? You can't come in either," and disappears inside.

Katie says that the chemical in the drinking water is trichloroethylene,[clii] the contaminant in the Erin Brockovich case and *A Civil Action*.[cliii] Six kids have cancer as do three teachers and some nearby residents, including a fifteen-year-old boy. But Katie has trouble getting people to sign petitions, one parent suggesting that they're afraid of losing their welfare checks. Others feel they're not sufficiently educated to fight City Hall. Katie's got Erin Brockovich herself on the case, however. Among other advice, Brockovich tells Katie to move.

I give Katie Joel Kupferman's number and Joel takes on another pro bono case.


Back to D.C. for a hearing of the Senate Committee on the Environment and Public Works, noting an oxymoronic "Industrial Park" on the way.

Over salad and mud pie, as per his new diet, Hugh shows me a letter from a mayor whom Hugh had found to be protecting polluters.

"Why would a mayor do such a thing?" the press had asked.

"Well, in the past in such situations," Hugh had replied, "it's been found that the mayor was on the take."

The letter to a mutual acquaintance says, "Tell Hugh Kaufman to watch his tongue or I'll cut it out for him."

The mayor was put away for ten years.

*Tuesday 8:30 a.m.* Arrive Environment and Public Works room and hand to such press as are already there a list of the questions which we've sent Hillary and her staff to ask Whitman.

EPA Region 2's Deputy Administrator Kathy Callahan gives me a friendly Hello which I return distantly. Adminstrator Jane Kenny sails by without a word. (*"I'll be damned if I'll let her snub me."*)

I'm wearing a T-shirt which features a charcoal rendering of a fireman planting a flag at Ground Zero. A play composed of interviews conducted by Stuyvesant students under the guidance of teacher Annie Toms offers an account of that flag which, we have been told, perhaps inaccurately, was from the school auditorium. Building Staff member Kerneth Levigion described:

*the brown wooden staff*

*the six-inch brass coupling that held the two pieces together*
*the gold fringe that went around the flag*
*the gold tassel dangling*
*off the top of it*
*and the eagle missing both of its wings.*
*Now it's*
*a strange*
*thing that I said to the*
*to The Spectator*
*(I dunno if you wanna use this)*
*but I said:*
*You know seein' that picture*

*seein' those wings missing*
*symbolizes*
*to me*
*the Tra-*
*the fact that the*
*Trade Center*
*is gone*
*okay*
*the wings symbolize the Twin Towers*
*they're both gone*
*but the flag is still waving.*[cliv]

The Senators' opening comments pay homage to ranking member Bob Smith who's just lost his primary. A beefy guy, Smith grows red with sentiment.

Christie sits down. She's shorter than on TV but not for the usual reason: disappointment at seeing one's hero in the flesh; it's because she's wearing flats.

The focus of her speech, she opens, is not to dwell on the past but rather, to present a vision for the future: As part of the development of Homeland Security, EPA is acquiring state of the art equipment and 75 new employees. They will be stationed in Las Vegas so if anything happens out west, EPA won't have to summon people from far away.

Hillary praises the EPA's response to 9/11 although she mentions that in the future, we have to figure out who's responsible for indoor air. She also makes a plea to extend the deadline for cleanup until the end of the year to which Christie offers her stock response, "That's up to FEMA."

Jeffords, who seems smitten with Christie, echoes the fawning praise while the other Senators fall in line behind him.

Not long after, the House holds a hearing on the Ombudsman in which Congressman Frank Pallone accuses his Republican colleagues of trying to put one over on him. He didn't learn of the hearing until the previous week and didn't get the testimony until 6:30 the previous night.  Chairman Gilmore objects that the Republicans got it at the same time.

Bart Stupak from Illinois points out that the Bush administration doesn't support superfund sites but goes out of its way to support big business.  Norwood says it doesn't help anyone for the attack dogs to use this forum as a political arena.

Somebody protests that the problem of people doing "too good a job" (the complaint about the Ombudsman's office) is rampant throughout this administration whose appointees take the ideal of loyalty to the point of not speaking up.

A walking illustration is EPA's lawyer, Robert Fabricant.  When Pallone asks him, "What about the Ombudsman's ability to hire and fire his own staff?  What about his authority over his own budget?" Fabricant answers with words to the effect of, "Ask him," passing the buck to the next witness.

"All right," sighs Pallone.  *"You're* not helping me out."


Data is coming out about the effect of 9/11 on Brooklyn where the number of respiratory patients doubled at some hospitals after the attacks and the winds bore the debris more than 80% of the time until the fires died out on December 14.  State Department of Environmental Conservation monitoring stations produced "some spectacular spikes" in particulates.[clv]

It's time to cut up my bedroom carpet for ultrasonication.  Neither I nor Jose the handyman get anywhere with scissors and end up tearing at the carpet (which I've wetted down) like animals.

The results come back at 79,333 structures per sq. cm. which is in the "area of concern" part of the spectrum.

OK, I'm concerned.  I throw plastic over the offending carpet, evacuate Alex to his Dad's and buy waterproof mattress covers, figuring that if they keep water out, they may also keep some asbestos in. Then I find a company that will perform an abatement which takes four burly Polish guys 22 hours.[23]

EPA has commissioned Toxicology Excellence for Risk Assessment (TERA), to organize a panel to review a document they've written on Contaminants of Potential Concern.

The backgrounds of TERA Board members and affiliates are such as would warm the hearts of the Koch brothers. One is the lead author of a study which states: "There is no convincing evidence that synthetic chemical pollutants are important as a cause of human cancer,"[clvi] going on to point out in the next sentence that regulating them is expensive. Others have worked for Rio Tinto mines[clvii] which has engaged in contamination of the environment by, *inter alia*, lead and fiberglass, both of which are Contaminants of Potential Concern being considered in the EPA document under review. Rio Tinto has also been accused of engaging in apartheid, keeping its workers in conditions that are "akin to slavery," and relocating residents to concentration camp-like settlements while its partner, Freeport McMoran, has been associated with murder, rape and torture.[clviii] And as of April, 2017, a lawyer for the company, which is run by Trump advisor Carl Icahn, has also been linked to ISIS and

---

[23] One test performed on the apartment post-abatement still shows a level of asbestos that is ten times higher than EPA claims to be achieving in Lower Manhattan. Appendix W; Testimony to the New York City Council; January 11, 2007

vigilantes attempting a coup in Indonesia.[24]
(Disclosure: I bought stock in Freeport McMoran years before learning any of this. If I remember correctly, the company was being touted for revitalizing the train system.)

Of the scientists to serve on the panel, Dennis Paustenbach earned over $300 an hour as an expert witness for Pacific Gas and Electric when the utility was sued for allowing poisonous chromium 6 to leach into ground water in the case portrayed in *Erin Brockovich.* To support his contention that a little chromium 6 never hurt anybody, he both drank chromium-tainted water and bathed in a Jacuzzi of it. Conflict of Interest issues compelled him to quit before the panel issued its final report.[clix]

A similar scenario played out with Paustenbach in the Toms River cancer cluster, a case brought by Jan Schlichtman, the lawyer who was played by John Travolta in *A Civil Action.*[clx]

While going to some pains to acknowledge the difficulties of the situation that EPA faced with 9/11, a number of the panelists nevertheless complain, "But we really don't understand what this document is for." So during the public comment period, we inform them that the document in question is actually being used *ex post facto* to justify the sorry cleanup that's already underway. And since they're from out of town, we also explain why air tests are not adequate and what needs to be done instead.

---

[24] Shocking Exposé Reveals Trump Associates & ISIS-Linked Vigilantes Are Attempting Coup in Indonesia; April 21, 2017; https://www.democracynow.org/2017/4/21/shocking_expose_reveals_trump_associates_isis

Mark Maddaloni, one of the document's authors, opens his presentation with a plea for mercy – "Before you all rake this over the coals," – and replies to the panel's requests for data with the lame, schoolboy's excuse to the effect that the dog ate it. ("That data's not in yet.")

By the end of day one, seeming to glean that EPA is taking them for a ride, the panel decide that both porous and hard surfaces need to be tested before an apartment can be given a clean bill of health.

That night, we get word that EPA is holding a press conference at 11:30 the following morning to announce how great the cleanup is going and the particularly good news: Only three apartments have tested positive for asbestos.

This is our nightmare: They do the wrong tests and voilà!

And is it simply coincidence that they're making their announcement when they know we'll all be otherwise engaged?

If, instead, it is a ploy, it fails. Joel, resident Jo Polett and I crash the press conference. EPA Spokeswoman Mary Mears seems startled but regains her composure. ("I'm a big fan of the First Amendment but this is an EPA conference so if you want to talk to the press, as I have no doubt you do, I ask only that you do it outside of this room and outside of this building.") Joel agrees and I say that whatever my lawyer wants is OK with me.

We talk to Channel 4 and CNN – a possible coup, since the press room is too small for TV cameras so we may have elbowed out EPA.

Then we return uptown for the rest of the TERA conference.

Something seems to have gone on at dinner the previous night because the panel is lining up more behind EPA. This may be because Bertram Price – a hunched, villainous figure with hands constantly washing over each other – has taken control, arguing against testing porous or even hard surfaces, in favor of only air testing for asbestos.

The panel is bent on finding a "signature" or "fingerprint" for WTC dust, a misleading metaphor, to my mind. Signatures and fingerprints are mere clues whereas the WTC dust is the criminal itself, the stuff that's going to make people sick.

Besides, how could there even be a signature or fingerprint?

*The World Trade Center was a...city with its own zipcode. Cities are not individuals and do not have signatures or fingerprints... When they burn, they produce many contaminants, each with its own signature or fingerprint. No one mixed the contaminants of 9/11 together in that great mixing bowl in the sky. They were dispersed to different places according to their weight, when they burned and which way the wind was blowing at that time.*

*Thus the search for a WTC fingerprint may prove to be as quixotic as the quest for the elixir of youth or the alchemical formula for gold. We certainly can't know in advance of representative testing whether there's a fingerprint. The only scientifically viable program... is one that tests for a broad spectrum of contaminants...[clxi]*

Even if a fingerprint is found, what do we do about all the other contaminants?

*...How... can we justify ignoring [lead]? That it lacks some ineffable, "Je ne sais quoi" marking it as uniquely WTC in origin? This is why the fingerprint metaphor is misleading and dangerous. The WTC was a building like*

*any other. The only unique thing about it is that it was really big. Apart from that, its lead was indistinguishable from any other lead. So it is disingenuous of EPA to ignore lead excesses in Lower Manhattan because the particles failed to arrive individually stamped "WTC."*[clxii][25]

The panel decide on a delicate blend of crystalline silica, fiberglass and a soupçon of I don't remember what else, (slag wool?) with a particular pH.[clxiii]

What happened to asbestos, their previous pet contaminant?

Anyway, if a fingerprint or signature is unique and irrefutable, why does the WTC fingerprint or signature keep changing?

Still other panels and medical forums sprout up at which we're obliged to testify lest we leave the impression that either:

a) there is, in fact, as EPA has always maintained, no problem

or

b) we've given up.

(But if there is indeed no problem, how come they're finding it so difficult to expose us to the usual one in a million extra cancer risk per contaminant?)

In scenes that evoke the movie *Groundhog Day*, a new crop of out-of-town scientists arrives to perform what they've been led to believe is a service for their country. Then we give them a crash course in reality.

When one of the panels, VERSAR, complains yet again about a sparsity of test results, with combustion expert

---

25 See Appendix M; Testimony to the World Trade Center Expert Technical Review Panel; September 13, 2004

Gary Hunt pointing out that EPA had only two samples of polycyclic aromatic hydrocarbons (PAHs) until January, it falls to Dr. Marjorie Clarke to tell them about 250,000 pages of data sitting in Edison, New Jersey. One of the EPA guys *who wrote the report on which the conference is based* says, "Really? Do you know how we could get it?" They wrote the report without it and are now asking an independent scientist on our side to help.

(When the VERSAR panel nearly unanimously recommends that tests of indoor air be done by an independent body rather than EPA, agency rep Matt Lorber's leg starts to jiggle violently until he bolts out of the room to pace up and down while shouting into his cell phone.)

More hearings at all levels of government are held as well, doing just what the name says: They hear. And they don't even do that convincingly. As often as not, elected officials deliver their own soundbites on the issue, then depart, leaving one lone committee member to nod sympathetically in between taking calls on his cell phone.

Sometimes the hearings are even openly described as arenas for us to voice our "concerns." As King Frederick of Prussia supposedly pronounced about his protesting subjects, "I let them say what they want and they let me do what I want."

*Thanksgiving*

With its usual Scroogelike timing, FEMA has chosen this weekend to close up shop. Beyond Ground Zero, Urban Justice and Nadler hold a press conference in which they reveal that FEMA hasn't been paying the rent on its post office box. As a result, hundreds of claims have been denied.

The following month, true to the federal government's tradition of committing its worst betrayals on national holidays when everyone's attention is otherwise engaged, EPA closes the hotline for cleanup.

We gather outside their building at 290 Broadway armed with Christmas carols duly warped to mark the occasion: "Clean our buildings' ventilation, Fa la la la la, la la la la. Or wind up in litigation, Fa la la la la, la la la la." "On the fifth day of Christmas, EPA gave to me: Five wet mops! Four pairs of long pants, three buckets, two wet rags and a home filled with toxic debris."

At Starbucks, where we've repaired following several press interviews, a guy at the next table says, "Excuse me, I've been overhearing your conversation but I can't quite make out what you're talking about. What are you all working on?"

"We're trying to get the EPA to do a proper cleanup after 9/11," someone says.

"Really? I saw something about that on the news this morning. The dark-haired woman said she had twelve times the normal amount of asbestos in her apartment."

He's talking about Nina Lavin. The incident confirms my belief that what people remember is graphic detail. The more we can give them concrete examples, cautionary tales of what can happen to people who live in contaminated apartments, the better off everyone will be.

125 Cedar Street has moved back in, EPA cleaning it twice because after the first attempt, they still had high asbestos readings.

This development gets the high-profile building, with Pat Moore's horrific photos of her apartment, out of the news.

*Citizens' Forum on the EPA Ombudsman
Congress*

Arrive six o'clock and make my way to a Quaker B&B recommended by Project for Government Oversight, one of the two organizations sponsoring the panel: $50 a night, no breakfast but also no tax, which is significant since hotel tax in DC is 14 and a half %. The door is answered by J., who's pleasant enough although later, when he and his wife are having dinner, they're both dure until they go into the kitchen, close the door and argue about whether a couple should be allowed to have their teenage son in their room. At fifty bucks a night, I don't blame the wife for taking a hard line.

In front of the bookshelves (numerous bibles; a tract on Mother Theresa) rests a coffee table on which a handwritten sign reads, "Please keep thy feet off the furniture." A basket on the stairs offers "No War in Iraq" buttons for the taking.

I call Hugh for a final update on the panel and tell him Danni at POGO said that they're going to be strict about the five minute cutoff. I've shaved my testimony to 4:45.

"Don't worry," Hugh says. "I won't let them cut you off. The WTC case is the biggest case; it puts everything else in the shade."

"Normally, Hugh, I'd be thrilled at the distinction but not in this case, boy."

"I know."

At 8:30 the next morning, Hugh rushes into the Dirksen Senate Building hearing room reporting sotto voce, "C-Span is here."

"Is this going to be live?"

"It might as well be," adds Lisette, who's come in on the heels of Hugh. "They don't edit it."

"No matter what happens?"

"No matter what happens. Don't worry. You'll be beaootiful... magnificent." She's imitating an Italian accent. "You've done this a hundred times; what are you worried about?"

"I have a nervous breakdown each time."

The Congressional panel consists of Mike Crapo (R-Idaho) and Nadler; a staffer from Senator Wayne Allard's office (R-Colorado) and Republican Congressman Jeff Miller from Florida.

Panelists include Margaret Williams, President of Citizens Against Toxic Exposure, who lives between two superfund sites near what is known locally as "Dioxin Hill."

I ask her how many in her community are sick.

"Everyone," she says.

Susan Shortz of Marjol, Pa., responds to the same question, "Most people are sick – the ones who haven't died, anyway."

In her community, where "[o]ver 500,000 cubic yards of battery casings are stockpiled and buried... [l]ead has been measured at levels as high as 250,000 parts per million in the soil."[clxiv]

Sandra Jaquith represents the community affected by the army's Rocky Mountain arsenal, "boasting the most contaminated square mile on earth."[clxv] Every year, the army asks Congress for exemption from environmental laws.[26] After taking five samples on a 900 acre site, she testifies, the army declared it safe. Even after they found a sarin bomb on it, they continued to invite school groups on tours... until they found nine more sarin bombs.

Deborah Sanchez, who lives 300 yards from the Shattuck Chemical Superfund site, testifies, "50,000

---

[26] EPA uses the army's special dispensation regarding toxics to suppress information on perchlorate, a byproduct of rocket fuel that's been getting into the lettuce.

"This is ridiculous!" Hugh erupts. "We're the country's janitors."

cubic yards of radioactive dirt was left uncovered and allowed to blow around our neighborhood."[clxvi] Salomon Brothers, the multibillion dollar company responsible, was fined $15,000.

One of the panelists testifies that EPA apologized to his community, explaining, "If we let your community push us around, we'd have to let every community push us around." Nadler and others smile at this in wry disbelief or maybe it's wry belief.

We have lunch with Bob Martin and his lawyer, Tom Devine, as well as Jeannie, a lawyer from Legal Environmental Assistance Foundation, Bob's new organization.

Hugh introduces Mark Herzgaard, "a best-selling author," who's interviewing Bob for an article to appear in Harper's.

But in response to questions, Bob is taciturn, explaining, "I've got one case going and another that could happen. Why don't you ask Hugh?" Hugh is also in litigation but when did that ever stop him from talking?

We learn that during the discovery period in his case, Hugh found out that EPA had secret files on four subjects:

1. People to be criminally prosecuted.
2. People to be fired.
3. Hugh
4. Bob

Hugh says that because of her husband's investments in Citigroup, Christie should have recused herself in any case the bank was involved in.[27]

"She'd be recusing herself all over the country," I say.

"Ah. Now you're getting to the point. Christie should never have taken the job of EPA administrator."

"Or her husband should have resigned from Citigroup," Jeannie adds. "Politicians do it all the time."

"But Christie needed the lifestyle," Hugh continues. "She's land rich but she needed that $600,000 income."[28]

When she was governor of New Jersey, he says, she cut its environmental program by 79% while Citigroup kept Monsanto from going bankrupt.[29] She also paid off

---

[27] When Citigroup itself was found to be financing terrorism, it was fined a mere $3000. Rex Nutting; Trading with the enemy; Apr 15, 2003; http://www.marketwatch.com/story/us-companies-quietly-caught-trading-with-the-enemy

[28] EPA criminal investigators are being pulled from their duties to take Christie's husband's rental car back to the agent or hold her seat at a restaurant. April 27, 2003; JohnHeilprin; https://www.washingtonpost.com/archive/politics/2003/04/27/criminal-agents-diverted-to-drive-epa-boss/1a1ad120-bff0-43d4-9fff-3306eba1e4e2/

[29] *Last year an Alabama court found Monsanto liable for pollution resulting from its production of PCBs near the town of Anniston in the 1970s. But the Environmental Protection Agency intervened, offering a deal to Monsanto and two successor companies that saved the corporations millions of dollars. As EPA chief Christine Todd Whitman leaves her post, many question whether her agency improperly derailed the state court process.* Whitman Leaves EPA Amid Pollution Lawsuit Controversy; Peter Overby; June 27, 2003; NPR; http://www.npr.org/templates/story/story.php?storyId=1313219

black ministers to keep their congregations out of the polls.[30]

As we part, I ask Hugh how to make the best use of the afternoon.

"Ed Towns' office signed on to the Ombudsman bill," he says. "That was very helpful. Turns out to be useful, talking to them. Why don't you go back?"

A 9/11EA member who watches the panel on C-Span says there were too many women. The panel needed more men in suits, "for diversity." She is not being ironic.


Call from Katie Acton: They're cleaning PS 65, probably because of the flood of articles and information that she's been forwarding to Congressman Anthony Wiener. The bad news is, you can't clean trichloroethylene. Hugh says they tried in California. It took twenty-five years.

Anyway, the parents who've spoken up about the contamination soon get a letter explaining that their kids are being moved to a different school, the vacated

---

[30] *At a November 9 Sperling breakfast, [Republican political consultant Ed] Rollins, boasting about how he had just helped win a governorship for New Jersey's Christine Todd Whitman, said the campaign had spent about $500,000 to suppress the black vote. He said GOP operatives had made payments to Democratic precinct workers in black areas on condition they sit on their hands on Election Day. And he said the Whitman campaign had contributed to church charities in return for black ministers keeping mum on the virtues of Democratic incumbent James Florio.*

*Rollins then backpedaled on his assertions...* January/February 1994; Insider Cynicism; Ed Rollins Meets the Press by Christopher Hanson; Research assistance was provided by interns Ken Davidoff and Jill Priluck.

places to be filled by new kids whose parents will presumably be clueless.

Governor Pataki has "good news!" 2005 is the date set for the reopening of Ground Zero. They're going to fast track the Environmental Impact Study in time to lay the cornerstone at the Republican Convention in September '04.

This means that a process which usually takes three years will be crammed into one.

Why?

Emergency!

However, the WTC site is getting federal funding so it has to adhere to NEPA, the National Environmental Protection Act. The developers get around this hurdle by segmenting the plot, allowing them to say that all the federal funding went to a bit over here and another over there. For the rest, regulations be damned; full steam (and diesel) ahead.

Brookfield Properties unfolds its plan for burying West Street. In his presentation, their representative uses the word "quickly" fifteen times. (See On the Draft Generic Environmental Impact Statement for Ground Zero, Appendix O; Testimony to the World Trade Center Expert Technical Review Panel, Appendix P.)

The bidding has closed on the contracts to rebuild Iraq. Why? Once again: Emergency!

The EPA Office of the Inspector General has leaked a report confirming the agency's egregious negligence about the contamination downtown, although they fall short of accusing them of "attempting to conceal data results."[clxvii] They also unearth the influence of the White House Council on Environmental Quality which changed cautionary statements about asbestos in at least one press release to reassurances. (See Conflict of

Interest, a 9/11 Windfall and the White House Council on Environmental Quality, Appendix A.) The conclusions of this branch of EPA itself offer an opportunity we can't afford to pass up to make the case once again for scientifically-based cleanup.

We are three activists in search of the action: Kimberly, Barbara Caporale and me. Also with us is Barbara's daughter, Rocky.

From the top of the hill at 79th street and the river, we spot a sporty crowd at the dock, standing in front of an impressively decked out sail boat, no pun intended. Some of the crowd have pads and cameras. Others are wearing blue jackets that display the EPA logo.

We stroll down *(Look casual!)* to the security gate where four guys with cell phones greet us pleasantly.

"Is this the Earth Day celebration?" Kimberly asks in her best Girl Scout voice.

"Sure is. Come right in," says Guy Number One.

In addition to Kimberly's guileless inquiry, it helps to have Rocky along. She does a dynamite impression of a five-year-old on a park outing.

Christie is addressing the crowd and doling out awards: Riverkeeper, South Street Seaport... We strategize on when to shout our complaints. Just three weeks ago, a hundred people got arrested for standing on a sidewalk. We will probably get more mileage out of waiting so that we can't be accused of spoiling the party.

Barbara applauds along with the crowd, hypocrisy not even required. Yay, Riverkeeper!

EPA spokesperson Mary Mears has spotted us. She edges over to a security guy and whispers at length. He glances at us and nods. Mears slinks away. The speeches wind down.

Caporale launches. "When will EPA do a real cleanup of Lower Manhattan? Beyond Canal Street and to include office- and workspaces?"

A large camera trains on her and Barbara goes on, afterwards explaining, "When you stop is when they grab you."

Kimberly and I add details at which point Christie looks around for the mike. But it has been dismantled and she won't stoop to shouting back.

She turns to get on the boat as Security Guy Number 2 consults with Guy Number 3: Is this public property? Do we have the right to do this?

Guy Number 3 comes over. "I'm going to have to ask you to leave. You need a permit. This is city property."

Being reasonable rabble, we do... but not before distributing the Daily News article from NYCOSH which Kimberly has brought along.

"Don't take that," Mears tells one of the recipients, "It's garbage."

The guy looks at it as though to check out its trashy qualities but doesn't hand it back.

## To 9/11 Environmental Action

This was a disheartening day. For a while, we were going strong in phase whatever-this-is of Operation Make Christie's Life a Living Hell. This time, hell took the form of raising the consciousness of the audience for David Letterman's Late Show on which HalfWhitman was to be a guest. (It was impossible to get tickets even using Diane Dreyfus' trick of dialling ten digits of the eleven digit number at 10:59 and the final one on the stroke of 11 a.m., when tickets went on sale.)

We'd decided to contact just three papers and NY1 for fear that if we did a wider press release, someone would tip off CBS. One reporter was openly hostile ("*She's not Administrator anymore*,") but the others, more hospitable.

We met at Starbucks where Kimberly gave each of us a stack of fliers and off we go to the Ed Sullivan Theatre.

A woman with platinum hair tells us we can't do this where the audience is lined up or she'll call the police. Kimberly disappears around the corner to scout out the other entrance to the theater.

"Get a lawyer," says Platinum.

"He's right over there," I say, pointing to Joel who's leaning against the wall in his neon green Lawyer's Guild cap, watching. But she may have a point, so I move to distribute somewhere else.

Another Lettermanette, as Kimberly calls them, now says we can't hand out literature under the marquee.

Someone calls the cops. A large specimen appears, shakes hands and agrees we have a First Amendment right to hand out our literature as long as we don't interfere with the line. And would we like him to set up a barrier in the street so we can be away from the marquee?

Kimberly, who's back from her reconnaissance mission, says, "That would be great."

More audience members arrive and we go back to work. A Lettermanette asks for a flier with which she vanishes inside.

Now here's where the disheartening part comes in.

Another Lettermanette stands between me and the audience pretending to count them – loudly. We have a shouting contest in which I proclaim, "EPA lied about the contamination of Lower Manhattan following 9/11," and Hitler Youth shouts, "Does anyone need to go the bathroom? You can go through that door."

And what is the audience reaction? "We don't care!" they shout at us.

A few on the line show interest but most are just there to have fun and mad at us for being such spoil sports. One guy, referring to Diane – who is dressed as Mothra, a moth that mutated after being exposed to the contaminants of 9/11 – yells, "Shoot the fucking butterfly!"

176

Now that the audience is safely inside, thanks to us, (they don't usually get let in for about forty-five minutes) we make our way around the corner where, unless someone's tipped her off, Whitman will be admitted.

A horde of paparazzi are crowding the stage door to see another guest on the show, Johnny Depp. Halfwhitman arrives and is swept past our "Boos" and jeers post-haste.

So if you're up at 11:30, watch Letterman. Let's see how funny Christie is.

*Later*

Well, she certainly wasn't funny but it's obvious our flyer reached its target because Dave was a lot harder hitting than we'd expected. His final question was, "What about the controversy surrounding EPA and 9/11?"

"There really isn't any," she said. "We told people to wear respirators but the problem was, we couldn't force them. Also we told people who had heart conditions not to work on the pile." She said a measure of her success at EPA is that the agency is being sued equally by people at both ends of the political spectrum.

Now she's gone to supervise elections in Cambodia.

"Boy," reflects Kimberly, "when this David vs. Goliath thing works, it's really a kick."

A rescue dog, Bear, has died, an autopsy revealing multiple cancers. The dogs worked closer to the ground than people but they also worked shorter shifts.

At a National Institute for Occupational Safety and Health conference, an Emergency Medical Services worker says that while they'd been expecting to see an explosion of cancer cases in ten to twenty years, five EMS workers have already been diagnosed, far above the average rate.

Joel Kupferman reports that Ground Zero workers have come to him asking, "Why am I spitting up blood?"

A NIOSH study of Stuyvesant faculty reveals that eight months after the disaster, 33% said they still had symptoms stemming from it.[clxviii] One of Alex' favorite teachers, Mr. Celestin, whom he had for French in ninth grade, dies of lung cancer at the age of 52.

Since going to school cannot be considered an occupation, NIOSH does not perform an equivalent study among the kids. The Parents' Association has stepped in, sending out a survey to which hundreds of parents respond. Two thirds have children who have manifested symptoms which they attribute to the environment at school that year. Anecdotally, we hear that one boy's lungs have collapsed while another student has had pneumonia. And a mother says that after she filled out the questionnaire reporting no symptoms, her daughter developed a rash that wouldn't go away.

Other parents continue to deny a connection to 9/11, one father blaming his son's nosebleeds on dry air at home.

Our fringey issue is sprouting legs. Suzanne Mattei of the Sierra Club publishes *Air Pollution and Deception at Ground Zero: How the Bush Administration's Reckless Disregard of 9/11 Toxic Hazards Poses Long-Term Threats for New York City and the Nation,*[clxix] bringing a new wave of national attention to the Bush administration's lies and their consequences.

As a result of negotiations between Senator Hillary Clinton and James Connaughton, the Chairman of the White House Council on Environmental Quality whose claim to fame came via editing EPA's press releases to change cautionary statements on asbestos into reassurances, the World Trade Center Expert Technical Review Panel is formed. (On Connaughton and his law firm, Sidley Austin, see Conflict of Interest, a 9/11

Windfall and the White House Council on Environmental Quality, Appendix A.) This final blue ribbon panel promises to establish, once and for all, the criteria for cleanup although of course, the longer it takes, the murkier the issue becomes. Before the government pays to clean toxic material, they need to make sure what the source is.

We discuss whether to participate and vote in favor since at least it will provide a forum to keep the issue alive.

Some testimony to this extended exercise in futility appears in the Appendix. Co-chaired by Dr. Paul Lioy of Rutgers University,[31] it fails – like all its predecessors –

---

[31] On Paul Lioy's tests, Dr. Cate Jenkins writes: "...USGS used a 20-to-1 ratio of water to WTC dust, and also used acidified water (pH 5.5) to extract the dust... Using a 20:1 ratio as well as using acidic water will lead to erroneously low pH levels. The study itself described taking the precaution to find outdoor samples that had been protected from rain, so as to reassure readers of their study that the original caustic WTC dust would not have been neutralized by contact with water and carbon dioxide from the air (a reaction called "carbonation"). However, if the study is read closely, before testing the samples for pH, the Rutgers team first added water to the samples, inverted the tubes several times, soaked them "several days" at room temperature, and then stored them in the refrigerator for an unknown time period before pH testing... Thus, **by their own admission, the Rutgers research team was intentionally and deliberately neutralizing the samples before testing the pH."** [emphasis mine.] May 6, 2007; FROM: Cate Jenkins, Ph.D.* GCB, HWID, OSW, OSWER, EPA; TO: Senator Hillary Rodham Clinton, Chair, Subcommittee on Superfund and Environmental Health; Congressman Jerrold Nadler, Congresswoman Carolyn Maloney COMPLAINT AND ADDITIONAL EVIDENCE OF pH FRAUD BY:

USGS, OSHA, ATSDR, NYC, EPA, and EPA-funded scientists

to reach an agreement on what might constitute a World Trade Center fingerprint, throws up its hands in frustration and disbands. The EPA conducts another "cleanup" which is no better than the first and even more widely ignored. (See "Ground Zero's Toxic Dust," Appendix F; "EPA's Latest Betrayal at Ground Zero," Appendix G.)

A lawsuit[32] brought by students, office workers and residents (of whom I am one) also comes and goes, meeting triumph in the lower court (See "Federal Judge Slams Whitman and EPA," Appendix H) but inevitably getting quashed at the appellate level. (See Lying to "Reassure" the Public, Appendix I.)[clxx] Ground Zero workers also file a lawsuit with a firm that some subsequently accuse of strong-arming them into settling.[clxxi] A number of well publicized documentaries by Heidi Dehncke-Fisher and Robert Greenwald, among others, bring the illnesses of rescue workers to prominence.

Over the ensuing years, we learn more of what was contained in the toxic morass of the World Trade Center disaster:

---

— 1. Falsification of corrosive pH data for WTC dust

— 2. Historical fraud by EPA of hazardous pH levels since 1980; http://www.journalof911studies.com/volume/200704/DrJenkinsRequestsSenateInvestigationOnWTCdust.pdf

---

[32] It's a common misconception that lawsuits are filed only to seek monetary compensation. However, we were suing, instead, for appropriate testing and cleanup.

[T]he Trade Center's 50,000 computers each contained four to eight pounds of lead while the smoke detectors contained radioactive americium 241. And Walter Hang, president of Toxic Targeting, an environmental database company, tells Democracy Now:

*[W]hen I saw the fire at World Trade Center number seven, I knew that underneath the building was a giant substation that controlled the delivery of electricity to all of southern Manhattan and I knew that there were huge transformers that were insulated with this oil that potentially could contain Polychlorinated Biphenals or PCBs, I knew there was a high voltage line from that giant substation to another substation in Brooklyn, and I knew if the building collapsed then the line would be severed and perhaps tens of thousands of gallons of oil would flow into the hall and catch fire... They found PCBs in dust in buildings at 32 times the amount that constitutes hazardous waste.*[clxxii]

The fluorescent bulbs, of which there were 500,000 at the World Trade Center, each contained 41 mg. of mercury, leading to mercury vapor concentrations in Lower Manhattan that were greater than those observed in non-industrial urban environments by a factor of 1,000 to 1 million.[clxxiii] One official suggests without a trace of irony that since the mercury vaporized, the elevated levels found in blood tests of Ground Zero workers are probably the result of eating tuna.

On December 31, 2003, the EPA Office of Research and Development in Washington releases a 160-paged report, dated October 2002, in the week between Christmas and New Year's when it's least likely to get press attention. On page 77, Daily News reporter Juan Gonzalez discovers that emissions of dioxins in and around Ground Zero in the two months following 9/11 were "likely the highest ambient concentrations that have ever been reported."[clxxiv] At Park Row near City

Hall Park, dioxin between October 12 and 29 averaged 5.6 parts per trillion/per cubic meter of air, or **nearly six times the highest dioxin level ever recorded in the U.S. At the pile, levels were "between 100 and 1,500 times higher than typically found in urban air."**[clxxv] [emphasis mine.]

EPA scientists maintain that dioxin exposure is usually associated with contaminated food rather than air. But this is because dioxin is usually *found* in food rather than air.

Finally, Dr. Cate Jenkins publishes several memos for which she suffers backlash within the agency.[33]

---

[33] The World Trade Center case does not mark the first time Dr. Jenkins has found herself embattled within her own agency.

During the late 1960s, Monsanto produced Agent Orange which contained dioxin and was responsible for illnesses among the Vietnam War vets as well as birth defects among their children. Monsanto workers were getting sick and dioxin levels around the factory at Times Beach, Missouri, were 100 times the limit considered safe. (A Chemical Conundrum: How Dangerous Is Dioxin? Jon Hamilton; December 28, 2010; http://www.npr.org/2010/12/28/132368362/a-chemical-conundrum-how-dangerous-is-dioxin)

Cate pointed out that the tests Monsanto used to show that dioxin wasn't a carcinogen were funded by Monsanto itself and scientifically invalid: The control group which was supposedly randomly chosen had, in fact, also been exposed to dioxin. http://www.greens.org/s-r/078/07-49.html

Once she publicly confirmed that the EPA was conducting a criminal investigation of Monsanto's fraudulent studies, writes William Sanjour, former head the EPA's Hazardous Waste Management Division, "'Monsanto constantly intervened at the EPA to block the investigation and to force the agency to discipline or even fire Cate. All these internal documents prove it,' he said, showing me a sheaf of letters on Monsanto letterhead." (The World According to Monsanto: Pollution, Corruption, and the Control of ...; Marie-Monique

Robin; The New Press (January 3, 2012)
https://books.google.com/books?id=UUIs-
x8MER0C&pg=PA84&lpg=PA84&dq=sanjour+%22internal+do
cuments+prove+it,%E2%80%99+he+said,+showing+me+a+sh
eaf+of+letters+on+Monsanto+letterhead%22&source=bl&ots=
ypMqczw7Vq&sig=SY3u4fNvXNtZs_3eIG_7OkVUuZU&hl=en&
sa=X&ved=0ahUKEwjqm_iGuJTPAhXHZCYKHeRJAV8Q6AEI
HDAA#v=onepage&q=sanjour%20%22internal%20documents
%20prove%20it%2C%E2%80%99%20he%20said%2C%20sho
wing%20me%20a%20sheaf%20of%20letters%20on%20Mons
anto%20letterhead%22&f=false)

Cate was relieved of substantive duties for over two years and sent to a figurative dungeon from which she filed a lawsuit for discrimination. In a 1994 paper "dedicated to the memory of my friend Captain Cameron Appel, U.S. Army Airborne Engineers, who died of cancer after serving two tours in Viet Nam and leaving behind a young widow with two baby children," Sanjour wrote:

*The judge ruled in Jenkins' favor... For the third time, EPA refused to accept the decision and continued to use taxpayer funds to appeal the case to the Secretary of Labor, who also ruled for Jenkins... This was the second EPA whistleblower case in less than a year that went all the way up to the Secretary and in both cases the Secretary ruled against EPA. The agency was getting a bad reputation with the Labor Department, so after two years of fruitless litigation, EPA management threw in the towel and promised to restore Jenkins to her old job until she won whistleblower status through the Department of Labor." (Ibid)*

Addendum: The beat goes on. As recently as 2017, a former EPA official has become a key figure in twenty lawsuits alleging that Monsanto failed to warn consumers its glyphosate-based herbicide might cause non-Hodgkin's lymphoma. Monsanto Cancer Suits Turn to EPA Deputy's 'Suspicious' Role; Joel Rosenblatt; February 27, 2017; https://www.bloomberg.com/news/articles/2017-02-27/monsanto-cancer-suits-turn-to-alleged-whitewash-by-epa-official

She reveals how EPA's manipulation of the pH scale deceived the public about the alkalinity of the dust, which had in fact attained the level of Draino:

☐ *U.S. Geological Survey falsifies its WTC pH data*
☐ *Research lead by Rutgers neutralizes WTC dust before pH testing*
☐ *EPA-funded research using NYU collected dust sample falsifies pH data*
☐ *ATSDR/NYC false health claims about caustic high pH WTC dust constituents*
☐ *UC at Davis finds 21% cement in smallest WTC dust, pH 11 to greater than 12*
☐ *No immediate pH tests at Ground Zero as required by regulation*
☐ *No pH tests of more corrosive dust subjected to heat at Ground Zero*
☐ *9/13/01 – EPA Admin. Whitman claims "below background levels," fact ignored by EPA Inspector General when finding "no evidence of false statements"*

*...The pH scale is logarithmic, which means that each change of one unit on the pH scale means a change in 10 times the acidity or alkalinity. However, pH tests are not always reliable predictors of the true ability to cause chemical burns to human tissues. In part this is because some materials, like mostly insoluble WTC dust, have a high "alkaline reserve capacity," the ability to release caustic levels of hydroxyl ions over extended periods of time as they slowly dissolve...*
*...The first official release of pH data by USGS to the public was through a report posted on the internet about 2/5/02... This report was altered and back-dated in*

*2004 to an earlier date, 11/27/01, making it appear that USGS had released the report in a timely manner…*
*…October 2002 USGS gives higher pH levels (12.3 and 12.4) for indoor dusts with no explanation*
*…In October 2002, USGS released different pH data at a scientific conference for the exact same indoor dust samples shown above ("WTC01-20" and "WTC01-36")…*
*The pH levels for the same samples were claimed to be 12.3 and 12.4 at the conference.* ***The 2/5/02 USGS report had given the pH of 11.8 for both samples. (A change of one unit in the pH scale represents a 10-fold change in the alkalinity.) There was no explanation provided for the change…***[clxxvi] *[emphasis mine]*

And lest there be any lingering doubt as to whether EPA's ineptitude in response to 9/11 was really just that, Dr. Jenkins also publishes a memo establishing that they, as well as New York City, were lying from day one. Both "deliberately concealed, altered, falsified, and deleted data showing asbestos levels that both EPA and NYC declared unsafe."[clxxvii]

## IF IT BLEEDS, IT LEADS

We had secured $20 million for cleanup of the schools of Ground Zero and convinced the parents of PS/IS 89 to delay return to their building. At least two parents also removed their children from Stuyvesant because of the information provided by activists. Our insistence on the importance of HVAC systems resulted in more buildings getting them cleaned. Finally, we'd brought the environmental devastation of 9/11 to the attention of the media, not only on the local level but also on the national and international levels, leading to a more skeptical general attitude to official reassurances in the wake of subsequent disasters.[34]

Yet we had always known that our issue would receive the attention it deserved only when the body count began to mount – in other words, when it was, in critical ways, too late.

Initially, Ground Zero workers had been given the run around.

*In the early days after the Trade Center fell, within two weeks, Mt. Sinai accompanied DC 37 to the Office of Labor Relations in New York City, and we said to them,*

---

[34] The chemical industry will have to adjust their advice: "Find a 'credible and comforting' person to drive the message of the chemical industry in times of disaster or in response to environmental/health issues. This person may not be your company CEO, it may be the fire chief, or the mayor..."

Rachel's Environment and Health News No. 779, October 30, 2003; Monique Harden, Nathalie Walker, "What the Chemical Industry Fears," Environmental Research Foundation, http://www.rachel.org/?q=en/node/5710; Accessed June 30, 2011.

*'Look, we need you to document all of the city workers who are at that site, and we need to set up a monitoring program.' They threw us out," [Lee Clarke, safety and health director for District Council 37] said.*[clxxviii]

And FDNY Paramedic Deborah Reeve didn't have her disability pension approved until a week after her funeral.[clxxix] Even as late as 2006, Mayor Bloomberg denied the connection between illnesses and 9/11.[clxxx]

However, once Ground Zero workers began to manifest serious symptoms in numbers that could no longer be ignored, they became supremely effective advocates as they combined world-reknowned heroism with undeniable suffering.

Each of their stories deserves a book of its own. But perhaps the most widely publicized is that of John Feal, the iron worker who lost part of his foot at Ground Zero. Not entitled to compensation because his injury took place beyond the mandatory first 96 hours following the attacks,[clxxxi] he spent the next fifteen years fighting for compensation and medical care for Ground Zero workers. When one of them appealed to his website for permission to place a plea for a new kidney, Feal denied the permission, instead donating his own kidney.

He was a superb spokesman not only because of his history at Ground Zero but also because he was not constrained by ties to a corporation or a union whose leadership was cozy with an opposed politician. Or if he was, he didn't let it stand in his way. Feal behaved like a man who had nothing to lose.

Non-Ground Zero worker victims such as Felicia Dunn-Jones and Marcy Borders, "the dust lady" of the iconic photo taken immediately after the collapse of the buildings, also died of causes related to their exposures to 9/11 fallout.[35]

As of the fifteenth anniversary of the attacks, there have been over a thousand deaths acknowledged to be World Trade Center related, and 37,000 illnesses. The mainstream media now publish predictions that by the twentieth anniversary, the number of deaths from the environmental fallout of 9/11 will exceed those on the day itself. This mushrooming effect will be due to the latency periods for various cancers and other illnesses having been reached so that an exponential rise may be expected to continue after that date.

Stuyvesant students fall ill as well but so far, neither the World Trade Center Health Registry nor any other entity has published comprehensive data on this population. Thus, as has traditionally been the case, we are relegated to anecdotal evidence: Amit Friedlander, who'd invited Bill Clinton to speak at graduation in

---

[35] Just as the EPA initially acknowledged only a few contaminants as World Trade Center related, health agencies initially acknowledged only respiratory, dermatological and gastro-intestinal illnesses. It has taken years of cumulative evidence to prove what a few activists maintained all along: That the neurological, endocrinological and circulatory systems were also being and would continue to be affected. Suzanne Mattei also points out: "Other health effects that may manifest in years to come could include impacts on reproduction (such as birth defects or fertility problems), immune system impacts and... learning disabilities. Immune system effects will be particularly difficult to measure because they may manifest only in the person becoming more susceptible to diseases that one would normally never trace back to a chemical exposure." Pollution and Deception at Ground Zero; How the Bush Administration's Reckless Disregard of 9/11 Toxic Hazards Poses Long-Term Threats for New York City and the Nation; http://www.gothamgazette.com/rebuilding_nyc/sierraclub_report.pdf

2002, was diagnosed with Hodgkin's lymphoma in 2006. In 2014, Michele Lent Hirsch wrote for the *Atlantic Monthly* about her quarantine following thyroid cancer radiation treatment.[clxxxii] A third cancer victim, whose diagnosis is less public, had a particularly difficult time finding a compatible bone marrow donor because of his racially mixed background. Parent Linda Lam tracked down an organization founded by a woman who'd been in the same straits.

Other graduates have seen a surge of asthma, chronic bronchitis and other illnesses. Lila Nordstrom, who founded the website Stuyhealth, became their spokesperson in the more than decade-long struggle to secure the permanence of the James Zadroga 9/11 Health and Compensation Act.

*"I found him lying on the floor, as I always knew I would," said Joseph Zadroga, father of Detective James Zadroga who died in January at the age of 34. "Tyler Anne's baby bottle was in his hand.*

*'I went in and told Tyleranne.*

*'She said, 'I knew he was sick. I just didn't know it would be this fast.'*

*'Four years old. Her mother had already died.*"[clxxxiii]

Named for the New York City police officer who died as a result of his exposure to 9/11 pollutants, the Zadroga Act met with obstruction in Congress for more than a decade. Finally, thanks to the efforts of Ground Zero worker advocates, some of whom were dying when they visited Washington, as well as comedian Jon Stewart, Congresspersons Carolyn Maloney, Jerrold Nadler and others, Senators Hillary Clinton and her successor, Kirsten Gillibrand, 9/11 Environmental Action under the directorship of Kimberly Flynn, Community Board 1, the New York Committee on Occupational Safety and Health and other coalitions that represented residents and office workers, it was included in "must pass" legislation of 2015. Blessed are the troublemakers.

The BP oil rig, Deepwater Horizon, exploded in the Gulf of Mexico, mirroring the environmental disaster of 9/11 in the initial downplaying of health effects; the denial of links between illness and pollutants; the attribution of symptoms to PTSD; the reliance on sensory perception (visual for World Trade Center contamination; smell for BP;) the argument that the pollution may have had a different source; and finally, a "cleanup" that served only to bury the problem beneath the ocean surface thereby exacerbating it. Hugh Kaufman warned residents of the dangers they faced as did Kimberly Flynn, who originally hails from Louisiana.[clxxxiv] During Hurricane Sandy, the New York Committee on Occupational Safety and Health advised residents on how to deal with the mold and other contamination that ensued. Catherine McVay Hughes, former Chairperson of Community Board 1, works on New York City resiliency in combating climate change.[clxxxv] (Interview with Catherine McVay Hughes, Appendix J.) Former Deputy Schools Chancellor David Klasfeld has died of a heart attack, age 58. And as of the fifteenth anniversary of 9/11, Christie Todd Whitman has apologized for EPA's "mistakes." So far, no equivalent "mea culpa" has been forthcoming from the wizard behind the curtain, James Connaughton.

On the third anniversary of the attacks, I was invited to speak on their environmental aftermath at the 9/11 Omission Hearings taking place at Symphony Space. There I met journalist Mike Ruppert whose website, Fromthewilderness.com, investigated 9/11 in relation to the bigger picture of Peak Oil and our economic paradigm which is based on infinite growth. As always, I passed on the new information to 9/11 advocates and other friends. These emails met with a wall of skepticism, as I'd anticipated, although by now, the impulse to laugh off the dire warnings was subdued.

Everyone's wiser now and more skeptical of authority although perhaps still not skeptical enough. Having come of age in the seventies, we'd been living the wrong movie: The one where after a long, hard slog, the plucky little guys prevail in the end. But at this point in history, rage and protest, however justified in substance and impressive in numbers, are not enough. The current "movie" is a global one and while some actors on that cosmic stage are profoundly criminal, all of us in the developed world are, to varying degrees, implicated.

The argument underpinning this thesis is laid out in *The Moron's Guide to Global Collapse.* It has to do with the cost, until now borne someplace out of sight or at a time which is also over the horizon, of the lifestyle we take for granted. But if we're to escape the effects of climate change and the multiple ways in which we poison our environment, it's critical to understand the big picture. Otherwise, with each new disaster, new outrage, new righteous cause, we will simply be reacting to symptoms rather than addressing the fundamental disease. (See How Science Was Abused to Perpetrate Lies After 9/11, Appendix S.)

So despite seeming to modulate to a distant key in the last few paragraphs of this account, here's the takeaway: Until we understand the root of our collective predicament – the unsustainability of our economic paradigm based, as it is, on fiat currency, fractional reserve banking and interest – environmental and other manmade disasters, even including literal wars, will become only more extreme. The infinite growth on which this economic paradigm is predicated cannot continue forever on a finite planet for in the end, it isn't money that counts. Money is nothing more than a symbol. Of what? Resources. If there isn't enough water or food or medicine or energy, it doesn't matter how many zeroes you tack onto your currency or who's holding the bills. As the environmental disaster of 9/11 has made excruciatingly clear, we sacrifice each other and ourselves on the altar of the economy.

# Appendix A
## Conflict of Interest, a 9/11 Windfall and the White House Council on Environmental Quality[clxxxvi]

*James Connaughton, Cheney's Boy Wonder[36]*

James Connaughton, the Chairman of the White House Council on Environmental Quality which coordinated with the National Security Council to edit EPA's press releases following 9/11, faced the music last Wednesday with a nimble tapdance.

Padded with cliché allusions to the "unprecedented" attacks and a homespun vignette about his son's fear that dad was dead, Connaughton's testimony at the Senate Hearing Into Federal Government Failures on [the] Environmental Impact Of [the] 9/11 World Trade Center Attacks deftly passed the buck, pointing out that there was a flurry of press releases; they were the work-product of many people, and that anyway, the public doesn't read them.

But in the course of this fancy footwork, (First the blame is over here, now it's over there) the Chairman slipped on the banana peel of a detail.

In response to a question about the EPA Inspector General's Report of 2003 which showed how the White

---

[36] *Cheney took full advantage of the president's cluelessness, bringing the CEQ into his own portfolio. "The environment and energy issues were really turned over to him from the beginning," Whitman says. The CEQ became Cheney's shadow EPA, with industry calling the shots. To head up the council, Cheney installed James Connaughton, a former lobbyist for industrial polluters, who once worked to help General Electric and ARCO skirt responsibility for their Superfund waste sites.* Six Years of Deceit; Tim Dickinson; June 28, 2007; http://www.rollingstone.com/politics/news/six-years-of-deceit-20070628

House CEQ "tweaked" EPA's press releases – for instance by changing cautionary statements about asbestos to reassurances and omitting advice to obtain professional cleaning – as well as why, (in order to reopen Wall Street,) Connaughton asserted that the 9/11 Commission later did a thorough investigation of the same issue coming to very different conclusions.

During a recess, this writer asked Connaughton if, by "thorough investigation," he was referring to the footnote on page 555 of the 9/11 Commission Report, the only mention the report makes of the environmental aftermath of the attacks.

"I am," he replied gamely. (His demeanour throughout the hearing was chipper, as of one who has nothing to hide; who is, in fact, eager for the chance to tell his side of the story.)

During the Commission hearings, Richard Ben-Veniste had regretfully told the parent of a Lower Manhattan student that the Commission would not investigate the environmental issue.

This writer relayed that information to Connaughton.

"They changed their minds after the Inspector General's Report came out," he asserted. "They did a thorough investigation, interviewing lots of people."

The footnote in the Commission Report containing the fruits of said "thorough investigation" is four paragraphs long. One paragraph reads in its entirety: "We do not have the expertise to examine the accuracy of the pronouncements in the press releases. The issue is the subject of pending litigation."[clxxxvii] (This writer is one of twelve original plaintiffs in one of the pending lawsuits.)

As for coming to very different conclusions from the Inspector General's Report, while it is true that the Commission Report's footnote offers Whitman some support, it also says:

*The EPA did not have the health-based benchmarks needed to assess the extraordinary air quality conditions in Lower Manhattan after 9/11. The EPA and the White House therefore improvised and applied standards developed for other circumstances... Whether those improvisations were appropriate is still a subject for medical and scientific debate.*[clxxxviii]

This writer then asked Connaughton about his less well-known but potentially even more explosive role as Chairman of the White House Task Force on Energy Project Streamlining which was established on the recommendation of Vice President Dick Cheney's infamously secretive National Energy Policy Development Group. The Task Force included representatives from 21 Federal agencies as diverse as the Departments of Defense, the Treasury and the CIA. (Two years later, its mandates were amended to include the security of pipelines.)

Connaughton frowned in concentration.

"Ah yes!" he said triumphantly, as though retrieving a bauble from the depths of memory.

"How does this position expand the normal powers of the CEQ?" this writer asked.

"It doesn't!" he asserted. "I inherited it."

The Task Force was created, and Connaughton appointed its Chairman, by Executive Order 13212 on May 18, 2001,[clxxxix] two weeks after Connaughton was appointed to the Council on Environmental Quality so it is difficult to understand from whom he "inherited" it.

Concerning why so many disparate agencies had to be involved, Connaughton said, "The Defense Department, because often the energy is located in other countries. The CIA? I don't know; I don't think they came to any meetings."

Serving at the pleasure of Cheney's Energy Task Force, Connaughton and the CEQ faithfully carried out the Vice President's environmental agenda of relaxing regulations (that is how "streamlining" happens) the better to serve business interests.

In fact, so lax did regulations become, they managed to offend Christine Todd Whitman, whom Cheney had brought into the EPA, a feat that is comparable to shocking Larry Flynt.*

"It was Cheney's insistence on easing air pollution controls," writes the Washington Post, "not the personal reasons she cited at the time, that led Christine Todd Whitman to resign as administrator of the Environmental Protection Agency."cxc

In response to the Inspector General's allegation that a major reason the CEQ downplayed dangers in EPA's press releases was the need to reopen Wall Street, much has been made of the fact that one smoking gun press release was issued after Wall Street re-opened; ergo reopening the markets couldn't have been a motive.

This reasoning is simplistic; bosses don't necessarily spell out their wishes. In an article entitled "Leaving No Tracks," the Washington Post quotes Paul Hoffman, a former Cheney Congressional aide, who says, "Cheney never told [Hoffman] what to do... He didn't have to.

'His genius is that he builds networks and puts the right people in the right places, and then trusts them to make well-informed decisions that comport with his overall vision."cxci

Through the CEQ, Cheney turns up again in the furor over climate change. When NASA scientists complained of the Bush Administration's censorship of the issue, (once again by editing press releases) the spotlight fell on one Philip Cooney, who reported to Connaughton.

### ...And the Horse He Rode In On

Before becoming the eager hatchet man of the White House's environmental policies, James Connaughton was a partner in Sidley, Austin, Brown and Wood, which has been ranked among the top five law firms representing the 250 largest companies in the U.S. for business litigation and as the top provider of legal services to the hedge fund industry.

Clients have included J.P. Morgan Securities, Deutsche Bank, Chinese National Offshore Oil Corporation, Monsanto and GlaxoSmithKline. Sidley Austin represented Searle when it was cleared of price fixing and Marathon Oil when the federal government was ordered to provide it with a refund for the infringement of drilling rights.

The ties between Sidley Austin and the Bush Administration are extensive. Besides Connaughton, partner Patrick Morrisey has served as the Deputy Staff Director and Chief Health Counsel to the House Energy & Commerce Committee while Sidley's Senior Government Affairs Advisor, Dean Clancy, is the former Program Associate Director of the Office of Management and Budget. According to the Washington Post, Clancy is a "'proclaimer" for the Separation of School and State Alliance, which favors home schooling over compulsory public education in order to "integrate God and education." In addition to opposing public schools, Clancy also opposes stem-cell research and federal taxes for which reasons Esquire magazine calls him a fanatic.

In 2007, President Bush appointed Sidley Austin partner Daniel M. Price, who had served in The Hague as the U.S. Deputy Agent to the Iran-U.S. Claims Tribunal, as Deputy National Security Advisor for International Economic Affairs.

Then there is Bradford Berenson who returned to Sidley Austin Brown & Wood after two years as Associate Counsel to the President.

According to his biography on Sidley's website, his responsibilities to the President "included work on judicial selection, executive privilege, and responses to congressional oversight efforts. In the aftermath of the September 11 attacks, he played a significant role in the executive branch's counterterrorism response. He worked on the USA Patriot Act, the military order authorizing the use of military commissions, detainee policy and anti-terrorism litigation, presidential action against terrorist financing, and the restructuring of the federal government to create a new Department of Homeland Security...

'He previously worked on the defense of complex white collar criminal matters...

Mr. Berenson has defended criminal cases at every stage of development, from corporate internal investigations and grand jury proceedings through trials, sentencings, and appeals, in areas as diverse as government contracts, environmental crime, health care, and public corruption."cxcii

### Conflict of Interest Alive and Well

At the White House, Berenson worked closely with Cheney's Chief of Staff, David Addington, and fended off critics who demanded the recusal of Judge Antonin Scalia, after he went duck hunting with Cheney, in the Sierra Club case demanding access to Energy Task Force records.

Conflict of interest objections were apparently waived in this case because the Government Accounting Office also hired Sidley Austin to sue Cheney to obtain a list of officials from Enron and other companies who met with the energy task force.

The ubiquitous Mr. Berenson also served as the attorney for former Rove assistant Susan Ralston during the investigation of White House ties to Jack Abramoff as well as for Kyle Sampson, Alberto Gonzalez' Chief of Staff. He defended the habeas corpus stripping provisions of the military commissions bill and has stated:

"[T]he Geneva Conventions do not apply to Al Qaeda terrorists." (p. 55)

He has also maintained that the "process that's now in place in Guantanamo is, in many ways, superior to an Article V process.... [The prisoners] all get annual administrative review board hearings, and this is far in excess of the international law obligations and the law of war obligations." (p. 55)

Like Connaughton, Berenson is a zealous executant of the Cheney philosophy, stating, "[W]hen we are at war, we weigh the risks to innocents entirely differently than we do when we are not at war. Grievous damage to the lives and liberties and property of innocents are a regrettable but daily function of a state of armed conflict, of warfare the kinds of injuries that are totally unredressable in war time, but which we would never tolerate in peace time, if we were not at war." (p. 17)

And concerning executive privilege, he stated: "It's the President in time of war, the executive branch that's responsible for our security." (p. 18)

Cleverly, he suggests that a little fascism wards off the prospect of worse: "Were there to be more attacks on the scale of 9/11 or God forbid worse, there would inevitably be a far more draconian response than we've seen thus far. And so in the name of preventing that kind of response, which the public would demand, and in the name of ensuring our ultimate victory over an Islamo-fascist ideology, a religiously inspired fascist ideology, that is as illiberal as any the world has ever seen, we all need to keep first and foremost in our minds the need to wage this war effectively and ensure that the forces of right and the forces of liberalism and democracy prevail in the end." (p. 20)

Sidley Austin, then, may be justifiably described as an éminence grise of the powers that be. But lest it be viewed as biassed towards the right, it is also the law firm where, as a summer associate, Barack Obama met his future wife, Michelle.

*How Sidley Survived 9/11 Not Only "Intact...."*

On 9/11, Sidley Austin, which had merged with Brown and Wood in May 2001, (the same month that Connaughton left for the White House) had its offices in the World Trade Center. In an article written in 2003, Sidley describes how it accomplished the feat of "surviv[ing] 9/11 with vital records and employees intact."cxciii

Some of these vital records which included client, personnel, vendor and services lists, backup tapes, floor plans with personnel locations identified, inventory lists of equipment, furniture, and supplies, procedures manuals, docket calendars, and blank checks, "were available because they were part of a planned dispersal in which they had been copied and sent offsite for safe keeping."cxciv Weekly computer backup tapes were also being stored in New Jersey.

The article is written in a breathless style, pausing to pay lip service to the dreadfulness of the day before going on to the myriad resourceful steps Sidley had taken to the benefit of their cherished clients.

Then comes the punchline. As far as Sidley Austin is concerned, September 11 had a silver lining made of real silver.

*...But Also With A Windfall*

In addition to all its other prudent measures, on September 1, 2001, Sidley had taken the extraordinarily felicitous step of not only renewing, but also of doubling, its insurance.

"When it was announced that the firm's insurance policies had just been renewed and doubled on September 1, 2001, applause filled the room. The insurance policies not only covered reconstruction costs for the files but for the organization's valuable art collection and personal effects as well."cxcv

This move joins a distinguished line of coincidences leading up to the attacks such as highly anomalous put options on United and American Airlines; numerous war games including "practice Armageddons" which diverted planes away from the East Coast and introduced chaff onto the radar screens to paralyze pilots who wanted to respond; as well as dozens of warnings to our intelligence agencies which are normally overlooked by the mainstream press.

Assessing its recovery plan from the attack, Sidley confesses that "some individuals listed as having supervisory roles in the disaster recovery plan ended up not having job assignments, which was frustrating to those sitting around on 9/11. Part of the problem stemmed from a lack of testing of the plan the year before."cxcvi

But despite the frustration, over all "the firm," to use a Grishamesque phrase, dubbed its recovery effort a success.


*One Minor Glitch*

And so the reader comes away believing, even after encountering this sentence: "By September 13, only one individual had not been located."

Written this way, the account relays the information concerning "only one individual," as an example of yet another triumph. What the article neglects to say, however, though it was published nearly two years after the disaster, is that the reason the individual was "not located" is that she was dead.

A telephone operator who dreamed of opening a candy business, Rosemary Smith was the only member of the firm not to make it out of the building alive.cxcvii And while Sidley mentions her elsewhere on its website and has apparently put up a memorial to her somewhere in its offices, it is difficult to understand what the writer of the article means by the phrase, "employees intact."

The "good news" about the firm's assets, however, seems to be abundantly accurate.

# Appendix B
## Sins of Omission:  Stories the Media Overlook
*Left Forum, John Jay College of Criminal Law, 2015*

Welcome to Sins of Omission:  Stories the Media Overlook...

My baptism into this topic, among others, came courtesy of 9/11.  Prior to that, I was an average politically correct, knee-jerk liberal New Yorker who believed, to the extent I thought about it at all, that the media, particularly our own New York Times, gave a fairly undistorted view – using the word "fairly" in both senses – of the important stories going on in the world.

But with 9/11, which took place while my son attended Stuyvesant high school located four blocks north of Ground Zero, I got a ringside seat to that circus in which the government practices sleight of hand while the media play the role of the gracious and accommodating magician's assistant.

As everyone now knows but few then believed, the kids at Stuyvesant, like Downtown's residents and office workers, not to mention the Ground Zero workers, were exposed to record-breaking levels of over 2000 contaminants which, it has been shown, the Environmental Protection Agency not only should have known about but did know about. (That subtle but significant distinction is a prime example of a story which the mainstream media have left unexamined.)

And yet their tricks in camouflaging the truth were, like the virtuoso magician's, not only abundant but also mercurial so that by the time the handful of activists following the issue figured out one, the magician had moved on to the next.

To quote no less a master sleight-of-hand artist than Karl Rove: "We're an empire now, and when we act, we create our own reality. And while you're studying that reality — judiciously, as you will — we'll act again, creating other new realities, which you can study too, and that's how things will sort out."[cxcviii]

With one or two isolated exceptions, the first being Juan Gonzalez of the New York Daily News, the media did not join us few activists in probing for data or asking such choice but telling questions as, "Why are you focusing only on asbestos? What about the hundreds if not thousands of other toxic substances released by the collapse of the buildings and the fires that were allowed to burn and smolder freely for at least three months?" Or, when a waste transfer station was placed yards from Stuyvesant in violation of state, local and federal law, "You say it's an emergency but there is no longer any hope of finding survivors so what's the emergency for which the health of the school's students, faculty and staff is being placed in jeopardy?"

Instead, in partnership with the government, the media practiced a, "Don't ask; don't tell" policy which was allowed to continue because the public had its attention glued to the sword-wielding, swarthy enemy in Afghanistan. That public is smarter now but as Karl Rove pointed out, it's too late: The government has moved on to even greater disasters – hurricanes, droughts and wars and besides, there's a whole new generation of suckers who've come of age since then.

Not only did the media remain compliant as lobotomy patients; they did so even in the face of testimony from experts and first hand witnesses at hearings being held at all levels of government.

How could this happen?

One way was that the federal government was allowed to control State and local hearings by demanding to be heard first since they knew that by lunchtime, a large portion of the TV press would have to leave to edit their stories in time for, say, the 5 PM news slot. Besides, the media were not interested in presenting a fair and balanced report; only in getting one or two sound-bites from someone with an official title.

At times, conflicting information was dutifully reported but buried deep in the article or the article itself was nestled in a low-profile section of the paper. In the case of the symptoms which manifested themselves early on, the news was conveyed couched in terms of "fear," thus allowing physical symptoms to be patronizingly blamed on psychosomatic factors.

And then there is the issue of access, the threat that if you don't play by the administration's rules, you'll no longer get those portentous sound-bites; your competitor will.

*The way to read the Washington Post, and I suppose this applies to any newspaper in any city that you live in, is certain reporters [have] certain beats. They develop certain contacts with certain politicians, and if you know that and if you know who they're talking to every day... you can just sort of know by whose by-line is on the story where their information is coming from. So you don't read it as this reporter's story, you read it as the politician using this writer to say something.*[cxcix]

(Update 2016: "[Jeff Bezos] recently secured a $600 million contract from the CIA. That's at least twice what Bezos paid for the Post this year. Bezos recently disclosed that the company's Web-services business is building a 'private cloud' for the CIA to use for its data needs." From Amazon, 'The Washington Post' and That $600 MIllion CIA Contract.[cc]

The issue of access or government favor has been going on at least since World War Two when reporters agreed not to reveal the end of the war in the European theater until it was announced the following day. The pact was broken by Associated Press correspondent Edward Kennedy because the military had broken it first, by allowing the news to be broadcast in Germany. Kennedy was fired and an apology not issued until 2012, when Kennedy's daughter published a memoir on the subject.[cci]

This stranglehold of the media by the government would be fine if it was understood by the public. But unlike the former Soviet Union, we still operate under the illusion that our press is free. And as Joseph Goebbels knew so well, it is easier to put over a big lie than a small one since the public will be unable to believe the media "could have the impudence to distort the truth so infamously."

In addition to the manipulation of the press by politicians, we have their handmaidens, the banks or corporations. According to the late, great researcher John Judge,

*...the ownership of all four major television networks, [was] secretly held, through interlocking directorates, by the Rockefeller family since the 1940s, [until it] passed openly into the hands of General Electric (remember, "what's good for GE is good for the country") for NBC, and to Capital Cities, Bill Casey's stock investment company, ABC is under their auspices.[ccii]*

In other words, specifically words which have been attributed variously to William Randolph Hearst and George Orwell: News is something someone doesn't want you to know. Everything else is advertising.

We see the results in the news about everything from climate change to the financial crisis.

Case in point:

While investigating HSBC bank, Peter Oborne, a reporter for the British paper the Telegraph, "said one former Telegraph executive told him HSBC was 'the advertiser you literally cannot afford to offend...'"

Oborne said: *Late last year I set to work on a story about the international banking giant HSBC.*

*Well-known British Muslims had received letters out of the blue from HSBC informing them that their accounts had been closed. No reason was given, and it was made plain that there was no possibility of appeal. "It's like having your water cut off," one victim told me.*

*When I submitted it for publication on the Telegraph website, I was at first told there would be no problem. When it was not published I made enquiries. I was fobbed off with excuses, then told there was a legal problem. When I asked the legal department, the lawyers were unaware of any difficulty. When I pushed the point, an executive took me aside and said that "there is a bit of an issue" with HSBC. Eventually I gave up in despair and offered the article to OpenDemocracy...*

*I researched the newspaper's coverage of HSBC. I learnt that Harry Wilson, the admirable banking correspondent of the Telegraph, had published an online story about HSBC based on a report from a Hong Kong analyst who had claimed there was a 'black hole' in the HSBC accounts. This story was swiftly removed from the Telegraph website, even though there were no legal problems.*[cciii]

In the middle of Oborne's efforts to get his story out, the Telegraph ran a story, which was known to be false, about a woman with three breasts. That's rule number one of the magician's playbook: "Look over here!" to distract the audience from your sleight of hand. And what better way to do that than with sex?

Oborne resigned from the Telegraph.

This is not an isolated instance. Here are a few more from other media giants:

Condoleezza Rice Testifies on Urging the Times to Not Run Article[cciv]
Google Reports Surge in Government Surveillance[ccv]
Why Didn't CNN's International Arm Air its Own Documentary on Bahrain's Arab Spring Repression?[ccvi]

The New York Times acknowledges some of its failures. An interview in the German magazine, Der Spiegel, with Times editor Dean Baquet contains the following exchange:

*SPIEGEL: One of your best reporters, James Risen, said in a speech that the mainstream "failed after 9/11." Do you agree?*

*Baquet: Yes, absolutely. The mainstream press was not aggressive enough after 9/11, was not aggressive enough in asking questions about a decision to go to war in Iraq, was not aggresive enough in asking the hard questions about the War on Terror. I accept that for the Los Angeles Times and the New York Times.[ccvii]*

By what mechanism is this across-the-board censorship possible?

In *The Afternoon of March 30: A Contemporary Historical Novel,* the late dean of the University of Montana School of Journalism, Nathaniel Blumberg, writes:

*The American news media have been deeply penetrated by our intelligence community. Confirmation of everything I have been saying on that score came less than two weeks ago, and I've been waiting for just the right moment to pass it on. It comes from no less a source than the New York Times. I would like to say that it was the lead story on page one but, alas, as usual it was buried at the bottom of the fourteenth page of the second section on June 9. That story, my good and patient friends, reports that the Central Intelligence Agency, in order to settle a lawsuit under the Freedom of Information Act, reluctantly disclosed – those are the words of the good gray lady herself – that journalists have been used in a variety of roles and missions. Among other duties, journalists provided cover or served as a funding mechanism, some provided nonattributable material for use by the CIA, some collaborated in or worked on CIA-produced materials or were used for the placement of CIA-prepared materials in the foreign media. Some journalists had even served as couriers and as case officers who secretly supervised other agents. And some – oh, it's been a long time a-coming – provided assistance in* **suppressing what the CIA termed a media item, such as a news story**.[ccviii] *[emphasis mine]*

Lest Blumberg be unknown to the listener, and therefore suspect, here's a quote from CIA Director Robert Gates in a memo entitled "Greater CIA Openness." According to the memo, the CIA Public Affairs Office:

*...has relationships with reporters from every major wire service, newspaper, news weekly, and television network in the nation. This has helped us turn some intelligence failure stories into intelligence success stories, and it has contributed to the accuracy of countless others. In many instances, we have persuaded reporters to postpone, change, hold, or even scrap stories that could have adversely affected national security interests or jeopardized sources and methods.* [ccix]

This control of the media by the intelligence agencies, which has been investigated in depth by no less than Carl Bernstein of Watergate fame, came of age following World War Two when patriotic Americans, including some journalists, were proud to do their part for Operation Mockingbird, the CIA's campaign to stamp out communism.

For that's the magician's ultimate distraction; better than soccer; better, even, than sex. The enemy: In the 1950's, a communist; these days, a terrorist. Bread and circuses, or what the CIA's Frank Wisner called "the mighty Wurlitzer" are fine as long as supplies last; but when things get tight, an electric shock by way of a terror attack can be counted on to galvanize the "sheeple" into obedience.

# Appendix C
Interview with Firefighter/Author Dennis Smith[ccx]
Author of *Report from Ground Zero*

The interview took place December 9, 2003, in Smith's apartment near ABC studios where his son, one of five children, was a producer. It was in an office at these studios that a baby was exposed to anthrax shortly after 9/11. (According to brief news reports, he recovered.)

We had already spoken on the phone about Smith's take on the health issues of firefighters at Ground Zero. But it turned out that he had intended some of his remarks to be off the record so he suggested a second interview in person.

He was a trim man, small by firefighter standards. The apartment was furnished in the muted tones of the 18th century, the shelves stocked with art books. Voltaire's desk rested against the wall. I knew it was Voltaire's desk because I'd asked; Smith had mentioned it in his book, *Report from Ground Zero: The Story of the Rescue Efforts at the World Trade Center.*

"It's from his house in Switzerland," Smith began, "but I don't think he ever wrote at it. Anyone who knows anything about Voltaire knows he dictated as he walked."

"What does it feel like to write at it?"

"I just do handwritten correspondence there, Ma'am. My computer is upstairs."

The polite firefighter in response to a woman's silly question. We'll get past my golly-gee gawking; I had to ask.

"I was concerned about what you wrote. I hadn't intended all that to be published."

I can imagine that concern: "Aagh!" It's a reaction one frequently encounters when it dawns on people you're writing a book; anything they say may be used against them. Considering which, Smith has been the consummate gentleman. Anyway, I don't want enemies, certainly not among the good guys.

"Sometimes I think I should wear a sandwich board that says, 'Warning: Memoirist at Work,'" I reply. "What would you like to say about being at Ground Zero?"

"We knew the place was unhealthy. What we don't know is how those carcinogens work together. Asbestos has a five to twenty year incubation period."

"Even forty."

"Forty. But we don't know if some of these contaminants can have an effect in two years." [Note: This interview took place in 2003.]

In our previous conversation, Smith has mentioned several cancers among Ground Zero workers which some medical professionals believe may be attributable to exposure to 9/11 contaminants. "I've heard people say that there will be a time bomb effect," he says now.

"You wrote that firefighters had trouble with their eyes. What was the diagnosis?"

"People's eyes got filled with microscopic pieces of dust. Many firefighters' eyes were caked shut. My eyes were caked. Others were so bad they had to go to the hospital to have their eyes opened. I used a spray bottle of a clear medicinal water. [The next sentence, which is indecipherable in my handwritten notes, mentions saline solution.] But that's nothing new for firefighters."

"Yeah. You talk in the book about how firefighters crawl through smoke, coughing 'til they're nearly unconscious, as part of their training. It's called, 'taking a beating' and it would violate OSHA [Occupational Safety and Health Administration] regulations."

"OSHA didn't exist at the time we were doing that. But the conditions for firefighters are definitely unhealthy. In New York City, there's a lung cancer bill for firefighters so that it's presumed to be caused by the job."

"Even if they smoke?"

"I think so. Do you smoke?"

"No."

"Does your son smoke?"

"No. My father smoked."

"Is he alive?"

"No. He died of a brain tumor at fifty-seven."

"That's not from smoking."

"The primary tumor may have been somewhere else."

"And metastasized, you mean."

"Yes."

"My children smoke. I'm always after them. But there's a myth that the lungs repair themselves in five years.

'At Ground Zero there was a group of doctors who'd created a cleansing system that consists of repeated saunas, exercises and vitamins. It was developed by L. Ron Hubbard. Of course some doctors say any firefighter would feel better after doing four saunas a day."

"Did insurance pay for this?"

"No. The Church of Scientology paid for it, for firefighters only. Their offices were down around Fulton Street. An ornate, yellow building from the 1890s. Do you know it?

'These people had a big heart. But they were also trying to prove something. Toxic metals tend to stay in the body. They don't digest out of the body. The [doctors doing the treatment] showed me towels of different color sweat – purple, yellow, red... Detoxification exists only in sweat according to them. The treatment took thirty days."

"Did you do it?"

"No."

"Why not? It sounds like a vacation."

"It seemed like work to me. It took three hours. You had to go on the treadmill... X and those doctors don't think much of the treatment. But these firefighters were desperate for some sort of relief. They couldn't walk upstairs."

"Did they go back to work?"

"On night duty or sick leave."

"You talked in your book about Mafia involvement in the fireproofing of the World Trade Center. Was that the asbestos or the other stuff?"

"The other stuff. The World Trade Center was under construction three years before they outlawed asbestos. There was spray-on fireproofing. You've seen it. It looks like rough caulking. It goes over the steel. What I was told – I'd have to go to my notes but the information was credible enough for me to write it – was that the steel had been lying around rusting for months. It had to do with the litigation with the Port Authority.

The beams were not adequately cleaned before the fireproofing was applied. It was put on top of rust. When it was tested in '93 after the first explosion, they hit it with a hammer and it fell off. They tried to reapply it but they couldn't get to the underbeam.

The litigation lasted from the day the WTC opened just about until '92 when Dibono was found in the basement of the South Tower."

In his book, Smith says that Louis Dibono, head of the company that applied the fireproofing, was part of the John Gotti family. He died from multiple gunshot wounds.

"That litigation was created by the Port Authority against this construction company," Smith continues. "There wasn't any settlement. The company went kaput."

"Would it have been possible to fireproof the building?"

"No. Local law requires a rating system. Steel can burn for two hours before it melts. The New York requirement is more than in the rest of the country. It has a three hour rating.

'Did you read the paperback edition of my book?"

"Yes."

"The last seven pages which were added later have that information. The National Institute of Standards and Technology were given a thirty million dollar grant. It was laughable to me because they came to the same conclusion I came to in my book. They found that the floors collapsed in the heat. The government has its heart in the right place but [studies] have to do with keeping people employed. I'd rather take that thirty million and put it in public schools. Even if you got ten kids to get A's instead of B's it would be worth it."

"How has 9/11 changed your politics?"

"If anything, it's made me more conservative because I recognize we have to rely on our own diligence to protect ourselves. This is true on the left as well as the right. It's laxity of government that's created chaos and almost all the ability of radical Islamists to wreak havoc. Bernard Lewis said we should have invaded Iraq in 1993 and [he cites other years] but we didn't and we paid that price."

"But the terrorists didn't come from Iraq."

"That's true. But if there's any good to come out of this invasion it's that it'll force those governments to reevaluate themselves. They've left most of their populations behind."

"That would take a long time, for them to change their thinking to such an extent."

"Fifty years... Did you see Hillary Clinton's fusillades yesterday? She said the Bush administration didn't have to embroider information. There was enough. If that's true, why didn't we go into Iraq when the Cole was bombed?"

"We should talk about masks. What kind of respirators do firefighters usually wear?"

"It's not a respirator which is forced air[?] This is a self-contained air tank."

"How long does it last?"

"The new ones, about forty-five minutes. The mask whistles when it's running low. You have to go out and replace it."

"Why didn't the firefighters wear masks at Ground Zero?"

"No one thought of the danger of ingestion. If you can breathe, they thought it was O.K. It's a shame. I think there's room for litigation among the first responders.

'Everyone assumed the environment was dangerous in terms of smoke and dust."

This apparent contradiction of his previous statement is probably resolvable by distinguishing between long-term versus immediate dangers. But this is not a trial and I let the contradiction pass.

"Even the bosses didn't wear masks. It was only in the second week the firefighters were asked to wear masks. You know, the mask weighs thirty pounds.

"Those first six weeks before the cranes did most of the work were intensive. To have masks was impractical. I used a filter mask when I took a body out after decomposition but generally not. Many firefighters purposefully didn't wear masks because they wanted to smell bodies."

"Some people say that because Christie Todd Whitman said the air was safe, rescue workers didn't feel it necessary to wear masks." (I am one of twelve original plaintiffs in a potential class action lawsuit [for cleanup] against Whitman and the EPA.)

"I don't think people felt that. Ground Zero was led by smart people, experienced in emergency services, or the police. They knew there's room for litigation against the city.

216

'In any emergency, you act beyond the norm to try to mitigate. Any act of heroism is against the norm. In my book I talk about the firefighters who knew they might not come out. Terry Hutton saying, 'I want you to know I love you.' Other officers said, 'We might not survive this.' All that is evidence they knew the buildings could come down. There were six examples."

"But firefighters go into burning buildings every day."

"You don't think when you go into a burning building that you won't survive. You have confidence in the people you work with that you're protected against flashover fires and holes. There are always indications a building is going to collapse. The chief is trained to look for cracks in the wall, separations in the bricks."

"So what would the litigation against the city be for?"

"For not insisting that everyone wear masks."

"They did insist at the Pentagon."

"Christie Todd Whitman explained – I don't remember if it was to my satisfaction or not – that she didn't mean the air was clear."

"If the city had said, 'You've got to wear your mask,' would the firefighters have done it?'

"I think so. Of course you'd have to have enough tanks and the facility to refill them."

"Lieutenant Manny Gomez testified he brought a mask. But he was told not to wear it for fear of panicking people." (He also testified at a hearing held by the EPA Ombudsman that there were many masks available but they went unused.)

"It doesn't surprise me. [On the other hand] I saw a chief begging men to wear masks. But the grief was extraordinary and the motivation. So it was hard to boss people around. The chief said, 'Put the mask on. The OSHA guys are here.' Some people did it."

"How does this make you feel about Giuliani?" In his book, Smith praises the Mayor.

"He didn't have much to do with that. He understood that the person who controlled the information was central to the memory. This was the first major attack on U.S. soil since 1812. When Hawaii was attacked, it wasn't a state.

'No one had the authority to say anything, not EPA, not DEP. Giuliani had to say everything in a way even the Governor couldn't."

"Did you think, based on what you saw, that people should be allowed to move back in?"

"Then I did." He emphasized the word "then" to imply he no longer thought so. "When you hit a piece of furniture," he hit the arm of the couch as Community Board 1 member Catherine McVay Hughes had hit the table to make the same point in her interview, (Appendix K) "thousands of dust particles get released into the air. You don't see them. But down there you could *see* the residue. It would cloud up like powder."

"How did it happen that they never found a doorknob – everything was atomized – but they found body parts?"

"They only found parts of 1250 people. So there was a huge number of people for whom no DNA was found. People who weren't atomized were protected by firefighters, by their equipment.

'It's a very peculiar thing, how many naked bodies were found."

"What do you make of it? The clothes were burned off?"

"Or torn. When those buildings fell, they imploded like a huge mixer. A body didn't have a chance to stay contained. The buildings fell at 600 mph. It took twelve seconds. But 292 bodies were found whole."

"What was being there like? I know you wrote about some of that in your book."

"I suppose what I didn't say are those things I felt shouldn't be said.

'The way the community of 9/11 worked, if firefighters from Chicago came, they'd be let in. I don't know if they were needed or not. But if they had gloves and boots, they were allowed to work.

'I remember one day seeing a bunch of policewomen; I guess they came down from some detail. Often people at the site weren't working in full protective gear but in shirtsleeves and hard helmets. They found a police officer's body. The way things worked in the services, they found a badge or a gun, they'd leave it to that service and give it a military aspect. These people chose to go into these buildings. They were taken with the same stature as they had when they went in. I wondered what was going through their minds as they carried the body. It's rare to see eight policewomen together."

"Why did the fires burn for so long?"

"You know how many long burning fires there are in this country? There are fires that have been burning for years. Tires are buried in a pit and it would cost 43 million dollars to get to them to put out the fire."

"Could the WTC fires have been put out sooner, say, by injecting nitrogen?"

"No. The Fire Department was aware of the ways to fight deepseated fires, how to dynamite the walls down. But they took them down piece by piece because it was safer to do it that way. They were also concerned with the integrity of the slurry wall."

"And the need to search for body parts."

"Yes. That was almost holy in the beginning, the care and prudence given to the lifting of every beam. After that, we needed the steel in order to find out why the towers went down, to be prepared the next time. There were grapplers that could lift the steel chunks. Then they also had a system of spotters with long-range telescopes and binoculars. Others sat in the trucks. It's not foolproof. But to understand empirically why the towers went down, the Fire Department knew you'd have to have the steel. When the Columbia went down, we spent 40 million dollars to find out why."

"And there are a lot more skyscrapers than spaceships. Some of that steel wound up in Third World countries: South Korea, India."

"China too. If I'd been Mayor or head of the Department of Design and Construction, I would've said, 'Let's rent a field in New Jersey and put the steel there for a couple of years.' Maybe they thought of that and the EPA said it wasn't a good idea. Who knows?

'Every beam was numbered and coded."

"You could see that?"

"Oh, yeah. When steel melts, it bends and weakens. It doesn't disintegrate like molten steel. It loses its ability to hold."

"So you weren't astonished when the buildings collapsed?"

"No. Anyone who's ever been in the WTC knows how big it is. You see ten floors on fire, that's ten acres."

Some experts have raised questions about the speed at which the towers fell and other evidence which they say suggests that a controlled demolition was also involved. "How are you going to fight a fire like that? Last time I was in the WTC, the June before, I was at an art exhibit and we had lunch on the roof: Windows on the World."

"Have you fought wild fires like the ones out West?"

"Sure. We've had huge brush fires in New York: Queens, Staten Island, the Bronx, Orchard Beach. None in Manhattan that I can think of.

'Those fires, the volume of fire, it's three feet high for two blocks then suddenly it's ten feet high for two blocks.

"When you study to become a firefighter do they tell you that at such and such a temperature, dioxin forms and at another temperature some other contaminant forms?"

"You take a course in it. You learn more about the ability of fire to reproduce itself. There's a phenomenon of air currents in a fire. You take thirty candles and put them one foot away from each other, they'll stay separate. Four inches away, they integrate at the top and grow to twice their size. Years ago I went to the Mutual Company factory, to their fire investigation lab to get fire ratings. They burn everything there. If you burn a strip of polyurethane holding it horizontally it burns slowly. The carcinogens it emits are extraordinary. They'd kill you in two minutes.

'But if you place the polyurethane vertically, say, a ten foot strip, the fire rises to the top in thirty seconds. That's what happened in that nightclub last year. The polyurethane was used as soundproofing. Polyurethane flat burns with the physical rules of radiated heat, say, from left to right. Vertically, bottom to top it burns like gasoline because heat rises. The natural instinct of heat is like water seeking its own level. As it rises it doubles its volume every sixty seconds. In polyurethane, it's twice as fast."

# Appendix D
## The Lingering Clouds Over Ground Zero[ccxi]
*(Articles and testimony may contain material overlapping with body of the book.)*

*October 16, 2004*

September 11 was a tragedy that has changed the course of history and the way we live...

Did Bush himself know about the air quality downtown? If he didn't, it was because he operated on a "Don't ask, don't tell" policy so that the buck would stop short of him...

The Commission Report deals with the envirodisaster of 9/11 in a footnote in which they refer to an interview with Sam Thernstrom, coordinator for the White House Council on Environmental Quality. He denies changing press releases in order to reopen Wall Street, explaining that the reasons for the changes were procedural. His story is corroborated by Christy[sic] Todd Whitman who told the initial lies.

John Gotti and Lucky Luciano have got their stories straight...

The White House's actions in response to the environmental aftermath of 9/11 reveal that Osama Bin Laden could not have stumbled on a more felicitous collaborator than George W. Bush.

1 http://delta.ucdavis.edu/news.htm
2 http://www.911ea.org /
4
http://www.nyc.gov/html/doh/html/alerts/wtc1.html

# Appendix E
## The EPA and a Dirty Bomb[ccxii]

*January 6, 2005*

The environmental disaster of 9/11 has ominous repercussions for all Americans: The arguably reckless way the government has responded (or failed to) sets a precedent for future disasters of even greater magnitude such as a dirty bomb...

It is impossible to know why the EPA, the federal agency in charge of remediating environmental disasters, took its cues from the C[ouncil on Environmental Quality.] However, the CEQ was far from an obscure backwater of the White House. As of a May, 2001, directive by Vice President Cheney's National Energy Policy Development Group, the Chairman of the CEQ chaired the Interagency Task Force on Energy Project Streamlining which included representatives from the Departments of State, the Treasury, Defense, Agriculture, Housing and Urban Development, Justice, Commerce, Transportation, the Interior, Labor, Education, Health and Human Services, Energy, Veterans Affairs, the Environmental Protection Agency, the Central Intelligence Agency, the General Service Administration, the Office of Management and Budget, the Council of Economic Advisers, the Domestic Policy Council and the National Economic Council.(3)

The policy of money before people which, as promulgated by the CEQ and the EPA, came to the fore after 9/11, has continued to drive the EPA's response to the disaster. The standards used during their initial cleanup, announced on May 8, 2002, after much pressure from community activists as well as Senator Clinton and the indomitable Congressman Nadler, exposed residents (schools and businesses weren't even included in the program) to a hundred times the cancer risk that had been used at "comparable" Superfund sites in the past.

Traditionally, EPA cleaned to a standard whereby approximately one person in a million would get cancer from the contaminant involved in any given disaster. In Lower Manhattan, they cleaned to a standard whereby approximately a hundred people out of a million (i.e. one in ten thousand) would get cancer from any contaminant involved in the disaster.

Although during the initial, delayed cleanup EPA focused almost exclusively on asbestos, there were hundreds of carcinogens and other contaminants released on 9/11 and during the fires which burned and smoldered for several months, including dioxin, lead, mercury and polycyclic aromatic hydrocarbons (PAHs). Their additive effects were not taken into account, much less their explosive synergistic effects about which little is known. However work performed at Mt. Sinai has shown that if someone is an asbestos worker and a smoker, for instance, the risk of cancer is not simply twice as bad as being one or the other: It's eighty or ninety times as bad.

At a City Council hearing in March, 2003, EPA's Dr. Paul Gilman (who resigned from the agency in November, 2004) was asked under what circumstances EPA had previously used the standard that put a hundred times as many people at risk of cancer. He responded: Where the area was sparsely populated or few contaminants were released. Clearly, neither of these criteria applied to Lower Manhattan.

Another reason EPA officials gave for using the more lax standard in Lower Manhattan was that the more protective standard was impossible to achieve because their instruments clogged. To anyone who challenged this excuse (isn't the clogging of the instruments an indication that there's a significant amount of potentially toxic dust?) they responded, "This disaster was unprecedented." In other words, "What do you expect us to do?" On the other hand, they also continued to maintain that there was no problem. (The EPA cleanup was dangerously flawed for other reasons too numerous to go into here but which included using tests that were designed NOT to find contaminants. They did, however, have more accurate tests performed in their own building.)[4]

They also based part of their cleanup of Lower Manhattan on a finding of visible dust – although their own literature prior to 9/11 discusses the dangers of *in*visible dust – in addition to proposing testing only where the dust had been visible from an airplane.[5])

It is no surprise, therefore, to read in a New York Times article about the advice the federal government is preparing to give states and local authorities on what to do after a dirty bomb, that antinuclear activists have complained, "the exposure allowed under the contemplated advice would create almost 100 times as much cancer risk as those usually allowed from other kinds of contaminants, like chemicals, or from radiation in other settings."(6)[ccxiii]

Why would the feds do this? The answer appears in an earlier article and sounds all too familiar:

*...an attack using conventional explosives to spread radioactive materials – a dirty bomb – would probably occur in a far more prominent location than a toxic-waste site or a power plant, and the need to resume using the site would be higher, said [radiation specialist for DHS] Mr. Buddemeier, in his presentation to a National Academy of Sciences group.*

*'When balancing the risk of radiation exposure against the benefit of returning to normal activity, the government safety recommendations will weigh the importance of the contaminated location to economic or political life, said a radiation scientist who works for one of seven federal agencies drafting the document.*

'*Thus a major train station, cargo port or building in Lower Manhattan might be reoccupied sooner than a suburban shopping mall, said the scientist, who asked not to be identified because the document had not yet been published.*"(7)[ccxiv]

In other words, EPA's standards prior to 9/11 have now been officially turned upside down: The more people who are likely to be exposed (since economically important areas tend to be highly populated) the greater the likelihood that standards designed to protect human health will be overlooked. If you live in the suburbs, the federal government will give your health high priority. But as soon as economic interests enter the picture, the bottom line trumps health and science.

http://landofpuregold.com/truth203.htm
http://64.233.161.104/search?q=cache:n8bNmIPC9HEJ
http://www.etf.energy.gov/pdfs/eo13212.pdf
http://msnbc.msn.com/id/3076626
http://64.233.161.104/
http://query.nytimes.com/gst/
http://www.projecttahs.org/tahsjsp/t

# Appendix F
## Ground Zero's Toxic Dust[ccxv]

*May 13, 2005*

EPA's new, supposedly improved sampling plan to test for residual toxic dust from the environmental disaster of 9/11 was released Tuesday evening to a response that ranged from "serious concern" on the part of Senator Hillary Clinton to dismay among community activists.

"[I]t appears at first glance that the EPA's long-awaited plan has been designed in a way that is fundamentally inadequate to determine the true extent of WTC dust contamination," said Congressman Jerrold Nadler of the Eighth District which includes Ground Zero.

"While we are pleased that EPA agreed to test workplaces as well as residences," said David Newman, industrial hygienist for the New York Committee for Occupational Safety and Health and a member of the WTC Expert Technical Review Panel which has been meeting with EPA for the last year in an effort to arrive at a scientifically valid plan, "that is a hollow promise if employers can bar access for testing."

Newman was referring to an aspect of voluntary testing which many community activists feel could make it impossible to get scientifically valid results: If EPA relies only on buildings whose landlords have volunteered to be tested, those are the buildings that are most likely to have been adequately cleaned. In office buildings, employees who are worried about what they may be getting exposed to at work will be at the mercy of the decisions of their employers who may be afraid of the liability issues that could ensue from testing.

Other problems with the plan include its reliance on a WTC 'signature' which would supposedly insure that contaminated dust that might be found in people's homes indeed came from the disaster. Community activists have argued that the contents of the buildings were diverse and that nature did not obligingly mix them together into a homogeneous blend. This belief is borne out by experience: Independent testing performed in the years following 9/11 showed some apartments to have high levels of antimony; others, high levels of asbestos or lead, etc.

EPA's initial plan as laid out by James Connaughton of the White House Council on Environmental Quality (the organization that changed at least one of EPA's press releases following 9/11, turning cautionary statements about asbestos into reassurances) was to use asbestos as a surrogate for all the contaminants that might remain in people's homes. This suggestion was denounced by organizations such as 9/11 Environmental Action and the Sierra Club as well as being severely critiqued by independent experts. Asbestos was then replaced by two 'signatures', one for the collapse of the towers, the other for the fires that burned and smoldered for several months. The fire signature idea was abandoned. The collapse signature has metamorphosed several times. A few months ago it was to be slag wool. The current plan adds gypsum and concrete; the latter a contaminant too heavy to have travelled far from Ground Zero. The chameleon nature of the WTC signature underscores the dubiousness of the whole 'signature' notion since the essence of a signature is its constancy.

Even if EPA were to arrive at a reasonable plan, there are still problems with the way it would be executed. Residents who took part in EPA's first cleanup, begun in September 2002, witnessed equipment that broke down, fans for air tests that were never turned on or, when they were turned on, were placed facing the wrong direction. Some community activists, including this writer, have argued for third party monitoring to prevent a repeat travesty.

# Appendix G
## EPA's Latest Betrayal at Ground Zero[ccxvi]

*December 1, 2005*

Doing an end run around the Lower Manhattan community with which it has been in supposed consultation concerning plans to test and remediate toxic contamination remaining from 9/11, yesterday the US EPA announced a 'clean-up' which represented several steps backwards.

The move outraged community advocates, scientists and elected officials.

"[T]he plan... fails to correct the major problems identified by EPA's Inspector General in 2003," said Senator Hillary Clinton. "For example, the plan does not include testing in north of Canal Street or in Brooklyn, in spite of the Inspector General's conclusion that the cleanup boundaries were not scientifically developed. In addition, the plan ignores many of the recommendations made by the World Trade Center Expert Technical Review Panel over the last 20 months."

"This sham plan is terrible in many ways," said Congressman Jerrold Nadler whose district includes Ground Zero. "It excludes workplaces; it does not address the problem of contaminated HVAC systems; it ignores buildings slated for demolition; it will not investigate whether areas have been re-contaminated; and it does not cover all the geographic areas known to have been showered with dust – and that's just for starters."

EPA's announcement followed the conclusions of an independent panel about EPA's plan to base testing for toxic contamination on the presence of slagwool, a building component which EPA chose to serve as a 'signature' for WTC dust. The independent scientists concluded that EPA's method did not support slagwool as a signature, thus corroborating what community advocates including the Sierra Club, 9/11 Environmental Action, the New York Committee on Occupational Safety and Health and the World Trade Center Environmental Organization, had been saying for years.

Doing an about-face from EPA's previous advocacy of slagwool Dr. Timothy Oppelt, Chairman of the Expert Technical Review Panel, told the Washington Post, "We would prefer to go further, but the science won't let us. We can't be whimsical."

It is debatable that whimsy is what the independent scientists had in mind when they wrote:

*The peer reviewers were skeptical that EPA's evaluation and interpretation of the study data were performed fairly. Peer reviewers pointed to several non-standard steps taken to enhance the study's ability to distinguish WTC dust from background dust. These steps could be interpreted as attempts to prove the method's success rather than to objectively evaluate its real-world potential for fingerprinting WTC dust.* [ccxvii]

Dr. Oppelt reiterated EPA's claim that the boundaries of the announced 'cleanup' were generous because they went beyond the heaviest dust viewed from a satellite in the days following 9/11. The relevance of satellite photography to toxic particles some of which can only be seen with powerful microscopes is questionable.

In the final coup de grace before he retires from EPA in January, Dr. Oppelt also disbanded the panel which will have its last meeting December 13 before it has addressed a major part of its mandate: unmet public health needs. The Health Registry, which had been

In the final coup de grace before he retires from EPA in January, Dr. Oppelt also disbanded the panel which will have its last meeting December 13 before it has addressed a major part of its mandate: unmet public health needs. The Health Registry, which had been given the floor on several occasions, is distorted by problems including lack of objectivity (it is based on self-reporting by participants rather than on medical tests) and conflict of interest. (The New York City Department of Health, under whose auspices the Registry is being conducted, initially told residents to clean their apartments using a wet mop or wet rag.) With the peremptory closing up shop of the Technical Review Panel, sick residents, students and office workers will be deprived of what has been their only forum for possible redress.

However, Congressman Nadler concluded that with its latest 'cleanup' plan, the EPA had in fact satisfied "its traditional internal goals: to obfuscate the facts, to deny the truth, and to produce a plan designed not to find any contamination."

# Appendix H
## Federal Judge Slams Whitman and EPA[ccxviii]

*February 6, 2006*

In a move that vindicates the activists and victims of the environmental disaster of 9/11, last Thursday, U.S. District Judge Deborah Batts blasted former EPA Administrator Christine Todd Whitman for her actions following the collapse of the Twin Towers and the five other buildings that were destroyed that day.

The case brought before her by residents, students and office workers who were exposed to thousands of contaminants including benzene, asbestos, mercury and lead, alleges violations of plaintiffs' Fifth Amendment right to protection against bodily harm. Concluding that Whitman's "deliberate and misleading" statements rose to the level of "shocking the conscience," Judge Batts' opinion leaves open the possibility that Whitman herself could be held personally liable for resulting damages.

Commenting on next steps lawyer Robert Gulack, a union steward speaking on behalf of the union at the SEC said, "What would happen if the EPA failed to contest this lawsuit further? The EPA would be compelled to finance medical monitoring for the victims of Sept. 11... to test and, where necessary, clean office buildings, schools, and homes in Lower Manhattan and Brooklyn. What would be so terrible about that? What responsible government agency would hesitate for a moment to do these things?" Gulack is a plaintiff in the case, having suffered permanent lung damage from his exposure to contaminants in the Woolworth Building downtown.

Although I represent Brooklyn in the case, it is as the mother of a student at Stuyvesant High School that I got involved in this cause. Because of the EPA's assurances that the air was safe, both my son and my ex-husband believed that our son should stay at the school. With the exception of Juan Gonzalez' article in the Daily News on October 26, 2001, there were few public warnings early on about the "toxic nightmare at Ground Zero." Gonzalez' article was considered a red herring, what one "expert" at the time brushed off as "yellow journalism." It took three months before I could gather enough data to convince my son and ex-husband otherwise. But it was during those three months, while the fires burned, that the air was the worst.

At a press conference held Friday by Senator Hillary Clinton about Judge Batts' decision, Congressman Jerrold Nadler whose district includes Ground Zero, said, "I hope that EPA's lies and wrongdoing will finally be laid bare for all to see, and that they will be forced – finally – to exercise their responsibilities: to clean up the WTC dust completely and provide medical treatment to all those affected."

9/11 Environmental Action's Kimberly Flynn added a reminder about 130 Liberty Street, formerly the Deutsche Bank building, which, like many other highly contaminated buildings downtown, is slated for "deconstruction." These demolitions threaten to become 9/11, the Sequel, exposing New Yorkers to the contaminants of 9/11 all over again.

# Appendix I
## Lying to "Reassure" the Public[ccxix]

*December 15-17, 2007*

Might it sometimes be appropriate for the government to lie in order to reassure the public? Asked this question during a Court of Appeals hearing yesterday in Benzman vs. EPA, the case brought by residents, students and office workers exposed to and in many cases sickened by the environmental hazards following 9/11,* EPA lawyer Alisa Klein answered, "Yes."

Competing interests such as the economy or the "return to normalcy" [sic] might supercede that of public health, she argued.

There's no question that Ms. Klein accurately represented EPA's position. In addition to their compelling urge to reopen Wall St. ASAP after 9/11, the protocols they have developed to respond to a dirty bomb also take into account the economic import of the area exposed, regardless of the fact that an area that's important to the economy will also be more densely populated.

Accepting, for the moment, the mind-bending reasoning that requires us to be reassured by a government which has admitted that it will lie whenever it feels like it, let us turn now to some situations in which said government has seen fit not to reassure us but in fact, to scare the sh*t out of us.

The lead-up to the Iraq war, when Condoleeza Rice dropped a metaphorical bomb into the conversation with her allusion to a mushroom cloud, comes to mind, as do the "Hoo-oo-oo – Be very afraaaaid" references at the time to chemical and biological weapons labs.

Ditto Iran, up until last week.

Then there are all those toys with kooties and that contaminated toothpaste from China. I'm not saying they're safe. I'm just wondering why they've garnered such prompt headlines while the press on American products such as Zonolite has traditionally been sluggish, never mind Agent Orange and depleted uranium. Some of the interests that have rightly decried lead-contaminated toys from China have, on the other hand, put up the strongest resistance to changing the lead laws in New York City housing, for example. (Also compare the press on avian flu with that on the numerous offenses of the American food industry.)

And remember the good old days of Homeland Security orange alerts and Osama's sneak previews? The ones that tended to come just before an election or some other sensitive event?

They don't fall into the category of reassurance but doubtless those in charge knew what they were doing those times also.

The government may not be consistent about wanting to reassure us but it certainly is consistently entertaining.

# Appendix J
## Catherine McVay Hughes
*Interview conducted c. 2003*

A vivacious mother of two boys who were five and
eight when the attacks took place, Catherine McVay
Hughes reminds one of Diane Keaton if the zaniness
were replaced with an engineering degree from
Princeton. The driving force behind the post-9/11
environmental initiatives of Community Board 1, which
encompasses Ground Zero, she would go on eventually
to chair the Board and be appointed by Governor
Andrew Cuomo to the Lower Manhattan Development
Corporation.

Q:  Were you home when the planes hit?

*A:  No, thank God. I was taking the kids to school in
Brooklyn at Packer. One of the science teachers said a
plane had hit the WTC but I couldn't believe it. Remember
when a plane flew into the Empire State building? I
thought it was like that so I started to go home.*

*The trains weren't running. A bunch of mothers wanted
to walk across the bridge but it was closed. I decided to
walk back to Packer. Then I called my husband, Tom, but
no one would pick up the phone. When I finally reached
him I told him we would stay in Brooklyn. He was going
to walk uptown.*

*We were lucky. He used to work in the WTC on the
104th floor. His vertical commute was longer than his
horizontal commute from our house. On a windy day, the
chairs rolled. They had someone whose only job was to
rearrange the calendars and pick up things that fell off
the walls.*

*In the backyard of Packer, it was snowing debris like
confetti at a ticker tape parade. After I got the kids, I went
to the ATM and took out as much money as I could. Then I*

*went to the hardware store and bought those little paper masks. I figured if we had to stay at someone's house, it would be a welcome gift. I took the kids to the Promenade and showed them the plume. I said, 'I don't think we're going home for a long time.' Then I bought water.*

Q: Where did you put all this stuff?

A: *In my backpack. I brought the water to a friend's house where we stayed the first night. Then I went out and bought food for everyone. Do you know how many kinds of tomato sauce there are? You want to get a common denominator that everyone will be happy with.*

*The household we were in turned off the TV because they didn't want their kids to get scared. So I didn't know for at least an hour when the first building came down. No one wanted to tell me. The woman we were staying with closed all her windows and put on her a.c. Then she put wet towels around the doors.*

*I didn't know if we still had an apartment. We slept on the floor in the basement. The next day, Tom picked us up. We went to my sister's house on the Upper East Side. All we had with us was the clothes we were wearing. You couldn't buy underwear because the stores were closed. And my sister has a daughter so my kids couldn't borrow her underwear.*

*I feel as though I could do an American Express commercial. Based on our address, they knew we were going to have unusual expenses in the next while.*

*The National Guard evacuated our building in Lower Manhattan but they had to break in. That's how a lot of debris got into some buildings. Two women stayed, though, to take care of their cats.*

*Our electricity and gas never went out. You have to write that because EPA makes the excuse about why they did so little testing, that there was no electricity. In some places it went out, but not all over. Our phone and DSL went out, though.*

*Tom was President of the Co-op so on September 12, he snuck back to the building. He didn't want to go up in the elevator because it could get stuck and no one would ever know. So he climbed fourteen flights of stairs and called to ask what I wanted.*

*We'd just bought cellphones the day before. We'd never had them before. He got my contact lenses and the insurance contract. Then he turned off all the computers and took pictures of the apartment.*

*I told him, 'You've got to get out.' We thought 1 Liberty Plaza and Hotel Millennium would fall. But the cellphone went dead. A lot of windows [in those buildings] got broken and you could hear the metal creak. Glass is a liquid so some windows bowed from the pressure of the towers' collapse but they didn't break.*

*The super didn't want to leave the building. He's an engineer from Russia. I think he used to work at Chernobyl. Tom ordered him to leave and find his wife and son.*

*One day there were ninety bomb threats.*

*It took an hour and a half to get to Packer from 86th Street.*

*My sister's apartment's really small so after a few days, we moved to the Marriott in Brooklyn. Everyone was staying there: firemen, displaced residents... A week later we had our apartment tested with wipes. We didn't have asbestos but I don't know what test they did. We did have pulverized glass. I was focused on asbestos so I was relieved.*

*Our insurance company said, "We don't guarantee air quality, just the contents of your apartment."*

*I went to Kinko's and bumped into a FEMA inspector. It was like a FEMA commercial. He said, "What's your address?" Then he looked it up on his computer and said, "I'm doing your apartment this afternoon."*

*It took four days for the insurance company to clean the apartment: seven people the first day, five people the next two and two the last. They took every book and wet-wiped and hepa-vacced it.*

*The FEMA inspector said, 'How about your sofa?' I hit the sofa like this,"* – Catherine slapped the table – *"and a cloud of dust rose. It was the FEMA inspector who told me we had to throw it out.*

*I have to feel very lucky, thinking about Tom, especially when the Times had an obituary for someone else called Tom Hughes...*

*Philip, my older son, said, "Mom, I want to move back home. Everyone else is moving." But I'm glad we didn't. The kids haven't gotten sick from this.*

Q: You have, though.

A: *Yeah, I have twitchy lung, hypersensitivity.*

Q: To what do you attribute that?

A: *To the four days I spent supervising the cleanup. They weren't wearing masks and I figured they must know better than I so I didn't wear one either.*

*After the Marriott, we rented an apartment in Brooklyn. Our apartment in Lower Manhattan was on the Evening News with Dan Rather. But it was hard to take pictures downtown because for months the whole area was being treated as a crime scene. The FEMA inspector told us not to expose the kids to the fires. He was the only one. So we didn't go home for five months.*

*When we finally went back, I watched them clean the outside of the building across the street. It looked so pretty, with a spray of particles. I guess it was glass.*

*This is a hard subject to get people interested in. ABC gave me a camera to record the life of a resident. But they didn't use the footage. They decided they wanted the wife of someone who'd died.*

# Appendix K
## Marie Christopher

Praised by US Representative Nydia Velazquez for her passionate advocacy for tenants' rights, Marie Christopher died of cancer in January of 2013.[ccxx]

The following is from an interview conducted c. 2003:

*We were in the frozen zone. I remember that day. It was particularly trying for me. I'm on the board of New York Tenants and Neighbors. I was two blocks from the World Trade Center; I saw the first plane hit. I called the office and spoke to Tom Waters who's now Executive Director. He said they were claiming it was an accident. I'm not watching TV; I didn't know.*

*When the second plane hit, I'm screaming at the top of my lungs. Those buildings were not going to stay up. Men don't listen. Tom had to run for his life.*

She sighed.

*Parents were panicking. I called my son's school. They said he'd have to stay. Normally, the playground would be filled with older people. Parents ran to the school and pulled their kids out. It was panic time.*

*You couldn't get visitors. You had to show ID to prove you lived there. My super went out. When he returned, they wouldn't let him park. He called the seventh precinct. My girlfriend who works on Grand Street had to leave her car on 14th. TA [Transit Authority] workers were forced to clean up the WTC. She cleaned the subways; she had to work on Stanton. She's gotten sick; her blood pressure's gone up and her sinuses have been affected.*

*People didn't go to work. One lady works for the Board of Health near the World Trade Center.*

241

*My son is autistic. People don't understand how difficult it is to have a program snatched out from under him.*

Q: Did you explain it to him?

A: *I don't know if he understood. He ate. They wouldn't let me back in. I threatened them with every police officer I knew.*

Q: How did you get in?

A: *They escorted me, which they could've done in the first place.*

*Everyone wanted to do their part but when it became inconvenient, they rethought that position.*

*My son's program lost a lot of money because 35 students couldn't go from downtown.*

*They don't have a clue. But not knowing is no excuse any more.*

*Some people were displaced [from their homes;] they have not been able to return because of the dust. People moved out, which put pressure on other parts of the city; the rent went up. We were denied family grant money. They cut it off at Delancey. Then they moved to Houston, west of Broadway. I believe it was deliberate because there's a lot of subsidized housing east of Broadway. It's not so affluent; not your white middle class. I feel it's important to preserve housing that is there; it's cheaper. They're taking the surplus in family grant [money,] 50 million from HUD and using it for people making $50-85,000.*

# Appendix L
## Testimony to the World Trade Center Expert Technical Review Panel

*April 12, 2004*
*(During Passover, a widely observed holiday in New York City, at which the question is asked: "Why is this night different from all other nights?")*

Why is this environmental disaster different from all other environmental disasters? The word "unprecedented" is used ad nauseam to describe it. But in crucial ways, the environmental consequences of 9/11 do have precedent and EPA has long-established protocols to clean up the contaminants that were released. Why are they not following them here? Why are they reinventing the wheel in the shape of a triangle? If this disaster was greater than its predecessors, all the more reason why state-of-the-art testing and cleanup should have been and still should be instituted ASAP.

# Appendix M
## Testimony to the World Trade Center Expert Technical Review Panel

*September 13, 2004*

Three points:

1.Deutschebank: Heavy metals coat the structural steel. During demolition, the bending of the steel will cause these metals to flake and powder which will pose a danger to residents (on top of the astronomical levels of contaminants in the building.) The building should be encased in Tyvek as was done after a release of asbestos in Gramercy Park. Similar protocols were used on the George Washington Bridge. Please recommend this to the Lower Manhattan Development Corporation.

2.This is a helpful EPA brochure called Protect Your Family from Lead in Your Home; it reads:

a."Lead dust which you can't always see can be a serious hazard." One wonders, then, why in its initial cleanup, EPA recommended visual inspection.

b.The brochure talks about the dangers of lead to children which include not only cognitive damage but also hearing loss. And it says that lead is also harmful to adults. "Adults can suffer from: difficulties during pregnancy; other reproductive problems in both men and women; high blood pressure; digestive problems; nerve disorders; memory and concentration problems," etc.

The WTC contained approximately 50,000 computers each made with between four and twelve pounds of lead. And none of these calculations ever take into account WTC 7 [let alone 3, 4, 5 and 6.] We know from previous testing (never mind common sense) that some of the lead landed in people's apartments. So two things are indisputable:

1. WTC lead is in people's homes.
2. It's dangerous.

How, then, can we justify ignoring it? That it lacks some ineffable, "Je ne sais quoi" marking it as uniquely WTC in origin? This is why the fingerprint [or today, the "signature"] metaphor is misleading and dangerous. The WTC was a building like any other. The only unique thing about it is that it was really big. Apart from that, its lead was indistinguishable from any other lead. So it is disingenuous of EPA to ignore lead excesses in Lower Manhattan because the particles failed to arrive individually stamped "WTC."

I also take issue with the statement that you already have the fingerprint for WTC dust. You only have it, possibly, for the immediate vicinity of the site since that's where the few samples being used to determine the fingerprint were collected. It's impossible to establish a universal fingerprint, if such a thing exists, before you've done representative testing.

2000 years ago, Cato the Elder ended each Senate meeting with the words, "Et Carthago delenda est." (*And Carthage must be destroyed.*) By the end of the year, the Senate took the hint and voted to destroy Carthage. Likewise at each panel meeting we say to you, "Having been destroyed, Carthage must be representatively tested."

# Appendix N
## 9/11 the Sequel
### *The Toxic State of Lower Manhattan*[ccxxi]

*February 3, 2005*

History is about to repeat itself, though on a smaller scale. 9/11 is scheduled to happen all over again. And again, it will happen all over Lower Manhattan.

While the whole world knows about the collapse of the Twin Towers (although the collapse of five surrounding buildings that day goes virtually unmentioned) and while the catastrophic health consequences from the dispersal of toxic debris and from the fires which burned for over three months becomes obvious as more people fall ill, the world outside of Lower Manhattan is not aware that at least three more highly contaminated buildings are scheduled for demolition in the near future. The United States Environmental Protection Agency, which was found by its Inspector General to have lied about the air quality after 9/11, continues to refuse to perform its legally mandated duty by taking the lead in the "deconstruction" of at least one of those buildings, the former Deutschebank at 130 Liberty Street.

Hounded by Lower Manhattan residents and advocacy groups such as the New York Committee for Occupational Safety and Health, 9/11 Environmental Action, the New York State Public Employees Federation and the New York Environmental Law and Justice Project, the Lower Manhattan Development Corporation which now owns 130 Liberty acknowledges the contamination of the building. Tests performed by Deutschebank in preparation for litigation found asbestos at up to 150,000 times normal background levels in addition to astronomical levels of other contaminants including dioxin, lead, polycyclic aromatic hydrocarbons (PAHs) and polychlorinated biphenyls (PCBs.) In addition, the use of the sprinkler system on 9/11 resulted in mold and the bacterium which causes Legionnaire's disease.

LMDC has assured the community they intend to abide by all city, state and federal regulations. However a deconstruction like this one is unprecedented in a residential neighborhood so those regulations do not go far enough. LMDC has hired a fleet of consultants and contractors to execute the deconstruction and related tasks such as air monitoring. According to Kimberly Flynn of 9/11 Environmental Action, this leads to a patchwork effect in which "everyone is in charge and no one is in charge."

Residents of 125 Cedar Street next door to 130 Liberty have testified to the urgent need for an emergency response plan which became highlighted a few months ago when windows fell out of the building. LMDC's recent suggestions have included calling 911. Joel Kupferman of the New York Environmental Law and Justice Project also points out that the building is next to subway grates and an emergency fan system which could potentially spread the contaminants at 130 Liberty Street to commuters.

Following 130 Liberty Street, Fiterman Hall, a Borough of Manhattan Community College building which is owned by the Dormitory Authority of the State of New York and is contaminated with dioxin, is also scheduled for demolition.

The final building in the doomed trio, 4 Albany Street, which is contaminated with asbestos and lead, is currently owned by Deutschebank which, being a private institution, is not obliged to engage in the same degree of public process as the other two entities. That demolition is already underway.

Other buildings downtown are also slated for demolition in the name of rebuilding and renewal. However, little is known about their levels of contamination.

3. http://query.nytimes.com/

# Appendix O
## On the Draft Generic Environmental Impact Statement for Ground Zero

*February 18, 2004*

This is a rush job. Although the rebuilding of Ground Zero will be one of the largest construction projects in the world, the usual three year Environmental Impact Statement process has been condensed to one for reasons that have nothing to do with the environment or public health. Once again, the reasons have to do with image and politics. In this respect as in others, the rebuilding process shows signs of repeating the reckless behavior of the cleanup operation.

The DGEIS consists in large part of sanguine projections into the future and assurances that where there are problems, they'll be handled appropriately "when practical."

Who determines what's practical? Who defines it and according to what criteria? During the cleanup, it was often found to be impractical to wet down dust – a measure mandated by science - during the winter for fear the water would freeze. Is that going to happen again? Will other actions protective of human health be considered impractical because they require too much time or money? Will it be considered impractical to enforce the rules against truck and bus idling? And *how* will those rules be enforced – simply through fines? Bus and truck companies are known to consider fines a necessary part of doing business and to write the expense into their contracts. The fines, therefore, don't deter anybody.

The DGEIS also asserts that P.M. 2.5 was not much of a problem outside Ground Zero. This, too, is false. For half the days until February P.M. 2.5 was higher at Stuyvesant High School than at Ground Zero...[ccxxii]

## Appendix P
Testimony to the World Trade Center Expert Technical
Review Panel

*February 23, 2005*

The Draft Generic Environmental Impact Statement
(February 18, 2004 testimony) assert[s] that the dioxin
levels until January 2002 – some of which were the
highest ever recorded, attaining to 170 times the
previous record – are "not expected to cause serious
long-term health problems."

Not expected by whom? There are many venerable
scientists who do expect serious long-term health
consequences. In this assertion, the DGEIS is engaging
in "averaging:" When levels are uncomfortably high,
dilute them over a larger time or space and they'll go
away.

OSHA action levels for lead have been exceeded at 130
Liberty St. yet so far as we know, no action has been
taken. The levels simply get posted to the website.

At the City Council hearing, Kevin Rampe (Chairman
of the Lower Manhattan Development Corporation)
spoke of applying for variances. This is troubling
because a variance is what you seek when you want to
avoid a regulation.

We've made some progress on Deutsche Bank but
even as we speak, 4 Albany Street is being demolished.
This has a private owner who is not subject to the same
kind of public process requirements as a state agency.
Nevertheless the public has a right to know how the
demolition is proceeding. We have reason to fear it may
fall short of what's necessary to protect the public
health.

Regarding the eternal issue of EPA taking the lead on the demolitions: EPA has taken to using the phrase but that's far from doing the deed. "Taking the lead" means taking responsibility; being the ultimately responsible party. What EPA means by it is that they're busy on the phone fobbing off responsibility onto other agencies. They've adopted an ever-so-polite stance of, "Department of Labor, you're such great experts in asbestos and you, Department of Health, are the authorities on lead; you must, of course, take the lead." Then when it's time for the lawsuits, we'll have a room full of agencies pointing fingers at each other. That's what EPA is counting on. Their pseudo-solicitous attitude of, "After you, Alphonse," in which they defer to every other agency on matters that fall squarely within their jurisdiction, is exactly not taking the lead. Politeness is fine in a business-as-usual situation but this is not business as usual. It's a potential public health emergency and you need to rise to the occasion.

## Appendix Q
Homage to the World Trade Center Expert Technical
Review Panel
*(In the triple meter of, 'T Was the Night Before Christmas)*

'T was two days after history changed its direction
as radically as a plane veering off course,
when mindful of Nasdaq and Dow's bottom line,
the White House, through Whitman, declared the air
"fine."
Returning to offices, schools and apartments,
the residents, with baited breath having waited,
let out that breath in relief, not understanding
that they'd have done better to have kept it baited.
For who would have thought, under such
circumstances,
the White House would lie, and to such a degree?
Americans couldn't begin to believe
that their leaders might poison them; call them naive.
They ignored the foul odor as harmless if gross,
like their symptoms the experts said would go away,
and armed with the buckets doled out by Red Cross,
they cleaned up their apartments that looked like
Pompeii.
A year later, confronting rage and litigation
from people who said we should not have returned,
EPA, in a moment of faux introspection,
came out with a document called Lessons Learned.
However the residents weren't appeased.
EPA and the White House kept feeling the heat,
so they set up a panel of experts to keep
the community busy and off of the street.
Five more buildings now face demolition and history
seems bent on repeating mistakes of the past.
Intervene, so years after this panel's adjourned,
your memoirs need not also be called Lessons Learned.

# Appendix R
Saving Private Capital
*A version of this ski was performed with SEC lawyer*
*Robert Gulack to observe the third anniversary of 9/11*

*Narrator:* September 11 was a unique tragedy in the history of our country. But while the victims' families and the rest of the world mourned, no one was harder hit than the nation's billionaires. For what was at stake for them was neither their lives nor their health from the record levels of contamination downtown; nor even the lives of their loved ones. The billionaires had been attacked where it hurt most:

*Billionaires:* (covering their crotches)  My portfolio!

*Narrator:* But the billionaires remembered what was truly important in life. And so, after a lengthy thirty seconds of soul-searching, ever valiant in the face of the hardship of others, they rallied to restore that one truly important thing.

*Billionaires: (to the tune of "Daisy, Daisy, Give Me Your Answer, Do")*
Wall Street, Wall Street, our love pure and true
We can hardly wait to reopen you
We don't care for public health
But only for our wealth
So we lie and cheat
Upon this street
Full of people that we can screw.

*Narrator:* Meanwhile, back at the ranch, aka the White House...

*Chairman of the Council on Environmental Quality is in his office, looking over some papers and frowning.*

*Enter Enviros 1 and 2. Enviro 1 holds a large sign. Enviro 2 holds papers.*

*Chairman (jaunty):* Well, everything's looking fine to reopen Wall St.

*Enviro1:* But Sir, there are dangerous levels of asbestos – see this press release?

*Enviro 1 shows Chairman sign that reads, "DANGEROUS LEVELS OF ASBESTOS."*

*Chairman:* Give me that. I'm just going to do a little editing.
He puts "NOT" in front of "DANGEROUS."

*Chairman:* There we go.

*Enviro1* (thrilled): Oh, thank you, Sir!

*Enviro 2:* But Sir, there's also antimony, lead, dioxin and some stuff I can't pronounce.

*Chairman:* Hmm.... Let me see that.

*Enviro 2 hands him paper which he looks at, frowning again.*

*Chairman:* (reading to himself) Antimony... no; arsenic, uh uh... Here's calcium, good. Dioxin, no... Lead, no good. Here's zinc, great!... And copper, good... Well it's very clear. The environmentally responsible thing to do with WTC dust is to recycle it... as cereal. Sprinkle it, bake it, do whatever you want but just (to the tune of Michael Jackson's "Beat it") Eat it, eat it.

*Enviro 2 (prostrate with admiration)* Oh Sir, now I understand why this administration is so reknowned for its brains!

*Chairman and Enviro 2: Duet to the tune of, "Mares eat oats and does eat oats."*

PCBs and VOCs, beryllium, asbestos
A kid'll eat gypsum too, wouldn't you?
Antimony, TCE, vanadium and benzene
A kid'll eat chlorine too, wouldn't you?

*Narrator:* So it was that in the face of danger to the nation and the people who had been attacked, the White House heeded a higher calling. They sacrificed more of the country's sons and daughters so that they could reopen that spiritual beacon to the world, Wall Street.

*All sing: (to the tune of Petula Clarke's Downtown)*

When the air's fine and you think it should be thicker
you can always go – downtown.
When you are healthy and you want to get sicker
take the number six – downtown.
Just listen to the White House with its bald
misinformation
Breathe deeply of the lead and other foul contamination
The air is more toxic there
You can forget all your troubles, forget all your cares
'Cause you're Downtown. Things are much worse
when you're Downtown. Get me a nurse
for you Downtown. Out in a hearse
for you there.

In a *Life Copies Satire* moment, a recent documentary contained the nugget – no doubt, like the rest of the documentary, a toxic admixture of truth and disinformation – that during Operation Paperclip, whose purpose was to cleanse the war records of former Nazis in order to take advantage of their scientific insights, Werner Von Braun's biography was "edited" to change the phrase "an ardent Nazi" into "not an ardent Nazi." I saw this documentary several years after writing the above skit. I don't know when it was made.

## Appendix S
### How Science Was Abused to Perpetrate Lies After 9/11:
### *A Cautionary Tale for the Approaching Peak Oil Disaster*[ccxxiii]

September 11 was, among other things, a Big Bang that signaled the birth of a new universe. As this universe unfolds, we're learning that it operates under laws which are antithetical to the ideals we grew up with. Human life is no longer sacred. Democratic ideals are not upheld; nor are any other ideals, certainly not those of health or compassion. The new universe upholds pragmatism above all else, even to the point of cynicism. For what is at stake now, given the arrival of Peak Oil and the depletion of water and other resources, is survival. Towards that end, the powers that be will tolerate all means necessary.

Whose survival? Not America's, much less the world's, but their own.

This new attitude of blatant indifference to human health, suffering and life itself first manifested itself in the environmental disaster of 9/11 which began when the twin towers and the other five buildings at Ground Zero collapsed and the fires ignited by the two planes burned and smoldered for three months releasing record levels of some of the most toxic and carcinogenic substances that flesh is heir to.

The World Trade Center was a city with its own zipcode. When it fell, hundreds of tons of asbestos were pulverized to particles of an unusually small size – which some scientists believe are especially dangerous to human health – and carried to Brooklyn and beyond. The towers also contained 50,000 computers each made with approximately four pounds of lead and that doesn't include the five other buildings that were destroyed. Tens of thousands of fluorescent lightbulbs each contained 41 mg. mercury per four foot bulb. Dioxin reached record levels. The smoke detectors contained radioactive americium 241. PCBs in the water attained 75,000 times their previous record. The alkalinity of the dust reached the level of draincleaner. A month after the disaster, Dr. Thomas Cahill of U.C. Davis found very- and ultrafine particles that were the highest he'd recorded of 7000 samples taken around the world, including at the burning Kuwaiti oil fields.

Yet a week later, EPA Administrator Christie Todd Whitman told the people of New York, "Good news. The air is safe to breathe." I should disclose that I am one of twelve original plaintiffs in a class action lawsuit [for cleanup] against Governor Whitman and EPA.

Whitman's announcement, she has maintained ever since, was based on the best science available at the time. Also ever since, science has been used in the service of lies and the economy at the expense of human life.

How is this possible? Science is objective. Instruments and facts don't lie.

It depends on who's using the instruments and what ax they're grinding. It depends on what facts are told and more pointedly, what facts are left out.


This is not the conference in which to discuss the fact that when Whitman told the people of New York the air was safe to breathe, not only did EPA lack the data to support that statement but EPA actually had data which contradicted it. Nor is this the conference to go into Whitman's potentially felonious conflict of interest in speaking about the World Trade Center at all when she owned shares of Port Authority stock and had sworn in her oath of office to recuse herself from cases in which she had a personal stake.

This is a conference about science so we will look at how science was used to promote the lies perpetrated by the EPA and the White House Council on Environmental Quality which edited at least one of EPA's press releases, replacing cautionary statements about asbestos with reassurances.

The technique was simple: Make a mockery of science. Perform scientific tests but use the wrong equipment in the wrong places the wrong way.

The technique was put into effect immediately, when EPA conducted its initial tests for asbestos.

First of all, query why they focussed so exclusively on asbestos. There were over two thousand contaminants released in the disaster, some of which had never before existed.

But even if this autistic focus on asbestos had been plausible, how could EPA's tests have come up with the wrong results?

Dr. Cate Jenkins, an EPA whistleblower, told the St. Louis Post-Dispatch that EPA had used 20-year-old instruments to conduct their tests. For every fiber of asbestos that EPA found, independent contractors found nine. The risk of cancer from the asbestos alone could be one person in ten.

EPA's Region 8 out West offered Region 2 in New York up-to-date equipment which they could conveniently summon from New Jersey. Region 2 said, "We don't want you fucking cowboys here."

Also EPA used a 1% standard for asbestos in the dust. But this standard was established for intact materials like water pipes. If a minute piece of the pipe broke off that contained more than 1% asbestos, that was considered dangerous because it might be inhaled.

EPA applied this 1% standard to Lower Manhattan where none of the material was intact. All of it had been pulverized. All of it could be inhaled. Furthermore, there was tons of dust.

Since 9/11, EPA has been nothing if not consistent. In addition to using out-of-date equipment, they have routinely advocated the wrong tests. For instance they advocated a wipe test for polycyclic aromatic hydrocarbons on soft surfaces whereas the test was intended only for hard surfaces. They resisted testing on horizontal surfaces where dust falls or in corners where dust was likely to be found, favoring vertical surfaces and countertops which had been frequently cleaned. They fought the use of ultrasonication, a sensitive test for asbestos which they themselves had developed. They based their determination of whether an area was contaminated on a "visual inspection" which means one of their reps would eyeball a given site and say, "Looks good to me." In some cases, this visual inspection was performed – I kid you not – from an airplane.

And how did they determine whether the dust they found was WTC dust? In one building, they asserted, "That's not WTC dust; WTC dust is grey and gritty;" in another, "That's not WTC dust; WTC dust is brown and fluffy."

Other abuses of science included EPA's writing off of deposits of magnesium because it's a nutrient. If only we'd known we were supposed to eat WTC dust instead of breathing it, perhaps everything would have turned out all right although I doubt it. People who ingested WTC dust now suffer gastro-intestinal as well as respiratory and other illnesses.

Then there was the issue of spikes.

When my son was twelve he wanted to be a magician. As he underwent his sorcerer's apprenticeship, I picked up some tricks of the trade. Rule number one is, when you're doing your sleight of hand, say, "Look over there!"

EPA and other authorities knew this trick too, and dismissed high levels as spikes or "outliers," thereby shoving unpleasant data under the carpet.

A corollary of this practice was "averaging" in which the "spikes" were averaged out over a lifetime or a large area and thus made to disappear.

The human body, however, doesn't average. When the lungs are exposed to too much water, you drown. When someone overdoses on drugs, the human body doesn't say, "I'll average this out over a lifetime." You die of an overdose.

Dr. Cate Jenkins has written several memos detailing other EPA lies. The latest [October, 2006] is subtitled:

Cover-up, corrosive alkalinity of WTC dust by EPA, OSHA and NYC Falsification of the health implications of the alkaline pH data Fraudulent reporting of pH levels for smallest WTC dust particles.

She shows how the Agency for Toxic Substances and Disease Registry and New York City relied on outdated texts that tolerated lead levels sixty times as high as those now considered safe. And she provides evidence of their lying and criminal malpractice.

EPA's execution of tests and cleanup was as shoddy as their research. In their so-called cleanup of 2002, residents found them performing air tests with the fan turned off or facing the wrong direction.

*****

Since 9/11, there have been several blue ribbon scientific panels which have convened to consult with EPA on next steps. At the first one, EPA neglected to tell the panel that the document on which they were supposedly conducting peer review was already being implemented downtown. The panel learned this from community members who were allowed to speak for two to three frantic minutes each in public sessions.

The final panel, which lasted almost two years, spent much of that time on a quixotic quest for a World Trade Center fingerprint or signature as though it were the fountain of youth or the alchemical formula for gold. For once the fingerprint was found, that would be it. If you had it, you had WTC dust and EPA would give you a cleanup, however shoddy. If you didn't have it, they wouldn't and you could get on with your life.

However a couple of us have always maintained that either metaphor was a snare. The World Trade Center was not a person; therefore it didn't have a fingerprint or a signature. Its contents were not stirred into a homogeneous blend in that great mixing bowl in the sky along with two eggs. There were over two thousand contaminants released and they were spread unevenly according to their various weights and chemical and physical properties as well as the wind conditions of the moment.

But the quest for the ever elusive fingerprint went on. First it was asbestos, then gypsum with a soupcon of, if I remember correctly, manmade vitreous fibers and a specific pH, then slag wool because in the dozen or so samples that one study had collected close to the site, slag wool, which is a component of glass, had been uniformly present.

One must ask, and one did, if a fingerprint or signature is unique and irrefutable, why did the WTC fingerprint or signature keep changing?

One must also ask, and many did, if the signature is determined to be a particular assortment of contaminants, what do we do about all the rest?

That question was never answered because EPA closed the panel process when an independent panel, commenting on their latest plan, in effect accused them of fraud.(1)

Let's go back to the assertion at the beginning of this talk that 9/11 was a watershed moment when the laws and precedents we previously relied on all got turned on their heads.

In the case of environemtal disasters what that means is this: Prior to 9/11, in the event of a release of toxic substances, EPA followed scientific protocol and conducted representative testing in concentric circles to determine the path of contamination.

But in the World Trade Center case they did no such testing. Instead, 9/11 set a new precedent for testing and cleanup: the quick and dirty method, a lick and a promise in order to get back to work ASAP. The cleanup standard they used in Lower Manhattan – a 1/10,000 cancer risk – exposed residents to a hundred times the cancer risk of previous standards. This is serving as a precedent for the new standards which they plan to implement in the event of a dirty bomb. Anti-nuclear activists have found that 100 times the usual level of radiation will be tolerated.[ccxxiv]

Why? Just as the Inspector General's Report of 2003 found that the White House CEQ edited EPA's press release out of the "need" to reopen Wall Street, EPA has matter-of-factly stated that if the area affected by a dirty bomb is important to the economy, human health will be sacrificed. Economic hubs tend to be highly populated. So the more people who are likely to be exposed to radiation because a particular contaminated site is important to the economy, the greater will be the haste to reopen the site.[ccxxv]

## What Lessons Can We Learn From The Environmental Disaster of 9/11?

The answer to this is the reason I felt it important to speak at this conference. What we can learn from the environmental disaster of 9/11 is that it is up to us to educate ourselves. We cannot trust the powers that be, the suits. We cannot bow to their supposed greater authority. To do that, knowing what we know, is to put our collective head in the sand and abdicate responsibility.

This lesson is of enormous importance as Peak Oil takes over the world. For the same scenario is playing out in this new arena. First the powers that be tell us there is no problem. Then, when the elephant in the living room grows too large, they acknowledge the problem but say, "Look over there!" and point to the tar sands in Alberta or to ethanol.

But will these solutions really work?

Just as after 9/11 it was necessary for the community – non-scientists – to teach themselves enough science to recognize rampant lying, in order to understand what's really happening with Peak Oil, it is necessary to do the math.

It's not hard math; about sixth grade level, if that's when you study ratios. So what does doing the math tell us?

The light, sweet crude oil we've been relying on to run the economy gives thirty barrels of oil for every one used to produce it. Around last December, the world's supply of that so-called easy oil went into permanent decline. Tar sands and heavy crude are not the same stuff. It takes steam, water injection or chemicals to extract them which in turn requires energy. And all the alternatives and renewables added up together don't come close to the Energy Returned on Energy Invested ratio for easy oil. The EROEI for ethanol, for instance, is 1.3; it barely gives back more energy than is required to make it in the first place.

With the decline in oil supplies, you might think, "Great; everyone will ride bikes." But oil is not just used for cars. It's a key ingredient of pesticides and fertilizers which, however much you might turn up your nose at their toxicity, are necessary to feed our current population of six and a half billion people.

Answers to the problems we're facing do not lie in British Petroleum's changing its name to Beyond Petroleum, or in politicians' soundbites offering easy answers. The devil is in the details. How much oil is necessary to keep the economy going? What will it take to sustain life as we know it?

The answers to these questions are not happy. The current economic paradigm is a Ponzi scheme that requires infinite growth. The earth is finite. There is no reconciling these two facts, not with all the renewables and nifty technofixes in the world, however useful those may be on a limited scale. But between the two, we have more control over the economy than over the finite resources of the earth so it is this that we must reform.

It must become localized rather than global. Peak Oilists are fond of pointing out that the era of the fifteen hundred mile Caesar salad is over. We'll have to rely on local food sources, grown within a hundred miles. And it would be better to transition to that lifestyle now than have it thrust upon us the hard way.

Why are people resistant to looking at these facts? Why do they persist in writing off Peak Oilists as fringey radicals, even as the Peak Oilists are being corroborated by headlines and world events?

Though more and more people have lost faith in George Bush and lies have been uncovered that make Watergate seem halcyon, the American people have not extrapolated. "Yes," they say, "there was the Downing Street memo, and the WMD never existed, and we invaded Iraq based on lies, and the government lied about the air quality following 9/11 and betrayed the heroes of Ground Zero who are sick and dying as a result, but the U.S. government caused the attacks? That's crazy. As for this Peak Oil business – if it's true, why aren't they talking about it on CNN?"

They're not talking about it on CNN because the Powers That Be at CNN don't want them to. They're keeping up the façade as long as they can while they clean out the cupboards. By the time you learn the cupboards are bare, it'll be a fait accompli. As ABC's Reuven Frank once said, "News is something someone doesn't want you to know. Everything else is advertising."

It's often said that those who do not know history are condemned to repeat it. What's happening now is that those who do know history are repeating it anyway, which is why history seems to be repeating itself.

It isn't repeating itself verbatim. Peak Oil isn't going to poison people; no one's going to get a deadly disease from it, at least, not directly. It's the structure of the drama that's being repeated. Again the powers that be are withholding the truth or actively lying. Again they are doing so "in order not to panic the public." Again the media are complicit or clueless. And again the public is trusting them anyway because that's what they've always done and doing the legwork themselves is just too hard.

*****

After 9/11, the people of Lower Manhattan were beguiled by the government, like children by the Pied Piper, to return to an area which every instinct told them was poisonous. They did this even as a few voices, some of them belonging to independent scientists, cried out, "This will kill you."

Some went back because they believed the government or they had nowhere else to go. But others went back because they were blinded: By wishful thinking because they wanted to go home; by ambition, because Lower Manhattan was where their jobs were; or by arrogance, smugly writing off the naysayers as fringey eccentrics because it is comforting to feel superior.

Some of these people boasted impressive achievements, advanced degrees, high IQs. But these credentials got in the way of their ability to perceive the truth. They were not open to the opinions of those who didn't represent an agency or have some sort of Good Housekeeping seal of approval. Who did we think we were?

What we can learn from the environmental disaster of 9/11 is that eight million Frenchmen *can* be wrong. The people who recognized early on how bad the air was and how egregiously the government was lying were a small minority. We lacked critical mass while the masses themselves were anything but critical. We had kooties. We were the kids whom the cool crowd looked down on. But we would rather have been proven wrong.

If any good is to come out of the environmental disaster of 9/11, it is as an innoculation against even greater disasters in the future. Those disasters will be both unique and universal. They will repeat history not in their superficial details – fascism does not always goosestep down Main Street wearing a brush mustache – but in their fundamental structure.

Those who lived through the lies and the terrible consequences of the environmental disaster of 9/11 must learn:

1. Truth doesn't always come dressed with the trappings of authority, or even wear a suit.

2. The smarter and more educated we are, the more we must be on guard against arrogance. We must keep an open mind and listen even to those from out in left field. Our lives depend on it.

*Notes*

1. [The independent panel raised questions as to whether] "... EPA's evaluation and interpretation of the study data were performed fairly. Peer reviewers pointed to several non-standard steps taken to enhance the study's ability to distinguish WTC dust from background dust. These steps could be interpreted as attempts to prove the method's success rather than to objectively evaluate its real-world potential for finger-printing WTC dust."[ccxxvi]

## Appendix T
Fire Claims Lives of Two Firefighters at Ground Zero;
Wall St. Journal Blames Community[ccxxvii]

*August 27, 2007*

The tragic fire at the former Deutsche Bank building
in Lower Manhattan nine days ago which took the lives
of two firefighters, Joseph Graffagnino, 33, and Robert
Beddia, 53, and which has already spawned two
criminal investigations, highlights problems about
which the community of Lower Manhattan has been
warning for years.

The company hired to perform the demolition of the
building whose chief claim to fame, post-9/11, was that
it had been contaminated with 150,000 times the
normal levels of asbestos among other toxic substances,
(which have since been reduced to a supposedly "safe"
level) has "apparently never done any work like it" nor
much of anything else since it was incorporated in
1983.

But while the John Galt Corporation has proven as
mysterious as the eponymous character in the Ayn
Rand novel, *Atlas Shrugged* – which opens with the
question, "Who is John Galt?" – this elusiveness has
allowed it to serve as an effective front for members of
Safeway Environmental Corporation whose contract had
been cancelled because of mob connections. One of
Safeway's owners, Hank Greenberg, is a two-time felon
who has been linked by the FBI to the Gambino crime
family. So it was no great surprise, when a building in
the process of demolition on Manhattan's Upper West
Side collapsed ahead of time, trapping pedestrians
including a seven-month-old baby, to learn that Safeway
Environmental was in charge.

269

Another firm involved in the demolition of the former Deutsche Bank, United Research Services, told Minnesota transportation officials that it would be able to fix flaws in the Minneapolis bridge that collapsed this summer.

A third firm, Bovis Lend Lease "presided over" nine major safety incidents in the past five years apart from those at the former Deutsche Bank.

On top of this shaky foundation (not the sort one wants when demolishing the equivalent of a former Superfund site) the NYC Fire Department failed to check the standpipes at the former Deutsche Bank building every 15 days as required by law. Thus the firefighters who went in on Saturday were unaware of the broken standpipe in the basement which prevented water from reaching the two trapped members of their company.

Lest the reader assume that last Saturday's tragedy might result in at least a temporary show of caution, the following Thursday two more firefighters sustained serious head injuries from debris that fell from scaffolding at the site.

Shocking as all these events are, they are no surprise to the community of Lower Manhattan which initially brought to the public's attention the shadowy connections of Safeway Environmental, protested the hiring of the equally dubious John Galt Corporation, highlighted unsafe conditions at the site such as windows falling out of the building and urged the City and the Lower Manhattan Development Corporation, which owns the former Deutsche Bank building, to put in place emergency plans both for the work site as well as for the surrounding area.

Yet when the fire broke out, many residents received no warnings or instructions.

It is therefore particularly galling to read an opinion piece in the Wall Street Journal as well as a letter in the New York Times which essentially blame Saturday's tragedy on the community's preciousness about any remaining environmental hazards in the building.

The Times letter, whose writer lives in Brooklyn, maintains that the community's concern for "every speck of dust and every fiber of asbestos" has delayed the demolition process and that somehow that delay caused the fire. For surely if the building had already been demolished, it wouldn't have caught fire, now, would it? And if you could go back in time and stop your grandparents from meeting...

The Wall Street Journal article compares the community's arguments (which are supported by scientific expertise as well as legal precedent) to "the endless debate and litigation we've also layered into efforts to surveil and prosecute terrorists."[ccxxviii] (That pesky Constitution again.)

The arguments put forth in these two pieces attempt to pit the interests of firefighters and site workers against those of residents, office workers and students. In fact, these populations have worked together effectively for six years and have always been able to see through the divide-and-conquer tactics of their opponents. They understand that such finger-pointing is designed to divert attention from the corrupt entities whose purported job is to protect the public but whose true purpose is to uphold the economy (particularly their own piece of it.) In this latter endeavor those entities have indeed done a heckuva job.

# Appendix U
## *September 11, 2011*

Today, on the tenth anniversary of 9/11, the cover of the New York Times Sunday Magazine features a glowering Alec Baldwin in suit and tie against a decorous black background. The attendant story is titled, "The High Art of TV."

This is fitting. For it was the high art of TV that took over what are fashionably known as the "memes" of 9/11: Those iconic images which will filter down into the collective conscious memory of that day.

I doubt that was the intended message of the Times but at least they are not pretending to pay homage. The top right hand corner of the cover, in the smallest print on the page, displays the 9/11 section: "A Liberal Hawk Recants," "Why Ground Zero Is Perfect Just as It Is Right Now" and "A Post-9/11 Free-for-All" along with two unrelated articles: "Laughing at Parents" and "Pie Don't Fly."

OK, they didn't forget. They've paid their lip service; "Now let's move on," they seem to say.

Meanwhile, over at the Huffington Post, the illustration accompanying the article on events to commemorate 9/11 is indeed of the Twin Towers but not on 9/11; it's the morning Philippe Petit pranced between them on a tightrope.

It seems as though this anniversary is being used not to remember but on the contrary, to paper over the memories of the attacks on those buildings with more whimsical ones about when they still stood. We're past 9/11 as personal memory and into the phase when it becomes history to pontificate on. Is there already an entire college course on it somewhere? Has a whole new area of "9/11 Studies" opened up a cornucopia for Ph.D. students on such hitherto unexplored subjects as 9/11: The Merchandising? Perhaps starting tomorrow, comedians will feel it's safe to launch the barrage of 9/11 jokes they've been itching to try out.

On a more somber note, the inbox is bombarded with articles concerning the second wave of 9/11 victims which, like the ripples from a stone dropped in a pond, is potentially a far larger group than the first: those bearing the brunt of the environmental disaster that ensued as soon as "the dust settled;" actually, long before.

The information in these articles is not new; it's a rehash, a fresh round of head shaking and hand wringing. By next week, it shall have receded again to the double-digit pages of the more earnest and less well-known newspapers.

But what is particularly disheartening about this milestone anniversary is the way it is embalming the memory in sweet-smelling lies. The names in the newspaper articles are all familiar; these people have been milling around 9/11 matters since day one. Trouble is, many of the ones who've now taken the reins of The Message were, on day one and in the months following, playing for the other side. Some of the doctors in charge of the care of Ground Zero workers, for instance, originally parroted the government's lies to devastating effect, for instance by telling parents it was safe for their children to return to school downtown.

All of this happened in the immediate aftermath of the disaster. That was the crucial period, when, if we'd had anyone with clout on our side, we might have been able to reach people to tell them that, contrary to what the government said and the media dutifully reported, it was not safe to return.

A few of us tried. They are the ones who matter to me, the real heroes to whom I'm forever grateful because even though in large part we fought a losing battle, we won a few victories ($20 million to clean the schools of Ground Zero, a thank you from a mother who'd taken her daughter out of Stuyvesant High School) and it was good to have a few buddies in the trenches.

# Appendix V
## Testimony to the New York City Council

*January 11, 2007*

I got involved in the environmental disaster of 9/11 as a Stuyvesant High School parent. In the process of working with other activists to get Stuyvesant properly cleaned, I learned of ultrasonication, a highly sensitive asbestos test developed by no less an authority than EPA themselves. Using that method, a cadre known as Concerned Stuyvesant Community found an astronomical 2.4 million structures per sq. cm. of asbestos in a carpet segment from the Stuyvesant auditorium.

Following that success, if you can call it that, I had ultrasonication performed on the carpet in my apartment in downtown Brooklyn, an act which led to my becoming a plaintiff in the class action lawsuit [for cleanup], Benzman vs. EPA. The result came back 79,000 structures per sq. cm. a gray area, according to the experts I consulted. (There are no established health-based benchmarks for ultrasonication.) I had the one bedroom apartment abated which took four burly men 22 hours. The apartment passed its subsequent air tests. But one of the tests showed a level of asbestos that was almost ten times higher than EPA claimed it was achieving in Lower Manhattan. Bearing in mind EPA's history of using the wrong equipment in the wrong places the wrong way, you may draw from this anomaly whatever conclusions you wish.

Councilmembers, this hearing has the air of a reunion. For over five years, EPA has shown up at hearings at all levels of government. Each time, experts and citizens who've been forced into de facto expertise have chastised the agency for innumerable flaws in innumerable plans. Each time, EPA has been sent back to the drawing board. And each time, after months of dragging their heels, they have emerged with a new plan that has outdone the last in scientific shoddiness. Then the process has started all over again.

The tail is wagging the dog. We should not be spending time on EPA's latest outrage. The appropriate response to environmental disasters is well-established: testing in concentric circles emanating from the center with cleanup to follow as warranted. In this case, the testing should be for a broad spectrum of contaminants since that's what was released.

# Appendix W
## HystericalMothers.com[ccxxix]

Ever tell your children the story of the boy who didn't eat his broccoli and died *the next day*?? (When he got hit by a car because he didn't *Look Both Ways*?) Does your daughter ignore your warnings that she might catch cold and have to miss the class play? Even though when you warned her to wear her kneepads skateboarding and she didn't, she scraped her knee so badly she had to get a shot? Do you think fear the underrated emotion and tell yourself it's what keeps rabbits alive?

Hysterical mothers, nags and anyone else who has railed against the force of will, *("I hate seatbelts!")* you are not alone.

When a huge horse showed up at the gates of Troy, Cassandra prophesied, "No good will come of this." The Trojans branded Cassandra nuts and what happened? The horse was full of *Greeks!* Who destroyed Troy!

When Lois Gibbs told people that their neighborhood was contaminated, the government said, "Everything's fine." What neighborhood was that? Love Canal!

When Monona Rossol and Drs. Cate Jenkins and Marjorie Clarke warned of the toxic soup which was the air of Lower Manhattan following 9/11, did people sit up and listen? Right.

But not all the doomsayers are hysterical mothers. None are hysterical and some aren't mothers or even women. Joel Kupferman, Hugh Kaufman, Congressman Jerrold Nadler and men on the staff of the New York Committee on Occupational Safety and Health also led the hue and cry following 9/11.

And many of the guys on the other side of the fence aren't men. Witness Whitman herself, the Darth Vader of Lower Manhattan who a few days after September 11, said, "I'm glad to reassure the people of New York that their air is safe to breathe."

So if not womanhood, what is it that distinguishes the hysterical mothers from the guys in suits?

That's right: It's the suits.

Juan Gonzalez may have been the first journalist to cry, "Toxic!" after 9/11 but he's not a bureaucrat. Hence, he doesn't wear a suit.

Joel Kupferman may be a lawyer but as he mostly hangs out at firehouses which are still contaminated from 9/11, again, no suit.

My high school friend Elinor was right: "The world is made in such a way that my mother always turns out to have been right."

So don't lose heart. Have the courage of your cautious convictions and remember the old adage: Just because you're paranoid doesn't mean they're not following you.

# Appendix X

*October 3, 2002*
*To Concerned Stuyvesant Parents*

Claire Barnett from Healthy Schools Network is testifying in D.C. about the Healthy and High Performance section of the Leave No Child Behind Act, which has been passed but not yet funded.

She and her guests from Maryland and Connecticut have decorated the room with posters: Mold blossoming on the ceiling; a classroom view of three kids with their hands up – all are wearing respirators.

One family has brought along their son who's in third grade but has only spent a total of five months in school in his entire life. The mold makes his face blow up (his parents show everyone the pictures) as though he's been in a fight.

First up to testify is Ramona Trovato from EPA. She's a va-va-voom vamp in a red dress and Jeffords is beside himself as the previous week, he had been beside himself over Christie. (Before the second panel give their statements, he launches into questions until an aide gently reminds him where we are in the hearing and he falls silent.)

Trovato talks about problems in schools which she maintains EPA has no authority over.

The next panel consists of Claire, green architect Alex Wilson and Lois Gibbs who was responsible for galvanizing the 800 families at Love Canal to leave.

We learn:

1. There are 1100 schools built within a half mile of a toxic waste site. Schools that don't have openable windows may have mold. These problems are cross-jurisdictional, involving the Departments of both

Education and Energy, neither of whom is at the hearing.

Wilson argues that green schools can save 40% on energy costs and that students who use daylight perform 26% better on tests than those who are at the mercy of poor lighting.

2. Asthma causes 14 million missed school days per year.

3. 40% of our schools are in unsatisfactory environmental condition. Kids in these mostly urban schools are about 5% more likely to die from these conditions. There are a million kids with elevated lead levels.

4. 14 million kids are in schools that threaten their health. Our schools are in worse conditions than our prisons.

Lois Gibbs talks about "school siting" on toxic dumps which only California has any legislation to prevent. EPA says they're working on a website that will give information on where toxic sites are but they don't have authority over indoor air. (At this, I look over at Hugh who's scribbling furiously in both senses of the word.)

According to Grayling White, a Tennessee father both of whose children have been incapacitated by the mold at school, (at the age of seven, his daughter had to undergo excruciating urinary tract tests) there are more regulations protecting the health of horses and chickens than that of children.

Hillary says that at some schools, kids have been contaminated by the lead at indoor shooting ranges including, in one instance, all the members of the rifle team. At another school there were multiple cases of testicular cancer.

5.  12 million kids are in Special Ed.  Since 1987, enrollment in the program has doubled.  Genetic factors account for only 10% of this increase; 28% is attributable to environmental causes.

The hearing adjourned, I lobby Jeffords and his environmental staffer, Geoffrey Brown, and meet Lois Gibbs.

"I'm sorry," she says, hearing I'm the mother of a Ground Zero student.  "We all said last year, 'Why are they sending the kids back so soon?'"

It's always unsettling to be pitied by the folks at Love Canal.

I ask her how that community doing now.

"Don't know," she says.  "They're all over the country.  No one's done a study or anything."

A mother from Maryland says her daughter has multiple chemical sensitivites because of the pesticide Dursban that was used at her school.

Claire takes us all to lunch in the cafeteria where the third grader (who's curious about the blue gorilla the unions put up at Stuy) eats a plate of chicken wings that I'd assumed were for both him and his father.  His mother says she's gained twenty pounds since homeschooling him.  Tomorrow, under a settlement that is being ironed out, he's to start going to a private school forty-five minutes down the highway.

Also with us is a teacher from that child's school and a woman who drove her to D.C. as her exposure to mold causes her to lose her equilibrium; if she turns her head to look back, she gets sick.  When we go lobbying after lunch, she stays downstairs since elevators also have the same effect...

# Appendix Y
## 9/11 Commission Investigative Hearing

*To 9/11 Environmental Action*

...Joel turns up in his bright green National Lawyer's Guild cap so when you're getting arrested amidst a hundred thousand people, you can pick him out of the crowd.

The first hour, the commissioners give their prepared speeches. A woman in the audience boos. Security escorts her out, Joel not far behind.

A staffer who's also followed the woman asks her, "Did you try contacting the Commission with your questions?" She sounds like a junior high school teacher who's taken a seminar in conflict resolution. "Because, you see, we want to hear what you have to say."

The woman stares at her, as though inwardly debating whether to ask the staffer if she is nuts.

The commissioners are staid, making Pataki, who follows them, look like Robin Williams.

He, in turn, is followed by Bloomberg who arrives flanked by his two archangels, Police Department Commissioner Ray Kelly and Fire Commissioner Nicholas Scopetta. Neither was in charge on 9/11 so they're not there for witness testimony but rather, to oblige the Commission's focus on the future.

David Lim, a cop who nearly died on 9/11, says that after the two planes hit, he left his "partner," Sirius, a labrador retriever, in his kennel and went up the stairs of Tower 2 where he called his wife. The hardest part was telling her he might not get out.

"But she's a good, strong, cop's wife," he explains. "She understood I had to do what I had to do."

On the fifth floor, he met a woman, Josephine, who'd walked down 72 flights and couldn't go on. A fireman picked her up, put her arm around his neck and with Lim, carried her down.

"You hear about cops and firemen not getting along," Lim said, "but that day everyone put rivalries aside."

The power was out but the stairs were lit by a neon stripe that had been painted on after the '93 attack. It looked eerie, Lim said.

When they got to the fourth floor, the floors above collapsed straight down like pancakes, the stairwell filled with black smoke and Lim thought he would die.

"My final thoughts," he said, "were of my family."

By this time, Lim was crying and men in the audience had taken out their handkerchiefs. Commissioner Jamie Gorelick wiped her eyes while other commissioners took off their glasses to wipe them.

The only reason Lim survived was that the stairwell acted like a "straw in a pancake."

Five hours later, he escaped. But he had lost his partner.

As everyone's just been through the wringer with Lim's testimony, the next speaker warns the "families" that his own testimony might be upsetting.

He was coming out of the men's room in the Pentagon when the plane ripped through the building "twenty seconds away."

He was so badly burned, including third degree burns, that the only place the medics could introduce morphine via IV was in his feet. For three days, maggots ate his rotting flesh.

The final speaker on that panel was a father who'd lost his son. He was grateful that when his son's body was found, it was intact. He touched his son from head to foot, maybe to convince himself he was dead or maybe because he missed him.

The speakers all have a lyrical tone as though to protect them from the terrible truths of their stories.

The next panel consists of a wife, Mindy Kleinberg, and a mother, Mary Fetchet. They have the immigration documents of fifteen of the hijackers. When asked for their destination, some had written, "California," or, "Hotel." One, said Kleinberg, had written, "No." Visas had been granted to dead terrorists.

Kleinberg also says that there were delays in scrambling the fighter jets of NEADS (North East Air Defense) of NORAD (North American Aerospace Defense Command.) The jets didn't fly at maximum speeds which would have enabled them to intercept the flights.

It's a conflict of interest, says one witness, to put the FBI in charge of preventing terrorist acts. They're rewarded after the fact, for solving them.

Jamie Gorelick, the sole woman commissioner, asked Kleinberg and Fetchet how, without being lawyers and having subpoena power, they'd collected so much information.

Kleinberg, a CPA who has become a fulltime mom to three children, says, "We got on the Internet and read everything. One article leads to another. We email each other all the time. We were obsessed." Sounds familiar.

Gorelick also remarks that ironically, before 9/11, the cafeteria at the Pentagon was called Ground Zero.

During lunch, Citizens' Watch, a 9/11 watchdog group, holds a press conference about its questions for the Commission. A major one is why the head of Pakistani Intelligence had given Mohammed Atta $100,000 dollars shortly before 9/11.

*Day two*: Self-congratulation from the Department of Design and Construction on the speedy cleanup and quick putting out of the fires. Maggie, if you submit testimony, you might want to include that paragraph about how they could've introduced nitrogen but didn't.

Commissioner John Lehman asks what became of all the steel.

"We knew it was contaminated with asbestos," says Holden, "so we thought it best to recycle it." (When the hearing is over, I tell Lehman about the email from South Korea asking, "Is this material contaminated?")

Lehman also says it didn't make sense for the Port Authority to have been exempt from city and state regulations when it was putting up a building in the middle of the city. The families applaud.

Following the hearing, I point out Sally Regenhard – mother of Christian Regenhard, a firefighter killed on 9/11, and Co-founder of the Skyscraper Safety Campaign – to NBC, saying she has a radically different take on the site cleanup and the actions of the Fire Department from what the Commission is hearing. They do a long interview.

# Appendix Z
## Outtakes

*May 30, 2002*

9/11 Environmental Action leaves our meeting a little after nine p.m., passing Ground Zero on our way to the subway. It is the last night of the cleanup and to mark the occasion, Beethoven's Ninth is being piped over the loudspeaker. As though in awe at the solemnity of the moment, the entire neighborhood falls silent.

*November 9, 2002*

In the spirit of transferring responsibility onto the public, the government has embarked on a campaign to educate us in how to catch terrorists. The program is launched, appropriately enough, at the Police Museum where about thirty chairs have been set out in what turns out to be an overly optimistic gush of enthusiasm. A third remain unoccupied.

As we sit around waiting for the lecturer, a cop comes out for what is known in TV as "audience warm-up."

"Y'all here to learn how to combat terrorism? All right! Gee, you guys are warming *me* up."

Good will all around. Almost.

Half an hour late, the lecturer, Lynda Marmara, arrives for a power point presentation.

Point one: If you see a terrorist about to detonate, call 911.

The audience nods as though in time to a familiar tune.

In fact, if you see any emergency, whether it's a crime or a terrorist about to detonate, you should call 911. 911 is for emergencies.

Good to know – but should we run away from the detonating terrorist before or after calling 911?

Point number two: Watch out for people behaving suspiciously. If they look around or look nervous. If they sweat a lot when it's not hot. (How about if they twist their long mustaches and laugh evilly?)

Look for anything out of the ordinary. Know what's normal for your neighborhood and if there's anything unusual, report it. For this, you don't have to call 911. You can call 1-888-nyc-safe.

What's unusual?

Someone wearing a trenchcoat in July. (If he's sweating profusely at the same time, does that count as two unusual things or do the sweating and the trenchcoat in July go together?)

Point three: Terrorists are more afraid of you than you are of them.

Wasn't that bears? Or cockroaches? Anyway, I have two possible responses: "So what?" and, "No, they're not."

Afterwards, NY1 asks attendees what they thought of the seminar. I tell them it was for six-year-olds.

Time to check out the museum.

There's a World Trade Center section with police mannequins sifting through simulated dust as well as a room set aside for fallen cops, displaying their badges and a steel cross on the wall with the motto: Fidelis ad Mortem ("Loyal Unto Death.") A recording, possibly taken from a service at Ground Zero, reads out their names.

A room with the rapsheets of famous criminals who all, for some reason, have nicknames; a history of gangs; a how-to display for counterfeiting money.

Highlight of the day, I shoot a gun – at a screen with actor-criminals running towards me and my imaginary partner. Some have weapons; others, not. You have to make instant decisions which I do badly, shooting every time (When am I ever going to get to do this again?) but usually miss. However, the cop in charge says I can now load a gun like a pro.

*November 12, 2002*
*Fire drill*

This morning a three hour seminar for fire safety chiefs was held at the Southgate hotel.

What a contrast with the joke of a police seminar on Saturday, maybe because that one was for civilians, translate: idiots.

This one had hundreds in attendance, many of them, standing. Then they had five speakers as opposed to the cops' one – who, by her own admission, was no terrorism expert – each with a particular specialty.

Highlights from the first hour:

In '93 it took five hours to evacuate the WTC but many skyscrapers only have a two-hour fire resistance rating.

Ladders don't go up beyond the 7th floor.

A retired fire chief tells us what he never could have said while still working for the department: That they can't extinguish fires in 20,000 sq. ft.

In 20,000 of the 800,000 buildings in New York, the radios don't work. (Unfortunately, the World Trade Center was among those buildings. The Motorola radios used that day, about which Mayor Giuliani had been warned, are partially responsible for the large number of deaths suffered by the fire department. )

*Account of "Listening to the City," a public forum on plans to rebuild Ground Zero*

...Those guys in suits are a scary bunch. At the end, they did a poll of how satisfied the audience was that they'd been listened to. 45% said, "Somewhat satisfied." About 33% gave a better ranking than that. Yaro said this means 80% of the people were satisfied. See the Spin Doctor spin. Spin, Spin Doctor, spin. A roar of protest rose in the room.

The high point of the day was hearing that the environment came in second on the list of concerns people have about downtown. What a change from a few months ago when they wrote us off as hysterics.

Here's an account from Marie Christopher of the Good Old Lower East Side:

"First there was the guy who had on a T-shirt that said, "Kill the Bastards." He was one of the good ones.

The lady sitting next to me said, "I don't think we should have low-income housing – the crime rate will go up.""

'I said, 'Let me get this straight: You think it's O.K. for black people to come into the neighborhood to serve you but it's not O.K. for them to live near where they work?'

'She said, 'Yes.' One of the other men agreed with her even though he lives in Mitchell-Lama housing that saved his ass 'cause he works for the Board of Ed and got laid off three times.

'Then there were the Nazis: A couple of guys from East Germany. When 'Kill the Bastards' got through with me, he started on them."

"Were they really Nazis?" I asked.

"Of course not. They were young.

'I was so sweet. I didn't curse or say anything I felt like saying. By the end of the day they all loved me."

She looked exhausted and forlorn.

# ENDNOTES

Most endnotes were researched in the course of writing this book rather than when the events took place and may be dated accordingly.

---

i http://fiscalpolicy.org/about-fpi
ii Stuyvesant High School Parents' Association http://www.stuy-pa.org/Environment/Sept11.htm
iii Ibid
iv An Administration in Crisis; Abigail Deutsch; The Spectator, The Stuyvesant High School Newspaper, Fall 2001.
http://events.nytimes.com/learning/general/specials/terrorism/stuy.pdf
v Ibid
vi Ibid
vii Maris Ip, Spectator;
http://events.nytimes.com/learning/general/specials/terrorism/stuy.pdf
viii Dylan Tatz, Ibid
ix Jeng Tyng Hong, Ibid
x Hamilton Davis, Ibid
xi Lindsay Kim, Ibid
xii Paul Banec, Ibid
xiii Laurence Wooster, Ibid
xiv Jessica Copperman, Ibid
xv Spectator; Ibid
xvi Spectator; Ibid (hard copy)
xvii Stuyvesant High School Parent's Association; September 11 Information; http://www.stuy-pa.org/Environment/Sept11.htm
xviii Ibid
xix Ibid
xx The Soldier and the Rap Star: A Tale of Two Post-9/11 Students Benjy Sarlin; Sep 8, 2011

http://www.theatlantic.com/national/archive/2011/09/the-soldier-and-the-rap-star-a-tale-of-two-post-9-11-students/244705

xxi Stuyvesant High School Parent's Association; September 11 Information; http://www.stuy-pa.org/Environment/Sept11.htm

xxii The Soldier and the Rap Star: A Tale of Two Post-9/11 Students  Benjy Sarlin; Sep 8, 2011 http://www.theatlantic.com/national/archive/2011/09/the-soldier-and-the-rap-star-a-tale-of-two-post-9-11-students/244705

xxiii Lower Manhattan High School Principal Doesn't Get Why You'd Want to Remember 9/11; John Tabin; September 2, 2011; https://spectator.org/27252_lower-manhattan-high-school-principal-doesnt-get-why-youd-want-remember-911/

xxiv Stuyvesant High School Parent's Association; September 11 Information; http://www.stuy-pa.org/Environment/Sept11.htm

xxv Swarna Chalasani; World Trade Center - Peripatetic Adventurer;  Profile published in THE NEW YORK TIMES on December 30, 2001. http://www.legacy.com/sept11/story.aspx?personid=130192

xxvi Monitors Say Health Risk From Smoke Is Very Small ANDREW C. REVKIN; September 14, 2001; http://www.nytimes.com/2001/09/14/nyregion/14ENVI.html?searchpv=nytToday

xxvii Ibid

xxviii NY Times quoted in January/February 2003; Air of Uncertainty; Susan Q. Stranahan; http://ajrarchive.org/Article.asp?id=2746

xxix N.Y. CAN BREATHE FREE – HEALTH EXPERTS SAY AIR QUALITY'S OK;  Barbara Hoffman; September 18, 2001 http://nypost.com/2001/09/18/n-y-can-breathe-free-health-experts-say-air-qualitys-ok-by-barbara-hoffman

xxx ANDREW C. REVKIN; op cit

xxxi Panel Traces Missteps in Aiding Post-9/11 Victims; Chief Leader - September 20, 2011; FLORA FAIR http://www.ufanyc.org/cms/contents/view/11716

xxxii http://www.ische.ca/users/phil-landrigan

xxxiii Public defender by Jane Whitehead
http://bcm.bc.edu/issues/winter_2007/features/public-defender.html#sthash.DNlJbU0n.dpuf
xxxiv City of Dust _ Illness, Arrogance and 9/11; Anthony de Palma, FT Press; 2011
xxxv COMPLAINT AND ADDITIONAL EVIDENCE OF pH FRAUD BY: USGS, OSHA, ATSDR, NYC, EPA, and EPA-funded scientists
— 1. Falsification of corrosive pH data for WTC dust; — 2. Historical fraud by EPA of hazardous pH levels since 1980; May 6, 2007; FROM: Cate Jenkins, Ph.D.* GCB, HWID, OSW, OSWER, EPA; To: Senator Hillary Rodham Clinton, Chair, Subcommittee on Superfund and Environmental Health; Congressman Jerrold Nadler; Congresswoman Carolyn Maloney;
http://www.journalof911studies.com/volume/200704/DrJenkinsRequestsSenateInvestigationOnWTCdust.pdf
xxxvi Testimony of Philip J. Landrigan, M.D., M.Sc.; Chair, Department of Community and Preventive Medicine; Professor of Pediatrics; Director, Center for Children's Health and the Environment; Mount Sinai School of Medicine; Impacts on the Health of Children of the September 11 Attacks on the World Trade Center Before the Subcommittee on Clear Air, Wetlands, and Climate Change; Committee on Environment and Public Works; United States Senate; New York City Monday, February 11, 2002
http://www.epw.senate.gov/107th/Landrigan_021102.htm
xxxvii What Was in the World Trade Center Plume? David Biello; September 7, 2011;
https://www.scientificamerican.com/article/what-was-in-the-world-trade-center-plume/
xxxviii Statement to Stuyvesant Parents by the Executive Board of the Stuyvesant Parents' Association  Monday September 17, 2001, 11:00 pm  http://www.stuy-pa.org/Environment/PAState09_17_01.htm
xxxix Pressure from Parents, Change of Plans; Abigail Deutsch; The Spectator; Fall, 2001;
http://events.nytimes.com/learning/general/specials/terrorism/stuy.pdf

xl Stuyvesant High School Parents' Association; September 11 Information; http://www.stuy-pa.org/Environment/Sept11.htm

xli THE PARENTS' ASSOCIATION OF STUYVESANT HIGH SCHOOL Bu l l e t i n; Issue 2 October 2001; http://www.stuy-pa.org/files/documents/PABulletin10-01.pdf

xlii Ibid

xliii The Cost of Breathing; September 9, 2016; Sonia Epstein; http://www.stuyspec.com/features/the-cost-of-breathing

xliv Exhausted by Diesel – How America's Dependence on Diesel Engines Threatens Our Health; National Resources Defense Council; http://www.nrdc.org/air/transportation/ebd/chap2.asp

xlv 9 chemicals identified so far in e-cig vapor that are on the California Prop 65 list of carcinogens and reproductive toxins; Center for Tobacco Control Research and Education; http://www.tobacco.ucsf.edu/9-chemicals-identified-so-far-e-cig-vapor-are-california-prop-65-list-carcinogens-and-reproductive-t

xlvi POLLUTION LOCATOR; Hazardous Air Pollutants Driving Cancer and Noncancer Risk Estimates; http://scorecard.goodguide.com/env-releases/def/hap_drivers.html

xlvii
http://academickids.com/encyclopedia/images/0/00/Stuy_100_gala.pdf

xlviii
https://twitter.com/kaitytong/status/737045967648763904

xlix Algorithmic Diagnosis of Symptoms and Signs: A Cost-Effective Approach; Douglas R. Collins; Wolters Kluwer; Lippincott Williams and Wilkins; https://books.google.com/books?id=G0156FR6WGgC&pg=PA354&lpg=PA354&dq=%22pseudotumor+cerebri%22+%22lead+level%22&source=bl&ots=WQoSwfuC1T&sig=PzbEJB7q4cn
-
PXzXW64YlHJCz78&hl=en&sa=X&ved=0ahUKEwjQtJb7wK_L AhWBmBoKHTBlBG8Q6AEIHDAA#v=onepage&q=%22pseudo tumor%20cerebri%22%20%22lead%20level%22&f=false

[li] Letter of February 7, 2002; quoted in Testimony of Jenna Orkin, mother of Ground Zero Student; http://www.epw.senate.gov/107th/Orkin_092402.htm

[li] EPA Is Doubted on Dust Testing As Asbestos Concerns Are Raised; Queena Sook Kim; The Wall Street Journal; Updated Sept. 25, 2001 http://www.wsj.com/articles/SB1001368607173149960; http://www.immuneweb.org/911/news/sept01.html

[lii] September 11 Digital Archive; Summary Report: Characterization of Particulate Found in Apartments After Destruction of the World Trade Center," September 11 Digital Archive, accessed July 31, 2015; http://911digitalarchive.org/items/show/2888; WTC2001.pdf

[liii] Air Today, Gone Tomorrow; Downwind from Disaster; New York Environmental Law and Justice Project; October 25, 2001; http://landofpuregold.com/truth30.htm

[liv] http://www.historycommons.org/timeline.jsp?env_imp_general_topic_areas=env_imp_WTCworkers&timeline=enviromental_impact_911_attacks_tmln

[lv] http://www.historycommons.org/context.jsp?item=a845sting ermissiles

[lvi] Pollution and Deception at Ground Zero; How the Bush Administration's Reckless Disregard of 9/11 Toxic Hazards Poses Long-Term Threats for New York City and the Nation; Suzanne Mattei; Sierra Club; http://www.gothamgazette.com/rebuilding_nyc/sierraclub_report.pdf

[lvii] Air of Uncertainty; Susan Q. Stranahan; American Journalism Review; http://ajrarchive.org/Article.asp?id=2746

[lviii] De Palma, Anthony; City of Dust; Pearson Education; FT Press; p. 76

[lix] What Was in the World Trade Center Plume? David Biello; Scientific American, Sept 11, 2007; http://www.scientificamerican.com/article/what-was-in-the-world-trade-center-plume/

lx Ground Zero Hazards; Environmental and Health Impacts of the WTC Bombing
http://911research.wtc7.net/wtc/groundzero/environment.html

lxi Federal Register CFR Part 763: p.15728; Management of Health Risks from Environment and Food: Policy and Politics of ...edited by Hajime Sato;
https://books.google.com/books?id=C8jAsxt0riUC&pg=PA141&lpg=PA141&dq=%22evidence+supports+the+conclusion+that+there+is+no+safe+level+of+exposure+to+asbestos%22&source=bl&ots=9LIFLipR_Z&sig=1N4TQDsDTUKfZiW-F9UjjnHiiFA&hl=en&sa=X&ved=0ahUKEwj2qpShgbnQAhUHbSYKHXCnDscQ6AEIGzAA#v=onepage&q=%22evidence%20supports%20the%20conclusion%20that%20there%20is%20no%20safe%20level%20of%20exposure%20to%20asbestos%22&f=false

lxii Are We Ready?: Public Health since 9/11; David Rosner, Gerald Markowitz; University of California Press;
https://books.google.com/books?id=jDtgS4NNWIIC&pg=PA29&lpg=PA29&dq=%22single+burst,+heavy+dose%E2%80%99+of+asbestos+could+be+enough+to+cause%22+asbestos+%22lethal+disease%22&source=bl&ots=-qPvr6-6Qj&sig=QDsH7qkAYIcbEG9ec48fXP83Vxk&hl=en&sa=X&ved=0ahUKEwjt5oaXgrnQAhUM7yYKHRBZD1IQ6AEIGzAA#v=onepage&q=%22single%20burst%2C%20heavy%20dose%E2%80%99%20of%20asbestos%20could%20be%20enough%20to%20cause%22%20asbestos%20%22lethal%20disease%22&f=false

lxiii NYC under an asbestos cloud; ANDREW SCHNEIDER, ©2002 ST. LOUIS POST-DISPATCH; January 13, 2002;
http://www.seattlepi.com/news/article/NYC-under-an-asbestos-cloud-1077322.php

lxiv Stuyvesant High School Parents' Association; Environmental Health and Safety Committee Status Report; October 26, 2001; http://www.stuy-pa.org/Environment/PAHealthSafety10_26_01.htm

lxv October 18, 2001 Letter to Parents from Stuyvesant Principal Stanley Teitel lxvi https://issuu.com/stuyspectator/docs/wtc; An "A" for Air Quality; Laura Krug with additional reporting by Abigail Deutsch http://events.nytimes.com/learning/general/specials/terrorism/stuy.pdf

lxvii Ibid

lxviii Ibid

lxix http://www.stuy-pa.org/files/documents/PABulletin6-01.pdf

lxx http://www.hoover.org/profiles/laura-krug

lxxi Right Wing Boycott Movement Links CPAC to the Muslim Brotherhood; Brian Tashman; January 5, 2011; http://www.rightwingwatch.org/post/right-wing-boycott-movement-links-cpac-to-the-muslim-brotherhood/

lxxii http://abigaildeutsch.tumblr.com/

lxxiii Environmental Health and Safety Committee Status Report; October 26, 2001; Letter from PA in resonse to BOE's November 5 letter; November 6, 2001 http://www.stuy-pa.org/Environment/PAltr11_06_01.htm

lxxiv Dr. Stephen Levin dead of cancer; Mount Sinai physician proved World Trade Center illnesses were real; NEW YORK DAILY NEWS; February 9, 2012 http://www.nydailynews.com/opinion/dr-stephen-levin-dead-cancer-article-1.1019463

lxxv "Dr. Stephen Levin, head of Mount Sinai Medical Center's Selikoff Center for Occupational and Environmental Medicine, said there is no safe level for asbestos. "There is always some increase in the risk of cancer in any exposure to asbestos," he said. But Levin and other experts said short-term asbestos exposure is not likely to result in serious health problems. Those most at risk are workers who handle the stuff daily for years and smokers. They risk lung-scarring, asbestosis _ the inflammation of lung tissue _ and cancer." ASBESTOS LEVELS IN GROUND ZERO AIR GENERALLY SAFE, EPA RECORDS SHOW; Alison Gendar, Susan Ferraro; NEW YORK DAILY NEWS; September 29, 2001;

http://www.nydailynews.com/archives/news/asbestos-levels-ground-zero-air-generally-safe-epa-records-show-article-1.926703
lxxvi
https://www.med.nyu.edu/environmentalmedicine/sites/default/files/environmentalmedicine/wtcProgram2001.pdf
lxxvii http://www.trinityschoolnyc.org/page/Curriculum-Detail?fromId=169521&LevelNum=833&DepartmentId=14356
lxxviii N.Y.U., Columbia Make A Mint on Real Estate; Matthew Schuerman; 05/01/06; http://observer.com/2006/05/nyu-columbia-make-a-mint-on-real-estate/
lxxix Statement of Dr. George D. Thurston, Sc. D. to the Committee on Environment and Public Works of the United States Senate Re: The Air Pollution Effects of The World Trade Center Disaster, February 11, 2002; http://www.senate.gov/~epw/107th/Thurston_021102.htm; quoted in http://www.journalof911studies.com/volume/200704/DrJenkinsRequestsSenateInvestigationOnWTCdust.pdf
lxxx Stuyvesant High School Parents' Association; Status Report; http://www.stuy-pa.org/Environment/01_1026_status.htm
lxxxi The Cost of Breathing; September 9, 2016; Sonia Epstein; Stuyvesant Spectator; http://www.stuyspec.com/features/the-cost-of-breathing
lxxxii Appendix C; World Trade Center Indoor Air Assessment; Peer Review Meeting; Observer Comments; http://www.tera.org/Peer/WTC/Appendix%20C%20Observer%20Comments.pdf
lxxxiii S. Hrg. 107-524, Part I; AIR QUALITY IN NEW YORK CITY AFTER THE SEPTEMBER 11, 2001 ATTACKS; FIELD HEARING BEFORE THE SUBCOMMITTEE ON CLEAN AIR, WETLANDS, AND CLIMATE CHANGE OF THE COMMITTEE ON ENVIRONMENT AND PUBLIC WORKS; UNITED STATES SENATE; ONE HUNDRED SEVENTH CONGRESS; SECOND SESSION ON AIR QUALITY IN NEW YORK CITY AFTER THE SEPTEMBER 11, 2001 ATTACKS; FEBRUARY 11, 2002;

https://www.gpo.gov/fdsys/pkg/CHRG-107shrg80397/html/CHRG-107shrg80397.htm
lxxxiv What is PM2.5 and Why You Should Care
http://blissair.com/what-is-pm-2-5.htm
lxxxv www.cleanair.org/diesel/health_effects.pdf
lxxxvi Report of the EPA Office of the Inspector General No. 2003-P-00012; p. 37;
https://www.epa.gov/sites/production/files/2015-10/documents/wtc_report_20030821.pdf
lxxxvii 'No Skeletons in My Closet!'; Wayne Barrett, October 23, 2007; http://www.villagevoice.com/news/no-skeletons-in-my-closet-6424044
lxxxviii
http://www.cuny.edu/about/administration/administrators/iweinshall.html
lxxxix http://www.stuy-pa.org/files/documents/PABulletin04-02.pdf
xc NYC under an asbestos cloud; By ANDREW SCHNEIDER, ©2002 ST. LOUIS POST-DISPATCH; January 13, 2002;
http://www.seattlepi.com/news/article/NYC-under-an-asbestos-cloud-1077322.php
xci *Exposure and Human Health Evaluation of Airborne Pollution from the World Trade Center Disaster*
https://cfpub.epa.gov/ncea/risk/recordisplay.cfm?deid=51929&CFID=72298698&CFTOKEN=12563981
xcii Here comes the judge? Freed may go for broke in Council race; Josh Rogers;
http://www.downtownexpress.com/de_260/herecomes.html
xciii For New Yorkers, Memory of Shared Loss; Michael Powell; September 11, 2003;
https://www.washingtonpost.com/archive/politics/2003/09/11/for-new-yorkers-memory-of-shared-loss/44302641-e67a-4d57-bb20-b24b4aca9d6d/
xciv S. Hrg. 107-524, Part I AIR QUALITY IN NEW YORK CITY AFTER THE SEPTEMBER 11, 2001 ATTACKS FIELD HEARING BEFORE THE SUBCOMMITTEE ON CLEAN AIR, WETLANDS, AND CLIMATE CHANGE OF THE COMMITTEE ON ENVIRONMENT AND PUBLIC WORKS; UNITED STATES SENATE; ONE HUNDRED SEVENTH CONGRESS; SECOND

SESSION ON AIR QUALITY IN NEW YORK CITY AFTER THE SEPTEMBER 11, 2001 ATTACKS; FEBRUARY 11, 2002 – NEW YORK CITY  https://www.gpo.gov/fdsys/pkg/CHRG-107shrg80397/html/CHRG-107shrg80397.htm

[xcv] Ibid

[xcvi] Ibid

[xcvii] Christie blasts Rudy on WTC air; Adam Nichols; June 23, 2007; http://www.nydailynews.com/news/christie-blasts-rudy-wtc-air-article-1.224008

[xcviii] Song by Tom Lehrer

[xcix] De Palma, Anthony; City of Dust; Pearson Education, FT Press. P. 77

[c] Testimony of Jenna Orkin, Ground Zero Parent; Ombudsman Panel, January 14, 2003; Stuyvesant High School, Toxic Site; Written Statements of Community Members Participating in the Citizens' Briefing on the EPA Ombudsman Issue; Topics: Energy and Natural Resources; Danielle Brian; Project on Government Oversight; http://www.pogo.org/our-work/testimony/2003/nr-epa-20030114.html#Jenna_Orkin_Ground_Zero_Parent

[ci] Trading Stocks The Week after 9/11 http://www.jamesaltucher.com/2011/05/trading-stocks-the-week-after-911/

[cii] New York City Health and Hospitals Corporation;  BOARD OF DIRECTORS MEETING; APRIL 19, 2012; http://www.nychealthandhospitals.org/hhc/downloads/pdf/board-packets/2012-04-board-meeting.pdf

[ciii] Pregnancies at Risk From 9/11 Debris; Naomi Lubick; Aug. 5, 2003 http://www.sciencemag.org/news/2003/08/pregnancies-risk-911-debris

[civ] Berger, Elizabeth: "Testimony Before the United States Senate Subcommittee on Clean Air, Wetlands and Climate Change;" February 11, 2002

[cv] Distant metastasis occurs late during the genetic evolution of pancreatic cancer; Shinichi Yachida,Siân Jones, Ivana Bozic, Tibor Antal, Rebecca Leary, Baojin Fu, Mihoko Kamiyama, Ralph H. Hruban, James R. Eshleman, Martin A. Nowak, Victor E. Velculescu, Kenneth W. Kinzler, Bert

Vogelstei & Christine A. Iacobuzio-Donahue; Nature 467, 1114–1117; 28 October 2010; http://www.nature.com/nature/journal/v467/n7319/full/nature09515.html

cvi https://answers.yahoo.com/question/index?qid=20110414135710AAoR9QK

cvii Waiting to exhale: Congress passes 9/11 health bill; Aline Reynolds; Villager Volume 80, Number 31 | December 30, 2010 _ January 5, 2011; http://thevillager.com/villager_401/waitingtoexhale.html

cviii MEMORANDUM to Affected Parties and Responsible Officials; Cate Jenkins, Ph.D; March 11, 2002; Status of air and dust asbestos testing after WTC collapse http://docshare.tips/jenkins-031102-asbestos-status-wtc_581ff700b6d87f6f998b480a.html

cix http://www.historycommons.org/timeline.jsp?timeline=envir omental_impact_911_attacks_tmln&env_imp_general_topic_a reas=env_imp_independentStudies

cx Senate Hearing 107-524] Part I; AIR QUALITY IN NEW YORK CITY AFTER THE SEPTEMBER 11, 2001 ATTACKS; FIELD HEARING BEFORE THE   SUBCOMMITTEE ON CLEAN AIR, WETLANDS, AND CLIMATE CHANGE OF THE COMMITTEE ON  ENVIRONMENT AND PUBLIC WORKS; UNITED STATES SENATE; ONE HUNDRED SEVENTH CONGRESS; SECOND SESSION ON AIR QUALITY IN NEW YORK CITY AFTER THE SEPTEMBER 11, 2001 ATTACKS; FEBRUARY 11, 2002 _ NEW YORK CITY; Asbestos in Manhattan, Cate Jenkins, Ph.D; https://www.gpo.gov/fdsys/pkg/CHRG-107shrg80397/html/CHRG-107shrg80397.htm

cxi September 13, 2001-September 19, 2001: EPA Building near Ground Zero Professionally Cleaned of Asbestos; Jenkins, 3/11/2002 pdf file; Kupferman, 2003 pdf file; Jenkins, 7/4/2003 pdf file; Air monitoring also reveals the presence of asbestos:

http://www.historycommons.org/timeline.jsp?timeline=envir
omental_impact_911_attacks_tmln&env_imp_general_topic_a
reas=env_imp_independentStudies
cxii

http://old.cehn.org/new_york_city_coalition_end_lead_poison
ing
cxiii

https://www.nycourtsystem.com/Applications/JCEC2013/b
io2013.php?ID=2375
cxiv The Deepwater Horizon spill may have caused 'irreversible'
damage to Gulf Coast marshes; Chelsea Harvey September
27, 2016; https://www.washingtonpost.com/news/energy-
environment/wp/2016/09/27/the-deepwater-horizon-oil-
spill-may-have-caused-irreversible-damage-to-marshes-
along-the-gulf-coast/?utm_term=.8f8e8fa100b4
cxv Trading in Disaster; CorpWatch, February 6, 2002;
Nityanand Jayaraman and Kenny Bruno
https://www.gpo.gov/fdsys/pkg/CHRG-
107shrg80397/html/CHRG-107shrg80397.htm
cxvi NYC under an asbestos cloud; ANDREW SCHNEIDER,
©2002 ST. LOUIS POST-DISPATCH; January 13, 2002;
http://www.seattlepi.com/news/article/NYC-under-an-
asbestos-cloud-1077322.php
cxvii Libby meets Manhattan: Connecting the dots between a
New York terrorist attack and a Montana mining disaster;
Paul Peters; Missoula Independent; August 02, 2007;
http://missoulanews.bigskypress.com/missoula/libby-
meets-manhattan/Content?oid=1138130
cxviii Schneider op cit
cxix Original article unavailable but referred to at:
http://ordinary-gentlemen.com/blog/2014/02/26/a-
standard-utopia/
cxx XCVIII S. Hrg. 107-524, Part I AIR QUALITY IN NEW YORK
CITY AFTER THE SEPTEMBER 11, 2001 ATTACKS FIELD
HEARING BEFORE THE SUBCOMMITTEE ON CLEAN AIR,
WETLANDS, AND CLIMATE CHANGE OF THE COMMITTEE
ON ENVIRONMENT AND PUBLIC WORKS; UNITED STATES
SENATE; ONE HUNDRED SEVENTH CONGRESS; SECOND

SESSION ON AIR QUALITY IN NEW YORK CITY AFTER THE SEPTEMBER 11, 2001 ATTACKS; FEBRUARY 11, 2002 – NEW YORK CITY  https://www.gpo.gov/fdsys/pkg/CHRG-107shrg80397/html/CHRG-107shrg80397.htm
cxxi Trade Center Debris Pile Was a Chemical Factory, Says New Study; September 10, 2003; The DELTA Group for the Detection and Evaluation of the Long-Range Transport of Aerosols; http://delta.ucdavis.edu/WTC.htm
cxxii EPA Ombudsman Quits Amid Controversy; Kelley Beaucar Vlahos April 23, 2002; http://www.foxnews.com/story/2002/04/23/epa-ombudsman-quits-amid-controversy.html;  Conflict of Interest for Christine Todd Whitman? Mark Hertsgaard; January 15, 2002; http://www.salon.com/2002/01/15/whitman_5/
cxxiii Harold O. Levy J.D; Executive Director, Jack Kent Cooke Foundation; http://www.bloomberg.com/research/stocks/private/person.asp?personId=36311416&privcapId=6477126
cxxiv https://en.wikipedia.org/wiki/List_of_Nobel_laureates_by_Secondary_School_affiliation
cxxv http://ic.galegroup.com/ic/uhic/ReferenceDetailsPage/ReferenceDetailsWindow?displayGroupName=Reference&disableHighlighting=false&prodId=UHIC&action=e&windowstate=normal&catId=&documentId=GALE%7CK1618002398&mode=view&userGroupName=penn63709&jsid=055ab01527bc52d5d9f333cf10a980c0
cxxvi Statement by Lucy Shaw, MSW, Research and Policy Initiative of the Community Development Project, Urban Justice Center and Hyun Lee, Director of Chinatown Justice Project, CAAAV to the City Council of the City of New York, Select Committee on Lower Manhattan Redevelopment; June 30, 2004; https://cdp.urbanjustice.org/sites/default/files/SelectCommitteeTestimony.pdf
cxxvii Volume 73, Number 7 | June 16 - 22, 2004; Why Westway sleeps with the fishes; Albert Amateau

http://thevillager.com/villager_59/whywestwaysleepswith.html

cxxviii EPA says toxic sludge is good for fish; Washington Times; June 19, 2002; http://www.washingtontimes.com/news/2002/jun/19/20020619-031957-2767r/

cxxix Written Statements of Community Members Participating in the Citizens' Briefing on the EPA Ombudsman Issue; January 14, 2003; http://www.pogo.org/our-work/testimony/2003/nr-epa-20030114.html

cxxx NYC couple still wait to go home; Geoff Gehman Of The Morning Call; http://www.mcall.com/all-a1_5artistsep08-story.html

cxxxi Red Cross defends handling of Sept. 11 donations; November 6, 2001; http://edition.cnn.com/2001/US/11/06/rec.charity.hearing/index.html

cxxxii How the Red Cross Raised Half a Billion Dollars for Haiti - and Built Six Homes; Justin Elliott, ProPublica, and Laura Sullivan, NPR; June 3, 2011; https://www.propublica.org/article/how-the-red-cross-raised-half-a-billion-dollars-for-haiti-and-built-6-homes.

cxxxiii Haitians Desperate for Help but They Don't Want it From the Red Cross; Peter Holley; October 13, 2016; https://www.washingtonpost.com/news/worldviews/wp/2016/10/13/haitians-are-desperate-for-help-but-they-dont-want-it-from-the-american-red-cross/

cxxxiv The Cost of Breathing; September 9, 2016; Sonia Epstein; Stuyvesant Spectator; http://www.stuyspec.com/features/the-cost-of-breathing

cxxxv TOXIC FIND SPARKS STUY HS DUST-UP; Carl Campanile; June 14, 2002; http://nypost.com/2002/06/14/toxic-find-sparks-stuy-hs-dust-up/

cxxxvi Few of Those Eligible Register For Cleanup Help Near 9/11 Site; KIRK JOHNSON; SEPT. 25, 2002; http://www.nytimes.com/2002/09/25/nyregion/few-of-those-eligible-register-for-cleanup-help-near-9-11-site.html

cxxxvii Ibid

cxxxviii Asbestos Spectre Haunts Manhattan; Laurie Kazan-Allen; http://ibasecretariat.org/lka_asb_spectr_manhat.php
cxxxixRebirth Marked By Cornerstone At Ground Zero; DAVID W. DUNLAP JULY 5, 2004; http://www.nytimes.com/2004/07/05/nyregion/rebirth-marked-by-cornerstone-at-ground-zero.html; For some, it's a day of protest; Joshua Robin; Errol A. Cockfield contributor; July 5, 2004; Newday
cxl MEMORANDUM DATE: August 29, 2002; SUBJECT: Stuyvesant High School Testing – EPA validates use of sonication testing – Brookfield CT school system using sonication; FROM: Cate Jenkins, Ph.D.
* https://www.scribd.com/document/45065998/Jenkins-082902-WTC-Stuyvescant-Carpet
cxli Marjol leader, Lukasewicz say O'Malley exaggerated role in cleanup; BORYS KRAWCZENIUK: May 14, 2015 http://thetimes-tribune.com/news/marjol-leader-lukasewicz-say-o-malley-exaggerated-role-in-cleanup-1.1881288
cxlii S. 606 (107th): Ombudsman Reauthorization Act of 2002; https://www.govtrack.us/congress/bills/107/s606/details
cxliii Jenna Orkin Testimony to the World Trade Center Expert Technical Review Panel, May 24, 2004
cxlivJun 23, 2011; Excavating the Past – 20 Years since the Discovery that Changed 290 Broadway; Elizabeth Myer; https://blog.epa.gov/blog/2011/06/excavating-the-past-20-years-since-the-discovery-that-changed-290-broadway/
cxlv GROUND ZERO HOUSING AID NOW AVAILABLE; Greg Gittrich; NEW YORK DAILY NEWS; August 16, 2002; "People closest to Ground Zero will receive the most money." http://www.nydailynews.com/archives/news/ground-zero-housing-aid-article-1.505627
cxlvi Misplaced health worries in a world of hazards; Orange County REGISTER August 21, 2002; JANE E. BRODY; New York Times News Service; https://mailman.mcmaster.ca/pipermail/cdn-nucl-1/2002-August.txt
cxlvii Ibid.

cxlviii IG CLEARS WHITMAN OF ALLEGED FINANCIAL CONFLICTS OF INTEREST; August 1, 2002 http://w.environmentalnewsstand.com/search/site/%22IG%20Clears%20Whitman%22%20

cxlix Written Statements of Community Members Participating in the Citizens' Briefing on the EPA Ombudsman Issue; January 14, 2003; http://www.pogo.org/our-work/testimony/2003/nr-epa-20030114.html

cl https://nadler.house.gov/press-release/congressman-nadler-introduces-clear-your-good-name-act

cli Mort de Patrick Bourrat, grand reporter à TF1; Didier FRANÇOIS; 23 décembre 2002; http://www.liberation.fr/medias/2002/12/23/mort-de-patrick-bourrat-grand-reporter-a-tf1_425587

clii Teachers consider boycott amid new PS 65 chem tests; Daniel Massey http://www.timesledger.com/stories/2002/34/20020822-archive633.html

cliii http://www.columbia.edu/itc/architecture/bass/newrochelle/environ/trichloro.html

cliv With Their Eyes: September 11th – The View from a High School at Ground Zero; Annie Thoms; HarperCollins

clv Bad Air Days From 9/11 Hit Brooklyn Hard; Paul Moses; November 13, 2002; http://www.newsday.com/bad-air-days-from-9-11-hit-brooklyn-hard-1.284564

clvi Misconceptions About the Causes of Cancer; Lois Swirsky Gold; Bruce N. Ames and Thomas H. Slone; in *Human and Environmental Risk Assessment: Theory and Practice;* Dennis Paustenbach, ed; John Wiley & Sons; 2002; https://toxnet.nlm.nih.gov/cpdb/pdfs/Paustenbach.pdf http://www.tera.org/about/2003%20annual%20report.pdf; http://www.tera.org/EcoTERA/EcoTERA.pdf "Dr. Pittinger...has evaluated chemical toxicity regulatory hazard classifications for the metals and mining industry (Rio Tinto...)" It's unclear when this affiliation to TERA began.

clvii Rio Tinto: Corporate Crimes; Corporate Watch; 05/05/2010 ; https://corporatewatch.org/company-profiles/rio-tinto-corporate-crimes;

"Rio Tinto has also seen significant labour conflict at its Rossing Uranium mine in Namibia, where concerns have long been raised about apartheid-style discrimination against black workers.7 Conditions at the mine and the Arandis camp where the workers live were described in 1979 as 'akin to slavery...'

Between 1989-1990 alone, it is estimated that 6,000 homes were destroyed and 24,000 people forcibly relocated to concentration camp-style 'care centres...' [Freeport McMoran] "there are countless cases of murder, rape and torture against residents..."

clviii Ibid;
www.cfmeu.com.au/storage/documents/rio/RT.pdf
clix PG&E Assailed in Hearing Over Chromium 6; March 01, 2003; Miguel Bustillo;
http://articles.latimes.com/2003/mar/01/local/me-chrom1
clx An Epidemiologist's Nightmare; George Johnson; April 1, 2013; http://blogs.discovermagazine.com/fire-in-the-mind/2013/04/01/an-epidemiologists-nightmare/#.V7yRZqj2ZLM
clxi Orkin Testimony May 24, 2004, op cit.
clxii Orkin Testimony to the World Trade Center Expert Technical Review Panel; September 13, 2004
clxiii World Trade Center Indoor Environment Assessment:Selecting Contaminants of Potential Concern and Setting Health-Based Benchmarks; May 2003;Prepared by the Contaminants of Potential Concern (COPC) Committee of the World Trade Center Indoor Air Task Force Working Group https://archive.epa.gov/wtc/web/pdf/contaminants_of_concern_benchmark_study.pdf Appendix B - 24.
clxiv Written Testimony of Susan Shortz, Throop, Pa., President of HELP (Halt Environmental Lead Pollution) and member of the Citizen Review Committee for the Marjol Site; For the Citizen's Briefing on the Ombudsman Issue; Citizens' Briefing on the EPA Ombudsman Issue; January 14, 2003: Danielle Brian; http://www.pogo.org/our-work/testimony/2003/nr-epa-20030114.html
clxv Written Statement of Sandra Jaquith, Rocky Mountain Arsenal, Site Specific Advisory Board; Ibid

clxvi Written Testimony of Deborah Sanchez, Administrator, Overland Neighborhood Environmental Watch; Ibid

clxvii UNITED STATES ENVIRONMENTAL PROTECTION AGENCY; OFFICE OF SOLID WASTEAND EMERGENCY RESPONSE; MEMORANDUM: July 15, 2004; NYC data concealed by EPA and NYC after 9/11,subsequently altered/selectively deleted by NYC; Reverses IG finding of "no evidence ... EPA attempted to conceal;" Cate Jenkins, Ph.D; https://www.scribd.com/document/45178178/Jenkins-071504-NYC-Doctored-Asbestos-Numbers

clxviii NEW YORK STATE ASSEMBLY STANDING COMMITTEE ON EDUCATION; ASSEMBLY STANDING COMMITTEE ON ENVIRONMENTAL CONSERVATION; ASSEMBLY STANDING COMMITTEE ON HEALTH HEARING TO ASSESS THE ADEQUACY OF NEW YORK STATE AND NEW YORK CITY'S POLICIES RELATING TO SCHOOL FACILITIES AND THEIR EFFECT ON THE HEALTH AND ACADEMIC PERFORMANCE OF STUDENTS Testimony of Marilena Christodoulou http://assembly.state.ny.us/comm/Ed/20040414/

clxix

http://www.gothamgazette.com/images/pdf/rebuildingnyc/sierraclub_report.pdf

clxx "Indeed, we have recently recognized the additional separation of powers concern - the right of federal agencies to make discretionary decisions when engaged in disaster relief efforts without the fear of judicial second-guessing"-that informs the Stafford Act's grant of discretionary function immunity to government officials engaged in administration of the Disaster Relief Act."

BENZMAN v. WHITMAN; United States Court of Appeals, Second Circuit.  Gail BENZMAN, Diane Lapson, Jim Gilroy, Anamae Gilroy, JoAlison Polett, Robert Gulack, Janice Fried, John Calder, Jenna Orkin, Kelly Colangelo, George Dinos, Brian Edwards, and Sara Manzano-Diaz, on their behalf and on behalf of all other persons similarly situated, Plaintiffs-Appellees-Cross-Appellants, v. Christine Todd WHITMAN, Stephen L. Johnson,and United States Environmental Protection Agency, Defendants-Appellants-Cross-Appellees;

Docket Nos. 06-1166-cv (L), 06-1346-cv (CON), 06-1454-cv (XAP); Decided: April 22, 2008; http://caselaw.findlaw.com/us-2nd-circuit/1239748.html#sthash.NdKGH4qb.dpuf

clxxi Lawyer accused of using scare tactics to get 9/11 victims to settle; Thomas Zambito; November 25, 2007; http://www.nydailynews.com/news/lawyer-accused-scare-tactics-9-11-victims-settle-article-1.256820

clxxii White House Pressured EPA Not To Warn Public About Health Effects of 9/11; August 12, 2003; http://www.democracynow.org/2003/8/12/white_house_pressured_epa_not_to

clxxiii Concern Over Mercury; Tests Show High Levels Near Site; Graham Rayman; June 6, 2002; Newsday; Air Today... Gone Tomorrow; http://landofpuregold.com/truth60.htm

clxxiv EPA REPORT BURIES A REVELATION; Juan Gonzalez; NEW YORK DAILY NEWS; December 31, 2002; http://www.nydailynews.com/archives/news/epa-report-buries-revelation-article-1.504682

clxxv Ibid

clxxvi UNITED STATES ENVIRONMENTAL PROTECTION AGENCY; OFFICE OFSOLID WASTE AND EMERGENCYRESPONSE; May 6, 2007; FROM: Cate Jenkins, Ph.D.
GCB, HWID, OSW, OSWER, EPA TO: Senator Hillary Rodham Clinton,Chair, Subcommittee on Superfund and Environmental Health; Congressman Jerrold Nadler Congresswoman Carolyn Maloney; COMPLAINT AND ADDITIONAL EVIDENCE OF pH FRAUD BY:USGS, OSHA, ATSDR, NYC, EPA, and EPA-funded scientists— 1. Falsification of corrosive pH data for WTC dust— 2. Historical fraud by EPA of hazardous pH levels since 1980 https://www.scribd.com/document/42238273/Jenkins-FBI-050607-WTC-pH-LIES-1stFBIcomplaint

clxxvii MEMORANDUM July 15, 2004; SUBJECT: NYC data concealed by EPA and NYC after 9/11,subsequently altered/selectively deleted by NYC -- Reverses IG finding of "no evidence ... EPA attempted to conceal"-- Evidence not considered or evaluated in 8/21/03 EPA IG report;

https://www.scribd.com/document/45178178/Jenkins-071504-NYC-Doctored-Asbestos-Numbers

clxxviii Panel Traces Missteps in Aiding Post-9/11 Victims; Chief Leader; September 20, 2011; FLORA FAIR; http://www.ufanyc.org/cms/contents/view/11716

clxxix Ibid

clxxx Ibid

clxxxi First responder fights back after losing foot to 9/11 accident; Yahoo! Laura E. Davis, August 16, 2011 https://www.yahoo.com/news/first-responder-fights-back-after-losing-foot-to-9-11-accident.html

clxxxii What Quarantine Feels Like: The experience of needing medical care while endangering the ones who give it; Michele Lent Hirsch; Nov 3, 2014 http://www.theatlantic.com/author/michele-lent-hirsch/

clxxxiii *Testimony of Joseph Zadroga to the Congressional Subcommittee on National Security, Emerging Threats and International Relations   September 8, 2006*

clxxxiv https://leanweb.org/issues/3-years-after-the-bp-spill-and-we-are-still-sick/

clxxxv Rising tides: Downtown flooding linked to climate change; YANNIC RACK; March 17, 2016; http://www.downtownexpress.com/2016/03/17/22510/

clxxxvi

https://challengingtherhetoric.wordpress.com/2014/10/01/253/

clxxxvii The 9/11 Commission Report: Final Report of the National Commission on ... https://books.google.com/books?id=UabGPLhbGckC&pg=PA555&lpg=PA555&dq=%22The+EPA+did+not+have+the+health-based+benchmarks+needed+to+assess+the+extraordinary+%22&source=bl&ots=KEYv0JOHNW&sig=_gAx2GQXrq0W70-BHi5qs_el3fk&hl=en&sa=X&ved=0ahUKEwjv67SWnLnQAhUBRSYKHff1CtMQ6AEIGzAA#v=onepage&q=%22The%20EPA%20did%20not%20have%20the%20health-based%20benchmarks%20needed%20to%20assess%20the%20extraordinary%20%22&f=false

clxxxviii Ibid

clxxxix Federal Register Volume 66, Number 161; August 20, 2001; Pages 43586-43587; FR Doc No: 01-20914; https://www.gpo.gov/fdsys/pkg/FR-2001-08-20/html/01-20914.htm

cxc Barton, Jo and Gellman, Barton; Leaving No Tracks; June 27, 2007; http://voices.washingtonpost.com/cheney/chapters/leaving_no_tracks/

cxci Ibid

cxcii http://www.sidley.com/notfound?item=%2Fnews%2Fpub&user=extranet%5CAnonymous&site=website; the original link is gone; an approximation may be found here: Neocons Braintrust US Atty Firings, Links to Bush (w/update) Valtin; Mar 19, 2007; http://www.dailykos.com/story/2007/3/19/313539/-

cxciii A disaster plan in action: how a law firm in the World Trade Center survived 9/11 with vital records and employees intact; Barr, Jean; 05/01/2003; http://www.freepatentsonline.com/article/Information-Management-Journal/102661044.html

cxciv Ibid

cxcv Ibid

cxcvi Ibid

cxcvii Rosemary Smith, 61, planned to open candy business; Staten Island Advance; September 11, 2010 at 1:00 AM, updated August 09, 2011; Date of Death 9/11/2001; Kiawana Rich; 10/21/2001 http://www.silive.com/september-11/index.ssf/2010/09/rosemary_smith_61_planned_to_o.html

cxcviii July 18, 2014; No, We Cannot Get Along; Missy Comley Beattie http://www.counterpunch.org/2014/07/18/no-we-cannot-get-along/

cxcix The CIA and Wash. Post - 2001 interview w/Deborah Davis; http://www.rigorousintuition.ca/board2http://www.zerohedge.com/news/2015-05-07/day-1945-reporter-fired-biggest-scoop-history/viewtopic.php?p=456789 cc Amazon, 'The Washington Post' and That $600 MIllion CIA Contract; Greg MitchellTwitter; December 19, 2013; https://www.thenation.com/article/amazon-washington-post-and-600-million-cia-contract/

cci On This Day In 1945: Reporter Fired For Biggest Scoop In History; Tyler Durden; 05/07/2015; http://www.zerohedge.com/news/2015-05-07/day-1945-reporter-fired-biggest-scoop-history

ccii September 30, 2007; JOHN JUDGE ON PROPAGANDA AND SOCIAL CONTROL; the article "Propaganda and Social Control" is from a booklet entitled *The Fourth Reich in America*, available from Flatland Books. Alex Constantine's Blacklist http://aconstantineblacklist.blogspot.com/2007/09/john-judge-on-propaganda-and-social.html

cciii Moment of Brutal Honesty: Political Commentator Quits Over HSBC Coverage, Accuses Telegraph Of "Fraud On Readers;" Tyler Durden; 02/17/2015; http://www.zerohedge.com/news/2015-02-17/honesty-shocker-telegraphs-political-commentator-quits-over-hsbc-coverage-accuses-pa

cciv Condoleezza Rice Testifies on Urging The Times to Not Run Article; MATT APUZZO; January 15, 2015; http://mobile.nytimes.com/2015/01/16/us/politics/condoleezza-rice-testifies-on-urging-the-times-to-suppress-leak.html?_r=2

ccv Google reports surge in government surveillance – et tu, Web? November 13, 2012; Jessica Guynn; http://articles.latimes.com/2012/nov/13/business/la-fi-tn-google-government-surveillance-20121113

ccvi Why didn't CNN's international arm air its own documentary on Bahrain's Arab Spring repression? Glenn Greenwald; 4 September 2012 http://www.theguardian.com/world/2012/sep/04/cnn-international-documentary-bahrain-arab-spring-repression

ccvii 'We Were Arrogant': Interview with New York Times Editor Baquet; Spiegel Online International; Interview Conducted by Isabell Hülsen and Holger Stark; January 23, 2015;

http://www.spiegel.de/international/business/spiegel-interview-with-chief-new-york-times-editor-dean-baquet-a-1014704.html

ccviii THE AFTERNOON OF MARCH 30: A Contemporary Historical Novel – November, 1984; Nathaniel Blumberg; Wood Fire Ashes Press

ccix How to Become Wealthy: Low Risk Strategies to Start a Business and Build Wealth; Charles G. Spender; Distributed by Lulu.com;
https://books.google.com/books?id=OgdnCwAAQBAJ&pg=PT49&lpg=PT49&dq=%22robert+gates%22+%22hold,+or+even+scrap+stories+that+could+have+adversely+affected+national+security+interests+or+jeopardized+sources%22&source=bl&ots=oEGW0Xs3wc&sig=M6kiD3oFcni7ZvBo2DUprxy3GK8&hl=en&sa=X&ved=0ahUKEwiT9oj8-Z3LAhXBFh4KHU0OC6IQ6AEIITAB#v=onepage&q=%22robert%20gates%22%20%22hold%2C%20or%20even%20scrap%20stories%20that%20could%20have%20adversely%20affected%20national%20security%20interests%20or%20jeopardized%20sources%22&f=false

ccx http://radicalacademy.com/studentrefscience6orkin.htm

ccxi http://www.counterpunch.org/2004/10/16/the-lingering-clouds-over-ground-zero/

ccxii http://www.counterpunch.org/2005/01/06/the-epa-and-a-dirty-bomb/

ccxiii Pending U.S. Advice on 'Dirty Bomb' Exposure Is Under Fire; MATTHEW L. WALD; DEC. 8, 2004;
http://www.nytimes.com/2004/12/08/politics/pending-us-advice-on-dirty-bomb-exposure-is-under-fire.html

ccxiv U.S. Plans to Offer Guidance for a Dirty-Bomb Aftermath; MATTHEW L. WALD; SEPT. 27, 2004;
http://www.nytimes.com/2004/09/27/politics/us-plans-to-offer-guidance-for-a-dirtybomb-aftermath.html?_r=0

ccxv http://www.counterpunch.org/2005/05/13/ground-zero-s-toxic-dust/

ccxvi http://www.counterpunch.org/2005/12/01/epa-s-latest-betrayal-at-ground-zero/

ccxvii

https://nepis.epa.gov/Exe/tiff2png.cgi/9101QEK3.PNG?-r+75+-g+7+D%3A%5CZYFILES%5CINDEX%20DATA%5C00THRU05%5CTIFF%5C00002169%5C9101QEK3.TIF; (peer review; other data could not be copied.)
http://nepis.epa.gov/Exe/ZyNET.exe/9101QEK3.TXT?ZyActionD=ZyDocument&Client=EPA&Index=2000+Thru+2005&Docs=&Query=&Time=&EndTime=&SearchMethod=1&TocRestrict=n&Toc=&TocEntry=&QField=&QFieldYear=&QFieldMonth=&QFieldDay=&IntQFieldOp=0&ExtQFieldOp=0&XmlQuery=&File=D%3A%5Czyfiles%5CIndex%20Data%5C00thru05%5CTxt%5C00000033%5C9101QEK3.txt&User=ANONYMOUS&Password=anonymous&SortMethod=h%7C-&MaximumDocuments=1&FuzzyDegree=0&ImageQuality=r75g8/r75g8/x150y150g16/i425&Display=p%7Cf&DefSeekPage=x&SearchBack=ZyActionL&Back=ZyActionS&BackDesc=Results%20page&MaximumPages=1&ZyEntry=1&SeekPage=x&ZyPURL
ccxviii http://www.counterpunch.org/2006/02/06/federal-judge-slams-whitman-and-epa/
ccxix http://www.counterpunch.org/2007/12/15/lying-to-quot-reassure-quot-the-public
ccxx The Lo-Down; Lower East Side Tenant Leader Marie Christopher Remembered; Ed Litvak; Lower East Side News; January 16, 2013;
http://www.thelodownny.com/leslog/2013/01/lower-east-side-tenant-leader-marie-christopher-remembered.html
ccxxi 9/11 the Sequel; February 3, 2005; The Toxic State of Lower Manhattan; Jenna Orkin;
http://jennifercw.blogspot.com/2005/02/911-sequel.html
ccxxii

http://www.gothamgazette.com/index.php/rebuildingnyc/1009-responses-to-the-enviromental-impact-statement#Skimming
ccxxiii Jenna Orkin; Lifting the Fog Conference, Berkeley CA; 11/11/2006.

ccxxiv
http://query.nytimes.com/gst/fullpage.html?res=9B04EED8
1231F93BA35751C1A9629C8B63
ccxxv http://www.counterpunch.org/orkin01062005.html
ccxxvi http://www.counterpunch.com/orkin12012005.html;
https://nepis.epa.gov/Exe/ZyNET.exe/9101QEK3.TXT?ZyAc
tionD=ZyDocument&Client=EPA&Index=2000+Thru+2005&D
ocs=&Query=&Time=&EndTime=&SearchMethod=1&TocRest
rict=n&Toc=&TocEntry=&QField=&QFieldYear=&QFieldMont
h=&QFieldDay=&IntQFieldOp=0&ExtQFieldOp=0&XmlQuery
=&File=D%3A%5Czyfiles%5CIndex%20Data%5C00thru05%5
CTxt%5C00000033%5C9101QEK3.txt&User=ANONYMOUS&
Password=anonymous&SortMethod=h%7C-
&MaximumDocuments=1&FuzzyDegree=0&ImageQuality=r7
5g8/r75g8/x150y150g16/i425&Display=hpfr&DefSeekPage=
x&SearchBack=ZyActionL&Back=ZyActionS&BackDesc=Resu
lts%20page&MaximumPages=1&ZyEntry=1&SeekPage=x&Zy
PURL
ccxxvii http://mikeruppert.blogspot.com;
http://www.911truth.org/fire-claims-lives-of-two-firefighters-
at-ground-zero-wall-st-journal-blames-community/
ccxxviii We Have Met the Enemy, Again; Daniel Henninger;
Updated Aug. 23, 2007;
http://www.wsj.com/articles/SB118783153423606105
ccxxix http://hystericalmothers.blogspot.com/

## Author Biography

Jenna Orkin is a writer and journalist whose short film, EnGaged:  Carolyn Gage On Stage and Off, has received a Top Indie Film as well as an LA Shorts Film award.

*Other Books by Jenna Orkin*

The Moron's Guide to Global Collapse
Writer Wannabe Seeks Brush with Death
Scout: A Memoir of Investigative Journalist Michael C. Ruppert

Made in the USA
Las Vegas, NV
08 June 2021